ISBN 978-0-332-36184-0
PIBN 10982659

English
Français
Deutsche
Italiano
Español
Português

www.forgottenbooks.com

Mythology Photography **Fiction**
Fishing Christianity **Art** Cooking
Essays Buddhism Freemasonry
Medicine **Biology** Music **Ancient**
Egypt Evolution Carpentry Physics
Dance Geology **Mathematics** Fitness
Shakespeare **Folklore** Yoga Marketing
Confidence Immortality Biographies
Poetry **Psychology** Witchcraft
Electronics Chemistry History **Law**
Accounting **Philosophy** Anthropology
Alchemy Drama Quantum Mechanics
Atheism Sexual Health **Ancient History**
Entrepreneurship Languages Sport
Paleontology Needlework Islam
Metaphysics Investment Archaeology
Parenting Statistics Criminology
Motivational

DL
AR.
h.R.

AND *fw*

COURT-KEEPING PRACTICE;

WITH NEARLY

TWO HUNDRED PRECEDENTS,

AND THE

ACT FOR AMENDMENT OF THE LAWS WITH RESPECT TO

Wills :

INTENDED NOT ONLY FOR USE IN THE OFFICE OF THE MORE EXPERIENCED PRACTITIONER, BUT SIMPLIFIED IN SUCH A MANNER AS TO ENABLE A TOWN OR COUNTRY SOLICITOR, PREVIOUSLY UNACQUAINTED WITH COPYHOLD OR COURT-KEEPING PRACTICE, TO TRANSACT WITH EASE ALL THE GENERAL BUSINESS IN

Admissions;
Purchases and Sales;
Mortgages;
Annuities; Leases;
Deeds for Benefit of Creditors;

Bankruptcy & Insolvency;
Wills, Partitions, and Enfranchisements;
Court-Keeping;
Adjustment of Fines, Fees, &c. &c.

———

BY ROLLA ROUSE,

OF THE MIDDLE TEMPLE, ESQ.

————

LONDON:

PUBLISHED FOR THE PROPRIETORS OF

The Legal Observer,

BY RICHARDS & Co.,

LAW BOOKSELLERS AND PUBLISHERS, 194, FLEET STREET;

AND SOLD BY SHERWOOD AND CO., PATERNOSTER ROW; ADAM AND CHARLES BLACK, EDINBURGH; AND HODGES AND SMITH, DUBLIN.

1837.

Spettigue, Printer, 67, Chancery Lane.

PREFACE

A WORK on Practice is useful to two classes of professional men :—to the experienced, in lessening fatigue, by allowing business to be transacted by clerks, which would otherwise require personal attention, and by facilitating the instruction of articled clerks ; and on the other hand, to practitioners having attention but seldom drawn to any particular branch of Practice, a work on that branch will be useful in affording the means of transacting any business connected with it, easily and accurately.

The present treatise has been prepared under the belief that Copyhold and Court-keeping Practice is most peculiarly within the principle of the above observation; and that methodising and simplifying the Practice, and embodying a full collection of precedents, would not only be found useful in business, but would dispel the prejudice which has long existed in the minds of many professional men, that Copyhold Practice is of a complicated nature, and cannot be understood without long study.

The object has been to treat of each branch of Practice in such a manner that reference need only be made to the part expressly relating to the point requiring attention; and such reference will at once give the Practice generally, each step to be taken according to its order and reference, by a number to the precedents in the Appendix. The plan of sections has also been adopted throughout the work, as affording much greater facility of reference than when merely given generally, or even if given by pages. A subdivision of such of the precedents as may be sometimes only wanted in part is also given, and will be found serviceable in instructing clerks to draw the more special documents or courts.

The following example will show the advantages of the system adopted.—Suppose a solicitor, previously unacquainted with Copyhold Practice, to receive instructions to act on behalf of an intended purchaser; he has merely to refer to the head "Purchase," and he will find under that head and the parts of the appendix referred to in it, all the Practice and Forms: comprising suggestions previous to the contract; the terms and form of contract; the abstract, its examination and sufficiency; requisitions on title; preparing and completing conveyance; obtaining admission, and adjusting the steward's fees; with forms of agreements, notices, conveyances, &c. The same observation applies to Mortgages, Leases, &c., &c.

In like manner all the information in *Court-keeping*

will be found under that head, with a full collection of Forms; so that a professional man, without having previously turned his attention to the subject, may be enabled, on obtaining a stewardship, to transact the business, make out his bills of fees, and enter his courts, with the ease and correctness of the more experienced practitioner.

The experienced Court-keeper will also be enabled by mere reference to numbers of sections, and the addition of a few words, to give such instructions to his clerk that all the general business of the court may be transacted without his being obliged to give his personal attention, except to the mere examination of the draft and entries; and he will also possess greatly increased facilities in making his articled clerks acquainted systematically with Copyhold and Court-keeping Practice.

Very great care has been taken in selecting the Precedents; and many points are suggested both as to the Practice and Forms, which have never been given in any work hitherto published on Copyholds, and which are also, many of them, applicable to freehold practice.

The rule for value of Copyhold Enfranchisements has never before been published; and attention is particularly directed to the suggestions on Purchase Contracts; the forms of such contracts; the practical suggestions on abstracts, requisitions, and replies; the peculiar arrangement of the Conveyancing Forms; the suggestions connected with Mortgage Securities, and the more special forms; the forms and points as to trusts for Creditors, Bankruptcy, and Insolvency; the providing for sale of copyholds under a will; the mode of obtaining Partition; the enfranchisement contracts; the arrangement of Court-keeping business, and Forms of Entries; and especially to the parts relating to Steward's Fees.

A full Analysis of the contents has also been given, with a view to turn the attention more immediately to the particular points on which information is desired; and throughout the work every care has been taken to combine methodical arrangement with practical suggestions, and precedents drawn from drafts in actual practice.

CONTENTS.

—◆—

ANALYSIS OF CONTENTS OF PART I.

PRACTICE ON ADMISSIONS.

Of Devisee.

Sect.

1. Extracts from will, and what to contain; delivery to steward, and what instructions required.
2. When admission should be taken, and remarks as to advantages of early admission.
3. Mode of taking admission, and as to admission by attorney.
4. Fee on admission by attorney.
5. Consequences of not taking admission at third court.
6. Steward's rights to fees before admission.
7. Fine not usually fixed before admission, and as to amount, and when payable.
8. Steward's fees.
9. Delivery of copy admission.

Of Purchaser.

10. As to admission being compellable, and general instructions by reference.

Of Heir.

11. Difference in instructions.
12. As to customary descent.
13. Mode of compelling admission.

Of Widow to Freebench.

14. Observation as to right.

PRACTICE ON PURCHASES.

PRACTICE ON MORTGAGES AND ASSIGNMENTS OF MORTGAGES.

ASSIGNMENTS FOR BENEFIT OF CREDITORS.

BANKRUPTCY.

WILLS.

PARTITION.

ENFRANCHISEMENT.

APPENDIX TO PART I.

PURCHASES AND SALES.

MORTGAGES.

ANALYSIS OF COURT-KEEPING PART.

—

FORMS.

PART I.

COPYHOLD PRACTICE.

COPYHOLD PRACTICE.

PRACTICE ON ADMISSIONS.

On behalf of Devisee.

SECT. 1. THE solicitor for a devisee will make extracts from the will, giving the date, name, and description of the testator; the parts devising the property to the party claiming; and, though not absolutely necessary, it might be as well to state the court in which and date when proved, as the steward's mention of the proof on the court rolls will frequently save expense in searching for the will in after transactions.

These extracts should be delivered or sent to the steward, with instructions for admission, either before or at the court wherein admission is intended to be taken. The instructions need not be in any particular form, and are usually in a letter to the steward, requesting that he will, at the next court, admit the party after the death of the testator under the will, of which extracts are sent.

2. The admission should regularly be taken at the first, second, or third court after the death, and which generally gives about a year's time; but as a fee of 6*s*. 8*d*. (and, according to the charge of some stewards, 10*s*.) is charged for each proclamation and entry, and the fees are otherwise enlarged by increased

1   B

length of admission, and as the steward, on be-half of the lord, frequently makes some abatement in the fine, or rather asks a somewhat less fine, if the tenant comes in soon, it is in general better to take an early admission; and a still stronger reason exists, which is, that the devisee has not a devisable interest before admitted. See *Wainwright* v. *Elwell*, 1 Mad. Rep. 627; see also *Wright* v. *Banks*, 3 B. & A. 664; *King* v. *Turner*, 1 Sim. & Stu. 545; and *Phillips* v. *Phillips*, 1 Mylne & Keen, 649.

3. Either the party attends personally and takes admission, or attends by attorney; and more fre-quently than otherwise (with a view to save expence) if the devisee's solicitor lives at any distance from the place where the court is held, he merely gives the steward the above instructions, and the steward's clerk, or any other person present at the court, takes admittance.

4. The steward's fee on admittance by attorney is 6*s*. 8*d*., whether the devisee's solicitor or the stew-ard's clerk attends.

5. Should the party not attend at the third court, the steward awards seizure, and issues a pre-cept directing the bailiff to seize the copyholds, and to make return at the next court; unless, therefore, the party should come in at the third court, the steward's fees will be very considerably increased on the re-grant at a subsequent Court.

6. Under 48 G. 3, c. 149, s. 34, the steward is entitled to demand payment of his fees before admis-sion; but this demand is scarcely ever put in force.

7. The lord is not bound to, nor does he gene-rally declare, the amount of fine till admission takes place; but such amount is by law limited to two years' improved value, deducting quit rent, but not land tax. (See *Grant* v. *Astle*, Doug. 722; also *Halton*, Bart. v. *Hassell*, 2 Strange, 1042. See also on the subject of fines, *Earl Verulam* v. *Howard*, 4 Moore & Payne, 148; *Wilson* v. *Hoare*, 1 B. & A. 350; and cases therein cited.) The fine is however

2

payable within a reasonable time after the court, usually three weeks.

8. The steward either at the court, or shortly afterwards, delivers or sends his bill of fees, the propriety of which the devisee's solicitor will see into, and should he be unable to adjust the amount with the steward, he will on behalf of his client make such a tender as he deems sufficient, and leave the steward to his remedy by action. It is however much to be regretted that the amount of fees charged by stewards differ very greatly, and that considerable diversity of opinion exists with regard to the amount of the different items which ought to be allowed. The principle which the Courts seem to lean to is that of giving the steward a fair remuneration for his services, and the most just way of so doing appears to be the allowing as much as in a liberal scale of conveyancing costs would be charged for the same work and skill. In the part relating to Court-Keeping (s. 431, &c.) some full observations and precedents of fees will be found; and reference to the following cases will be found useful on this head: *Everest* v. *Glynn*, 6 Taunt. 425; *Attree* v, *Scutt*, 6 East, 476; *Garland* v. *Jekyll*, 2 Bing. 293; *Rex* v. *Rigge*, 2 B. & A. 550.

9. The steward is bound to deliver the copy admission on demand at the expiration of four months, and at all events to make it out by that time. (See 48 G. 3, c. 149, s. 33.) This duty, however, is too frequently neglected, till repeated applications are made for the copy, notwithstanding the penalty imposed by the Act.

Admission of Purchaser.

10. The instructions will comprise the extracts from the bargain and sale, if under an executorship, with the production of the original for presentment by the homage; but where a surrender is passed, it will in itself contain sufficient instructions. The fees will be found in s. 431, 432, &c.; and it might

3   B 2

be remarked, that except by custom, a lord cannot compel admission of surrenderee during life of tenant; but, it should be added, that such custom is pretty general. Section 3 to 9 will also apply in general to admissions of purchaser.

Admission of an Heir.

11. In this case the only difference will be the substitution of a particular description of the party claiming, and of his right for the clause from a will.

12. It must be borne in mind, that the descent is in very few manors to the eldest son, but according to the particular custom of the manor, which should be ascertained by application to the steward, or from other authentic information, before instructions for admission. The custom in most manors is that of borough English, being to the youngest son; but in some manors gavelkind descent prevails, which is in favour of all the sons equally. The customary descent only extends as particularly named, and not to collaterals; thus, the eldest brother, or the eldest son of the eldest brother, will succeed in default of children. See *Ratcliffe* v. *Chaplin*, 4 Leo. 242; S. C. Godb. 166; 12 East. 62; *Roe* d. *Berbie* v. *Parker*, 5 T. R. 26; and see generally on this head Scriven on Copyholds, 34, &c.; and 1 Coventry on Copyholds, 223, &c.

13. Should the steward refuse to admit, but which however it would be against his interest to do, application may be made to King's Bench for mandamus to compel him. See *Rex* v. *Brewer's Company*; 4 Dowl. and Ry. 492.

To a Widow's Freebench.

14. Except by custom, the widow is not dowable (*Brown's case*, 4 Co. 22 a); but by custom of very many manors she is entitled to one-third of the copyholds which her husband stood admitted to at the time of his death, as freebench, and in some

manors to other portions, and in some manors has a freehold dowable right.

15. On ascertaining the custom, the only instructions will be the name and description of the widow, and the common instructions for admission (s. 1.)

To a Husband's Curtesy.

16. The same observations apply to this as to dower.

Admission on behalf of a Minor.

17. In cases of minors, it is usual for the party to be admitted by any person attending, and a guardian appointed at the Court (usually the surviving parent, or guardian named in the testor's will).

18. The mode of enforcing admission and paying the fine will be found in the part relating to Court-Keeping (s. 415), and where also is quoted the Act giving the power to the guardian to obtain repayment of the amount paid on admission.

19. In other respects the instructions must be similar to those on other admissions under a will.

Admission on behalf of Joint-Tenants or Tenants in Common.

20. The only additional observations in these cases will be the urging a full consideration of the question as to the fees which the steward may charge, and a reference to the subsequent part of this part relative to fees, 431, &c. to the case of *Attree* v. *Scutt* before cited, and the cases therein referred to, which will give full information as to these admissions.

In the case of joint-tenants, it was recently decided that the practice of charging two years as a fine for first life, one year for second, half year for third, &c. was correct. See *Wilson* v. *Hoare*, 1 B. & A. 350. Of course tenants in common only pay the amount of the usual fine between them; as on each life falling, another fine will be payable for his share.

5

PRACTICE ON PURCHASES.

___

The Contract or Treaty for Purchase.

21. In treating for the purchase of copyholds, the following points should be attended to:—The ascertaining whether the property is subject to a fine arbitrary (two years on death or alienation), or a fine certain; as, unless specified, the former will be presumed—the amount of the quit rent and land tax—and whether liable to heriots (for the learning on which see Scriven on Copyholds, 423, &c., and Coventry, 298, &c.) The purchaser should also learn that there is no level rate or other charge payable under a local but under a public act, as in *Barrand* v. *Archer*, 1 Simon 433, compensation was refused on such a charge.

22. The purchaser should object to take timber by valuation, the right to the timber, except in certain cases, being in the lord; (see on this subject Scriven on Copyholds); but the tenant being entitled to fell timber for repairs, some amount might be allowed, though a purchaser should not agree to specifically take by valuation.

23. The next point to be attended to will be the time from which the purchaser is to be entitled to the possession and the rents, and where *possession* is required, care should be taken to stipulate for such actual possession.

24. Connected with this is the provision for payment of interest in case of non-completion of the purchase at the time fixed, the rate of which is usually five per cent., but the purchaser might urge that four per cent. would be more just, and press for the inser-

6

tion of that amount in the agreement ; he should also object to the insertion of the words "*from whatever cause arising*," in the interest clause, as he ought in fairness to only pay interest when the delay arises from his default ; and the case of *Esdaile* v. *Stevenson*, 1 Sim. & Stu. 122, decided that with such a stipulation, even where the delay was occasioned by the vendor, the purchaser would be liable to pay interest agreeably to the condition ; and though circumstances might occur in which a different decision would be given, yet great difficulty would be thrown on the purchaser by such stipulation.

25. Where the purchaser is desirous to have the property accord strictly with the description, it might prevent difficulty were the agreement to state his intention not to accept compensation in the event of the vendor being unable to convey the precise property or interest contracted to be sold.

26. The proper stipulations should be made for delivery, at the vendor's expence, of an abstract of title certified by the steward, the making a marketable title, and the delivery of copies of admissions and other acts of Court and documents forming the title ; though in default of express stipulation to the contrary, the vendor would be bound to deliver copies.

27. It is highly desirable to have an abstract certified by the steward as the most certain way of getting an abstract free from misrepresentations or concealments.

28. In purchasing at an auction, a deduction should be made to meet the expence thrown on the purchaser under the conditions of sale, for copies, certificates, affidavits, production of court rolls, &c., and the purchaser should be guided in his biddings accordingly, so as to prepare for the additional expence.

The Agreement.

29. The terms of contract being settled, the agree-

7

ment is to be prepared, and forms embodying most of the terms likely to require attention will be found in precedents Nos. 271 and 227.

30. Two parts of the agreement should be written on plain paper, and signed by the parties, each taking one. If thought advisable, the agreement can, if of the class requiring a 20s. stamp, be stamped within twenty-one days, without payment of any penalty; (see Stamp Act, 55 G. 3); or afterwards on payment of penalty of 5l., and the usual practice is to omit the stamp, except where difficulties are expected from the other party.

31. Should the purchaser have made his own contract, and entered into an agreement made by the vendor's solicitor, the first step will be to obtain the duplicate agreement, or should none be delivered, a copy of the agreement must be procured from the vendor's solicitor.

32. The usual practice with regard to the expense of the purchase agreement is for each party to pay half, but of course this is open to alteration in making the contract.

33. Should the purchase have been made at an auction, the purchaser will have the auctioneer's agreement for delivery to his solicitor, and which can be stamped in the same way as a common agreement.

34. It would be very advantageous that a solicitor on receiving the purchase contract from his client, should, where the purchase is of any considerable amount, shortly explain to his client the effect of the contract on his will and disposition of his property.

35. He should particularly draw his attention to the circumstances, that without republication of his will, the newly purchased estate will not pass; that the heir will, on acceptance of the title, be entitled to enforce the contract at the expence of the personal estate; that the taking a conveyance to uses to bar dower will require a republication of the will,

8

though this only applies to a freehold part; provision should be made for giving the value of the estate to the party to whom he intended to give the estate, in the event of the contract being rescinded; even buying a different interest in the property, where before he had a partial interest, would also render a republication necessary, and the gift of such previous interest should be extended by sufficient words. (See on this subject Sugden's Letters, p. 19 & 20; as to devise before surrender see *Lady Foljamb's case*, 1 Ch. Ca. 39.) Attention must however be given to the alterations which the bill now before Parliament will effect, should it become a law.

36. The purchaser's solicitor will, when he has perused the purchase agreement, apply to the vendor's solicitor for the abstract of title.

37. The question then arises as to the abstract he is entitled to require, and whether he is entitled, in the absence of express stipulation either way, to an abstract certified by the steward; or bound to accept an abstract of the documents which the vendor's solicitor holds, or with the contents of which he is acquainted, and to compare the same with the court rolls himself, in order to ascertain its correctness; and if the latter should be deemed the practice, who is bound to pay the expence attendant on such comparison.

38. In support of the former position, it appears by Sugden's Vendors and Purchasers, ch. 9, that " the vendor must at his own expence furnish the purchaser with an abstract of his (the vendor's) muniments, and deduce a clear title," and that " the abstract ought to mention every incumbrance whatever affecting the estate." Now the title of the vendor is on the court rolls, and without having an abstract of all such parts of the rolls as apply to the vendor's estate, it is very doubtful whether a certain and correct abstract can be obtained of all the different steps of the title and of all the incumbrances; particularly as a previous conditional surrender or mortgage will not be

referred to in a subsequent admission, a copy of which may be held by the vendor, and an abstract of whose documents may give an apparently clear, though in fact an incorrect, title; whilst an abstract of the court rolls would give an incumbered, though actual title. To deduce a " clear title," and mention " every incumbrance," it appears that an abstract of the court rolls would be required. Independently of Mr. Sugden's authority, it seems conformable to reason that the abstract furnished by a person having in his possession all the transfers and charges on the estate, and not interested in misleading either party, should be far better than the abstract of partial documents prepared by the solicitor, interested in the concealment of objections to the title; and as it will appear clearly that an examination of the court rolls is requisite, it would, on the ground of economy alone, be preferable that the steward's abstract should be prepared, than that the vendor's solicitor should prepare a probably imperfect abstract, and that the subsequent additional expence of the examination with the court rolls should be occasioned.

39. The practice however inclines to this. The vendor prepares the best abstract he can from the documents in his possession, or the knowledge which he possesses of the contents of the documents of title, and either gets the steward to certify the abstract, or the purchaser has to examine the abstract with the court rolls; the steward's charges, and other expences in such examination usual in freehold cases being payable by the vendor.

40. A difficulty sometimes occurs by the steward refusing to allow a comparison of the abstract, contending for the practice first alluded to; but in such case, as it seems clear that the vendor is bound in the absence of stipulation to the contrary, to furnish the purchaser with the production; the purchaser's solicitor should give him notice accordingly. (See form post, 273.)

41. The mode of obtaining inspection is by man-

10

damus, as to which, and generally as to right to inspection, see Tidd's Practice, 499, 1052; *Stracey's Case*, Latch. 182; *Rex* v. *Lucas*, 10 East, 235; *Rex* v. *Town*, 4 Maule & S. 162; *Crew* v. *Saunders*, 2 Str. 1005; and *Bateman* v. *Phillips*, 4 Taunt. 162; and see general rule in Moore & Scott's Repts. 430.

42. A difficulty also frequently arises respecting the amount of the steward's fees, on allowing an inspection of the rolls, either generally, or with a view to the comparison of the abstract; respecting which, some observations will be made in 391, 392, 393, 431, &c.

43. The purchaser's solicitor should get the undertaking of the vendor's solicitor to pay the charges of the steward, in order to guard against difficulty on settlement of the purchase. As to propriety of the amount, see form, No. 274.

44. Having obtained the abstract, and made an appointment for examination with the writings, the next step will be

The Examination of the Abstract.

45. Where a steward's abstract is delivered, and the date of the steward's certificate is very recent, there will, unless the purchase is to a considerable amount, be very little necessity for examining the abstract with the court rolls, further back than such certificate; though of course it would be of advantage to do so; but it will be necessary to examine the abstract with the documents in possession of the vendor's solicitor, in order to ascertain that there are no covenants, agreements, or other documents, affecting the equitable title, throwing a doubt upon the absolute property in the vendor, and the freedom from annual payments, rights of way, &c.

46. Where the abstract is prepared by the vendor's solicitor, the purchaser's solicitor should not only carefully examine it with the writings held by the vendor's solicitor, but also with the court rolls; and as the steward will seldom give much assistance

11

where he is deprived of the emolument arising from drawing the abstract, the inspection of the court rolls must also be carefully made; or the better plan is, where the steward will do so for a moderate fee, to have him certify the abstract as being correct up to the certificate; though such certificate, where the vendor pays for comparison with the court rolls, would it is presumed have to be borne by the purchaser. This certificate would be of use on a future sale, with a view to save the expence of a fresh examination, by inserting a stipulation in such future contract, that a certified abstract should be deemed sufficient.

47. The importance of a careful examination of the abstract with the rolls, will be shewn by reference to a too common practice; where there are copyholds on several manors appearing to have been for many years held as one estate, and the vendor's solicitor has some of the documents of each, what is wanting in one manor exists in another, and he is thereby enabled to draw partly from documents, and partly from guess, a set of abstracts which to a careless observer appear as if regularly drawn from documents; and if pressed as to the sources from which he gives the title, he refers to the court rolls, or professes that he was guided by former abstracts.

48. It frequently happens that the writings are held by a mortgagee, in which case the abstract will most probably have been obtained from the steward, although the vendor's solicitor may sometimes prepare it from any drafts or extracts which he may have, or from an old abstract, in which case it is necessary that particular attention should be paid to the examination.

49. When the writings are held by a mortgagee, Mr. Coventry states in his Conveyancing Evidence, that such possession is deemed the possession of the vendor, and that consequently the purchaser must bear the expense of examining the abstract; but it is submitted that such rule would be liable to this.

12

qualification ; that if the mortgagee lives at a distance from the vendor, the expence of the purchaser's journey should be paid by the vendor, as the former purchases on the faith of having to attend at the office of the vendor's solicitor, and it would be as unjust to make him take a long journey to examine writings held by a mortgagee, as if held by another party ; and the practice inclines to the position here stated.

50. Attention to the following points will be of service in comparing the abstract with the writings, the importance of doing which properly, cannot be too strongly urged.

Commencement of the Title.

51. *By Purchase.*—Where the title commences with a purchase, using the word in its common acceptation, it will be under a surrender, or a bargain and sale from executors, or assignees of a bankrupt.

52. If under a surrender, notice particularly the statement in the admission, of the previous admission of the surrenderor, in order to see that there appears nothing throwing a doubt as to his power to surrender, or raising a suspicion that an estate tail existed; or if he is stated to have taken admission after a recovery, it would be prudent to see that the recovery was correctly suffered and the entail destroyed. It should be remarked, that though a recovery could only be suffered of copyholds under a custom, yet in most manors the custom exists.

53. If under a bargain and sale from executors, it would be requisite to inspect the will, in order to see the manner in which the power was given, that a surrender to use of will was made, and that the will was subsequent to such surrender, or the surrender, to uses declared or to be declared.

54. With respect to a bargain and sale under a bankruptcy, at such a length of time there would be little occasion to refer back.

55. Of course it will be ascertained that the ab-

13

stract states correctly and with sufficient fulness, the parties, their acts, the parcels, and the grant; and that no exceptions or reservations are omitted to be abstracted.

56. *By Will.*—Where the first document is a will, it would be right to ascertain that there existed a previous surrender to its use, either previously to date of will, or to uses declared or to be declared, as previously to the Act of 55 G. 3, such surrender was requisite, although Courts of Equity would supply it in certain cases in favour of child, wife, or creditor. See 1 Preston on Abstracts, 204 ; 1 Coventry's Copyholds, 178, &c.; Scriven's Copyholds, 275, &c.

57. It should also be seen that the contents are fully abstracted so far as relate to the property in question, and it would be right to notice the way in which the will appears to be attested, though a will of copyholds does not require three witnesses, or the formalities attendant on freehold will. See 1 Coventry's Copyholds, 168; Scriven, 302; and see Precedents of Wills, *post.*

58. When the first party admitted appears to have been a minor, the appointment of guardianship in the court rolls should be referred to, in order to ascertain his age, which is generally there stated, with a view to the being satisfied that at the time of the next step in the title, he was competent to perform it.

(59.) When the will is that of a married woman, the previous surrender to the use of her will should be referred to, in order to see whether such surrender was by her and her husband, and whether she was separately examined, as such examination was requisite in order to render the surrender operative during her marriage ; and a surrender to will before her marriage, would be suspended by her marriage. See *George* d. *Thornbury* v. *Rippon & Dowling,* Amb. 627, 473 ; Scriven, 144, 272.

60. *Under a forfeited Mortgage.*—The admission of the mortgagor and his surrender should be

14

referred to, in order to see his competence to mort-gage, and also the mortgage bond, if existing, should be inspected, as also any other documents affecting the mortgage, in order to see that the mortgage has not been recognized as subsisting within the last twenty years.

61. *Under a Descent.*—The previous admission of the last owner should be referred to, and it may be seen whether a surrender to will existed; it should be also seen that there is nothing on the title implying that a will existed. Some observations as to, proof of heirship and intestacy, will be found in the, parts relating to requisitions on the title. In the recent case of *Stevens* v. *Guppy*, 2 Sim. & Stu. 439, it was decided, that when the title commences with the, heir, who claims on the ground of a will being defec-tive, the purchaser is entitled to have such will produced, or evidence given of its contents.

62. *Under surviving Joint Tenant.*—Care should be taken to see that neither party made a sur-render to will, as such surrender would sever the joint tenancy. See Scriven, 151, 273; and *Gale* v. *Gale*, 2 Cox, 136. The following case also occurred to the writer, connected with some manorial property in which he was interested. The parties were admitted as joint tenants, and afterwards each surrendered to the use of her will. On the death of one, the writer required the admission to a moiety, and the party intitled to admission, although a barrister of some standing, and a trustee only under her will, felt bound to concede the point and take admission. This is a point of considerable impor-tance, but very likely to escape attention, from the, habit of considering surrenders to will as mere matters of form.

63. *On the Examination of the Abstract generally,* the following observations will apply.—It would be as well to state in pencil or red ink the day of the inspection, and place, with a view to the question of expence;, and in the margin the exact documents

15.

produced should be stated, as for instance, "Plain copy will produced,"—"Office copy will produced," —"Probate,"—"Pedigree," (a copy of this ought to accompany the abstract,) "Affidavits as follow," (stating them,) "Steward's copy admission," "Plain copy admission," "No copy produced," "Copy surrender," "Bargain and sale," &c.

64. Should any papers appear which are not mentioned in the abstract, note down every one of them, with a view to their careful examination and delivery on completion, thus, "Mortgage bond produced," "Deed of covenant," "Purchase agreement," &c. Carefully read through all the deeds of covenant, take a minute of any contents not abstracted, and if too long to take at the examination, and yet requisite on the title, note the circumstances and outline of contents, or apparent object of the deed, with a view to requiring a supplemental abstract.

65. Particular care should be taken in the examination of deeds of covenant and other documents affecting the equitable title; as frequently rights reserved to other parties, liabilities for joint-rapair of pumps, walls, &c., payment of annual charges, and other points tending to affect the property, are only to be discovered by such careful examination; and unless discovered before completion of the purchase, great difficulty will be experienced by the purchaser in getting redress, and the solicitor justly blamed for negligence.

66. The indorsements on mortgage bonds should also be carefully looked to, and also all warrants to enter satisfaction on mortgages should be read through, as some only extend to a partial discharge of the amount, and others only discharge part of the mortgaged premises. Any deeds of covenant for production should be carefully perused, and the contents alluded to, stating all the documents to which they apply, as it may afterwards appear prudent to call for all such documents, in order to see that they

16

do not incumber the property or affect the title, as the statement in the deeds will be deemed notice to the purchaser of their contents.

67. Should the original copies of admission not be with the writings, the vendor's solicitor should be asked to account for their absence, and his reply noted down; and as respects the later copies, and particularly the copies of the vendor's admission, it is absolutely necessary that a satisfactory account should be given of the possession, since the case of *Winter* v. *Anson*, 3 Russ. 493, decided that the copy may be deposited in the hands of a creditor, and will in the hands of that party create a lien on the estate.

68. Should the vendor's solicitor name the party holding them, it would be proper to see such party, and compare the abstract with the copies; at the same time stating the purpose of the examination, and requiring a statement from him of his claim or disclaimer of right, and the solicitor should note down accurately his reply.

69. Should the vendor's solicitor state that the copies were lost, such statement should be noted, with a view to requiring an affidavit or other evidence of the correctness of the statement.

70. On the general principle, the expense of going to the residence of such party would be payable by the vendor, he being bound to produce the writings for the purchaser's inspection, and the purchaser being bound at the vendor's expence to go to such place. See generally on this head, Sugden's V. & P.; and Coventry's Conveyancing Evidence.

71. Having carefully examined the abstract with the writings, the next point for consideration will be its sufficiency as respects the comprising all the documents of title, and extending over a proper period, and up to the time of purchase; and should the purchaser's solicitor consider that the abstract is defective in any of these points, he will apply to the vendor's solicitor for a supplemental or amended abstract.

17

72. *Supplemental Abstract.*—This should comprise all the documents omitted in the abstract previously delivered, and extend the title so as to cover the required period, and embody all the documents and matters of title up to the purchase ; and this abstract, it is presumed, the purchaser's solicitor will be entitled to examine, in the same manner as the original abstract.

73. *Amended Abstract.*—It may happen that the abstract, though mentioning all the documents of title, has not abstracted them with sufficient fulness, and that from their length, the purchaser's solicitor was unable at the time of examination to make the requisite additions ; in which case the purchaser's solicitor will return the abstract to be amended by the requisite additions, shortly adverted to in the note made by the purchaser's solicitor on examining the abstract, and which, when completed, will be examined as the supplemental abstract.

74. Should the vendor's solicitor refuse to deliver a supplemental abstract, the purchaser's solicitor should submit the abstract to counsel, with his notes of the documents which he requires to have abstracted, and act on his advice as to the waiving the supplemental abstract, or taking proceedings to enforce its delivery; and at the same time he might instruct the counsel, in the event of his not deeming the supplemental abstract essential, to peruse and advise on the title. A similar practice should also be adopted with respect to abstracts deemed not sufficiently full. In small purchases, and where the vendor's solicitor is thought likely to interpose difficulties, it will be prudent for the purchaser's solicitor to take the best notes he can on the examination of the abstract, and rest satisfied with such notes instead of a full abstract.

75. *Perusal of the Abstract and requisitions thereon.*—The perusal and requisitions will next require attention on behalf of the purchaser. Except in purchases of small amount, the more usual practice is

18

to submit the abstract after its examination to counsel for perusal; but as it frequently happens that from a desire to avoid expence in small purchases, or where there are copyholds on several manors, the solicitor himself peruses the abstracts and prepares the requisitions on them, the following observations will facilitate such perusal and requisitions.

76. It should be remarked at the outset, that from the much greater simplicity in copyhold than in freehold titles, the difficulty on copyhold requisitions is much less than on freeholds, except where there exists a complicated equitable title, as in cases of property held by brewers and other partnerships.

77. On copyhold abstracts, difficulties, as often if not more frequently arise, on questions connected with the documents to the possession of which a purchaser is entitled, and the expence of copies, than as to the title; the questions likely to arise on the former heads will therefore be first considered.

78. With regard to the right of the purchaser to copies of the acts of court, in the simple case of an entire purchase, when the vendor holds the stamped copies delivered by the stewards, no doubt can exist that the purchaser is entitled to have them on completion of the purchase.

79. The other cases will be those when the copyholder only sells part of the estate, sells to different purchasers, or in which the vendor, though selling the whole of his copyhold, either never had the copies or has lost them.

80. When a copyholder sells part, the rule appears to be that in default of express stipulation, the purchaser will be entitled to the possession of the stamped copies, if his portion of the property is the greater in value; and if less, the vendor will be entitled to the possession, on delivering copies (of what kind will be afterwards considered) at his own expence, entering into a covenant to produce the documents of title; such production to be at the expence of the purchaser. Sug. V. & P.; *Berry* v. *Young*, 2

19

Eep. Ca. 640. The authority given relates more particularly to freehold deeds; but it will be borne in mind that the original copies are equally evidences of title, and that consequently the principle would apply in the present case.

81. When the vendor sells to several purchasers, the rule appears to be that the largest purchaser shall have the stamped copies, and that the other purchasers are entitled to other copies and covenants for production at the expence of the vendor; but generally in such cases the vendor has the prudence to guard by his conditions of sale against his being subjected to such an expence.

82. Considerable difference of opinion exists relative to the kind of copies to which purchasers are entitled where the original steward's copies cannot be delivered; and a case came within the writer's own knowledge, where the opinions of three different counsel were taken on the point in the same sale, and each of them expressed a different opinion as to the copies to be delivered, though all agreed that the purchaser was entitled to copies. The first thought that the purchaser was entitled to copies on the same stamps as those originally delivered; the second, that he was entitled to copies on attested copy stamps; and the third was of opinion, that by the delivery of the stamped copies the steward complied with the Stamp Act, and that any subsequent copies should be on plain paper; and when it is considered, that on any question requiring legal proof of the title, the steward could be subpœnaed, and thus the original rolls produced, it would seem that the latter opinion must be most consonant with reason.

83. With regard to the expence, no doubt seems to exist that the expence should be borne by the vendor in the absence of stipulation to the contrary.

84. The importance of accounting for, the possession of the original copies has been before alluded to, and it may be proper to again suggest that in all cases where the later copies, and particularly that of

20

the vendor's admission, are not forthcoming, the loss or destruction should be most satisfactorily proved; and it would be satisfactory, not only for immediate use, but as a protection on a future sale, to have an affidavit made, explaining the circumstances of the loss.

85. In framing requisitions on titles, proof of the identity of the present with the former description should be required, though, since the late case of *Long* v. *Collier*, 3 Russ. 267, less strictness on this head need be adopted than previously. Should, however, the property be part freehold and part copyhold, the purchaser should, unless precluded by the conditions, require the vendor to set out in the best way he can the copyhold and the freehold parts; and in some cases it would be of advantage to prevail on the steward to present a map, shewing the copyhold, and have it entered on the Court rolls, even should the purchaser have to pay his fee for so doing.

86. The production of all the documents on the abstract and affidavits, or declarations under 5 & 6 W. 4, c. 62, verifying pedigrees. heirships, &c., with certificates of all the births, marriages, and deaths in the title, should be required; and where there appears any doubt as to the age of a party which might affect any act forming part of the title, an affidavit or declaration in proof of age should be given. Also affidavits of identity of persons where requisite; also that equitable interests should be discharged by release, or surrender and release, if from a married woman. On surrenders under a power of attorney, proof should be required that the party was living at the time of the surrender being passed. When a right arises under the will of a married woman, it should appear that subsequently to her marriage she, with her husband, surrendered to the use of her will; as a previous surrender would be inoperative, and the late statute of 55 G. 3, would not appear to operate so as to dispense with her separate examination. The points touched on in the

21

parts relative to the abstract generally, and its examination, will also suggest most of the other matters usually becoming the subject of requisitions.

87. The requisitions being drawn, are to be copied on foolscap or brief paper, according to the length, and sent to the vendor's solicitor for compliance.

88. On obtaining his replies they should be perused, and when not satisfactory, the purchaser's solicitor will of course again urge a full compliance with such requisitions as he does not feel it proper to dispense with. In some cases it may be prudent to lay the requisitions and replies before counsel to advise on the necessity for further compliance.

89. Hitherto it has not been necessary in copyhold purchases to search for judgments; but the abolition of arrest for debt bill making copyholds liable to judgments, the practice on searches under that bill, being passed, will be similar to that on freehold purchases. See Sugden's Vendors and Purchasers; and a reference to the act, from its special provisions, would also be advisable.

90. Should the vendor's solicitor refuse to comply with any requisitions which the purchaser's solicitor deems indispensable, it will be requisite for the latter to adopt means for enforcing compliance, either by an action on the contract, or which is better, by a bill for specific performance. See Sugden's Vendors and Purchasers, c. 4, s. 3. When the vendor's solicitor, either in the first answering the requisitions, or in the subsequent correspondence with regard to them, appears anxious for delay, it will be prudent for the purchaser's solicitor to have the purchase-money, if lying idle, paid into a particular bank, appropriated to the purchase, and to give notice to the vendor, or his solicitor, of those circumstances, with a view to avoid the payment of subsequent interest (see form 275, 295); but where the contract provides that interest shall be paid on delay in completion, from whatever cause arising, the only course for the

22

purchaser beyond the legal remedy, would be a bill for specific performance.

91. In purchases under the directions of a Court of equity, the purchaser must, at his own expence, procure a report from the master of his being the best bidder, and get such report confirmed; the practice on such report and confirmation will be found in Sugden's V. & P., c. 2, s. 1, and the Books on Practice in Equity.

92. The purchaser should not obtain the report till satisfied of the title, (See Sugden V. & P.)

93. He may also obtain an order to pay his purchase money into Court, and be let into possession (Sugden V. & P., c. 2, s. 11); and also if an incumbrance exists, he may, after notice, apply to the Court for leave to pay off incumbrances, and to pay residue into Court, but this can only be done when the parties consent.

94. Till the purchaser is satisfied with the title, he will take care not to obtain possession, except with a stipulation that such act shall not be deemed an acceptance of the title.

95. This observation does not however apply to cases where at the beginning of the contract, and before the title is at all enquired into, possession is given.

96. Should the vendor refuse to comply with the requisitions. and yet require completion of the purchase, he will either proceed at law, or more generally in equity, for specific performance; and if the sale be under the Court, by motion for payment of purchase money, after obtaining and confirming master's report of purchase; in either case the purchaser should obtain a reference as to the title—(see Sug. V. & P., c. 4, s. 3; and the different works on Chancery practice).

97. Even after confirmation of report in favour of title, if a new fact appears, by which the title is affected, the title will be referred back to the master; *Jeudwine* v. *Allcock*, 1 Mad. 597; and where it ap-

23

pears that the vendor's solicitor was previously acquainted with such defects, the case of *Dalby* v.
Pullen, 1 Russ. & Mylne 296, will be found to
strongly confirm this position.

98. Should the contract be rescinded on a sale
under a Court of equity by the biddings being opened
(see Sug. V. & P.); and the purchaser have paid his
money into Court, he would be entitled to receive it
with his costs; but should it at his application have
been laid out in the funds, he would have the stock,
whether of less or greater value.

99. When either party fails to perform the contract, the other, if he means to rescind the contract, should give a clear notice of his intention. *Ar-
miger* v. *Clark*, Bunb. 111; *Whitby* v. *Cottle*, 1 Sim.
& Stu. 174.

Drawing Conveyance.

100. The next step will be to prepare the draft
conveyance, which being at the purchaser's expence,
will be prepared by his solicitor.

101. Warrants to enter satisfaction on conditional surrenders, deeds of covenant for production,
or such other documents as are to be paid for by the
vendor, will be prepared by his solicitor.

102. In common cases the most usual conveyance will be a surrender, (forms for which will be
found in Appendix, Nos. 276 to 295); with a deed
of covenant or bond for title, (also in Appendix, Nos.
296 & 297,) and the following points may be useful
in preparing copyhold conveyances.

103. As a general practice, make the wife of the
vendor a party to the surrender; for although she
would in most manors be only entitled to freebench
of the property remaining in her husband at his
death, yet her joining, will prevent a captious objection by a future purchaser, and the present purchaser
incurs no expence; the only additional fee of 6s. 8d.
in consequence of her joining, being payable by the
vendor.

24

104. Where a new description of the property would be advisable, insert such description, as well as the old one, in the surrender, taking care to give the new as the actual description, and the old as the description of reference; for the reason stated in 1 Preston on Abstracts, 85.

105. In preparing the deed of covenant or bond, little difficulty can be experienced, as similar rules will apply relative to the covenants as would be adopted on a sale of freehold. The usual forms will be found in the Appendix.

106. Any surrenders and releases from interested parties, are usually, prepared by the vendor's solicitor, who will also prepare the deed of covenant for production when his client has to bear the expence; and when the purchaser has to bear the expence, the releases may be drawn from precedents 298 to 300, and with which forms the purchaser can compare the drafts sent by the vendor. The deed of covenant will be as in freehold cases.

In purchases of Executors

107. It will be prudent to recite the will fully, and to state the court where, and the time when it was proved, as a mode of facilitating any future references to the will. Of course, the executors can only be compelled to enter into the same covenant as in freehold sales, being that against their own incumbrances.

108. Where legatees would be the parties to a freehold conveyance, it might be prudent to make them directing parties to the bargain and sale, or to see that they sign the proper legacy discharges; and the case of *Johnson* v. *Kennett*, 6 Sim. 384, deciding that a purchaser was bound to see to application of money in payment of legacies, when debts and legacies charged and debts paid, would induce the exercise of that percaution, whenever the usual receipt clause is omitted. A surrender and release from the heir after admission of the purchaser, would in some cases

be prudent, and to obtain which, a power of attorney from him to an indifferent party to surrender and release might be advisable.

109. It should be borne in mind in preparing these conveyances, that if there be words of devise in the will, the executors must be admitted and surrender; and if the words of the power are defective, the heir must be admitted and surrender, in addition to the conveyance by the executors; or at least a surrender and release should be obtained from the heir after admission of purchaser. Forms will be found, No. 301 and 298, &c.

Under a Bankruptcy.

110. Previously to the Bankrupt Act of 6 Geo. 4, the conveyance of copyhold property under a bankruptcy was simply by bargain and sale from the commissioners, making the assignees parties, acknowledging payment, and releasing: but since 6 G. 4, the conveyance is by bargain and sale from the commissioners, making the assignees parties; and in such bargain and sale is contained an authority to some party (very frequently the bankrupt, and sometimes the purchaser's solicitor) to surrender to the purchaser; and under such bargain and sale and surrender, the purchaser is admitted. The forms of bargain and sale, exhibit, affidavit of execution, and surrender, will be found in the Appendix 302 to 305, and 288.

111. The rules as to enrolment of proceedings, and bargain and sale, will be found in the Bankrupt Act, 6 G. 4, and the different works on Bankruptcy Practice. In the Appendix, No. 305, will be found the opinion of an eminent conveyancer as to the mode of conveyance where the property was mortgaged by bankrupt for more than the value, and one of the assignees was dead, and also one of the commissioners. This will assist in drawing most of the more complicated conveyances under a bankruptcy.

26

Under an Insolvency.

112. Where the owner has taken the benefit of the Insolvent Act, the following will, under the Insolvent Debtors' Act, 7 G. 4, c. 57, s. 20, be the mode of conveyance. The assignment by the provisional assignee to the assignee or assignees, shall be entered on the court rolls of the manor, and thereupon the assignee may surrender to the purchaser. See also sec. 245 ; and surrender, 290.

Of Property mortgaged.

113. The conveyance will be by a surrender from vendor and a warrant to enter satisfaction on the mortgage.

114. This warrant will be prepared by the vendor's solicitor, and sent to the purchaser's solicitor for approval. Forms will be found in Appendix, No. 306, &c.; or should it be intended to let the mortgage remain, notice should be given to mortgagee of the conveyance.

115. If the property is in mortgage and sold under an executorship, the mortgagee will be made a party to the bargain and sale, acknowledging receipt; and a warrant to enter satisfaction will also be obtained, as in common cases, for the purpose of entry on the court rolls.

116. In cases of bankruptcy the like practice will take place. See Appendix, No. 302, &c.; and when mortgaged for more than value, see sec. 111, and 305.

Of Equitable Interests.

117. Forms of conveyance will be found in Appendix (Surrenders and Releases), and it will be borne in mind that though the legal estate in copyholds cannot be conveyed except by the customary modes of assurance, equitable interests may be bound by deeds or contracts:—1 Preston on Abstracts, 203, &c., and see Scriven and Coventry on Copyholds.

But it should be added, that there appears no mode of conveying the contingent interest of a married woman; as a contingent interest can only be barred by contract, and a married women cannot bar her interest by contract.

Under Sale by Tenant in Tail.

118. The form of a conveyance under Abolition of Fines and Recovery Act, will be found in Appendix, No. 294 & 5, being that substituted for the previous customary recovery. The importance of carefully perusing the act, so as to make the conveyance come within its provisions by any requisite alterations, need scarcely be adverted to.

Under Sale by Joint Tenants or Tenants in Common.

119. The conveyance in this and the following three cases will be found in Appendix 279, 280, and 296 or 297.

On Sale of Reversions or Remainders.

120. See Appendix No. 285 and 296 or 297; and it will be borne in mind that the lord having a tenant, cannot compel admission till such tenant's death. See *Rex* v. *Lord of Manor of Oundle*, 1 Adol. and Ellis, 283,

Of a Life Interest and Copyholds for Life.

121. See Appendix, Nos. 282, 3, and 4, and 296, or 297.

Of a Moiety or other Share.

122. The form of conveyance will be found in Appendix, Nos. 286, and 296 or 297.

Under Chancery.

123. In addition to preparing conveyance, purchaser must obtain masters' report of purchaser, and obtain the confirmation of report. See Sug. V. & P. c. 2, s. 1, and the different works on Chancery

Practice. The forms of conveyance will be found in Appendix, No. 291.

Premises part freehold and part copyhold, and as to Leaseholds.

124. When an estate, part freehold and part copyhold, is purchased, the conveyance is generally by a lease and release or other usual conveyance of the freehold, with either a covenant to surrender the copyhold whenever called on, and adding covenants for title both of freehold and copyhold, or, which is better, to have a concurrent surrender, and refer to the same in the freehold conveyance, adding covenants for title as well to copyhold as freehold. A form will be found in Appendix, Nos. 311, 276, &c. It is in general better to convey leaseholds separately by the common assignment, as being less confused in form, and with care, even less expensive than a lengthy and involved draft, comprising all in one conveyance. An inspection of the drafts combining all three conveyances given in Mr. Coventry's work on copyholds, will prove the truth of this observation, for though he has taken great pains to simplify the drafts, they are still very objectionable. Mr. Serjeant Scriven appears to take the same view of the case, having abstained from the insertion of any such precedents in his work.

Conveyance by Attorney.

125. In the absence of express stipulation, the purchaser is not compellable to accept a conveyance by attorney; but under an assignment for benefit of creditors, it is usual to make such stipulation. See forms, 292, and 296 or 7, 312, &c.

126. In such cases the purchaser should require proof that the party is living at the passing such surrender; and it would be prudent to have the surrender passed and money retained or deposited till such proof is obtained.

29

Notice to Tenants.

127. It will be as well to prepare a notice to the tenants of the sale, to be signed by the vendor at the completion.

Proceedings subsequent to drawing Conveyance.

128. The draft conveyance being prepared, is to be copied and sent to vendor's solicitor for perusal; and if to save time the draft be sent before all the requisitions on the title are disposed of, it would be prudent to endorse the draft to the following effect : " For the perusal of Mr. C. D., on behalf of the vendor, subject to compliance with the requisitions on the title," to prevent the sending the draft being deemed a waiver of objections to the title.

129. At the time of sending the draft conveyance for perusal, the purchaser's solicitor should urge the immediate preparation of any deed or document which practice requires to be drawn by the vendor's solicitor, and which drafts the solicitor, when he receives, will peruse and take a copy of, or at least of the material parts. The expence of this perusal ought perhaps in strictness to be paid by the vendor, but this is not usually required; and as the purchaser gets the document, it is not very hard to call upon him to pay his solicitor's charge for perusal.

130. It will be better not to return any such drafts received from the vendor's solicitor till his return of the draft conveyance, as it may happen that some modification required by the vendor's solicitor, may render it necessary to alter the draft sent by him.

131. Of course, any alterations in the drafts must be matter of negociation ; but except in special cases, where the drafts would be settled by counsel, there is much less difficulty or fear of difference in copyhold than in freehold conveyances.

132. Should the solicitors not agree on the settlement of the drafts, the better way is to mutually name a counsel to whom they may be sent for settle-

ment, or else resort must of course be had by one party to proceedings to compel performance; but in sales under a court of equity the draft is settled by the master in case the parties differ.

133. Should it be deemed advisable to alter the drafts after their return, they should be sent to the solicitor for the other party for reperusal.

134. The drafts being settled, the next steps will be the engrossments, the sending the same to the vendor's solicitor, the obtaining and examining his engrossments, and the arrangements for completion.

135. Either immediately on settlement of the drafts, or a reasonable time before the completion, the purchaser's solicitor will have his drafts engrossed on the proper stamps. (See Appendix.)

136. Surrenders and bonds are usually engrossed on paper, bookways, and in some cases releases; but deeds of covenant and bargain and sale, on parchment. A duplicate, or duplicate copy of the surrender, is also made to keep with the writings, and on such duplicate is endorsed a receipt to be signed by the steward on the delivery of the original. This receipt may be in the following form:—" Received this day of   , 1837, the original of which this purports to be a copy, to be presented and enrolled at the next Court." " A. B. steward, or C. D., deputy steward."

137. The engrossments will then be sent to vendor's solicitor for perusal, requesting him to return them with his engrossments, and make an appointment for completion.

138. It frequently happens that the steward resides at a distance from both vendor and purchaser, and consequently that it would be inconvenient to attend at his office to complete; in which case the usual course is for the vendor's solicitor to obtain an authority from him to take the surrender as his deputy, which is usually granted on payment of a deputation fee of one guinea for each surrender taken, and if power granted to separate deputies as to parties re-

31

siding at different places, then a deputation fee from each.

139. The deputation is obtained by merely writing a letter, requesting that the party may be allowed to take an absolute surrender from A. B. &c., and requiring no power of attorney, a verbal authority or answer by letter being sufficient.

140. The purchaser's solicitor should require the vendor to obtain such authority to take the surrender as deputy in order to prevent delay; and he ought not, in scarcely any case, to rely on a mere covenant to surrender, but obtain an actual surrender at the time of completion.

141. The vendor's solicitor is under the usual practice entitled to have the completion at his office; and consequently, should the steward reside in the same place, he will not generally deem it right to incur the expence of an authority to take the surrenders as deputy steward, but will make an appointment with the steward for the parties attending on him, or his attending at the office of the vendor's solicitor.

142. On receiving the vendor's engrossments, the purchaser's solicitor will examine them with the drafts, and return them, making a final appointment for completion.

143. Warrants to enter satisfaction require no stamp, the receipt being given on the collateral security; they are drawn in duplicate on foolscap, one to be kept, and the other to be given to the steward for presentment, and on such delivery he will give a receipt on the duplicate in the following, or a similar form:—" Received the   day of the warrant of which this is a duplicate, to be presented and satisfaction entered at next Court." " A. B. steward, or C. D., deputy steward." The usual steward's fee is 13s. 4d. on each common warrant, and which is payable by the vendor.

144. Having made the appointment for completion, the purchaser's solicitor should make out an account of any costs he is entitled to receive from ven-

dor's solicitor, as for examination of writings, fees to be paid to the steward on satisfaction, of conditional sums, examination of femes covert, &c.; also of the interest his client should be called on to pay, and of any proportion of rent to be paid either way, amount of abatement, &c.

145. The purchaser's solicitor should also make out a list of the writings to be delivered up, should they not all clearly appear in the abstract; and it will be as well to note down all the drafts and engross-ments. A memorandum of the signatures to be ob-tained to the engrossments will frequently be useful, as sometimes the points requiring attention at the com-pletion are so numerous that some escape attention, and cause much subsequent trouble and difficulty.

146. It will frequently save much trouble at the time of completion, to settle all questions of pay-ments, allowances for interest, costs, rent, &c. before the day of completion, so as to limit the attention on that day to matters free from question.

147. Frequently also the engrossments are sent to the vendor's solicitor for completion before the day fixed, and this is of course requisite when the parties are numerous, or cannot attend on the day fixed for completion.

148. On attending the completion, the purchaser's solicitor will first go through the list of documents to be delivered up, and see that they are all ready; he will then see that the conveyance is properly exe-cuted and surrender passed, and the notices to the tenants signed; and he will also have both parts of the surrender and warrant to enter satisfaction de-livered up to him, that he may obtain the steward's receipt, and will require payment of deputation fees, and fee on examining feme covert on surrenders, and the fee on presenting satisfaction on conditional sur-render: he will also take the bargain and sale, if the conveyance be by such deed; and when under a bank-ruptcy he will also obtain the surrender as in a com-mon case.

33   c 5

149. Having seen that the writings are ready for delivery, and the conveyance properly completed, he will hand over the purchase-money and interest to the vendor or his solicitor, or the mortgagee, as the case may be; and also pay or receive any costs which, under the conditions of sale or general practice, are payable either way, and the like as to portions of rent, abatements, or valuation monies.

150. If possession is to be given, he will take care that it is done at the time of payment; and if from distance such cannot be done at the moment, perhaps the following memorandum might be useful:—" Memorandum: Having sold and conveyed the estate called C. at A. which I now occupy, to Mr. E. F., I hereby acknowledge that he is entitled to the possession thereof." Dated, &c.

151. The purchaser's solicitor will serve the notices on the tenants as soon as convenient after the completion, and will deliver the surrender to the steward with any warrant to enter satisfaction, taking his receipt; and will direct him to send notice of any subsequent courts, so that admission may be taken in due time—instructions for which will be found in s. 4 to 10. In purchases of equitable interests, a notice must also be served on the party holding the writings.

152. In purchases under executorships, where no surrender is passed, the better way will be to apprize the steward of the deed, and request him to inform the solicitor of the subsequent courts.

153. On completing the purchase, where the amount is considerable, or the solicitor may think that his client has particular views with respect to its disposal by his will, he should again draw his attention to the necessity for a republication of his will, by pointing out the party to whom it will go, in the event of no republication or addition of a valid codicil taking place.

154. The purchaser's solicitor will in due time obtain the copy admission from the steward, and de-

34

liver it to his client.   The term allowed by the Stamp
Act for preparing the copy, is four months.

PRACTICE ON SALES.

Preliminary Matters.

155. Before proceeding to a sale, whether by auction or private contract, it would be very desirable to
inspect the title, with a view to supply any evidence
which may appear requisite, and to guard by the conditions of sale, or the purchase contract, against objections being raised which it would be difficult to
meet, or which could only be obviated by incurring
an expence which would press heavily, and might
with sufficient care be avoided.

156. In large sales it would frequently be very advantageous to have the abstract previously prepared
and submitted to counsel to advise on the conditions,
as they may frequently be so worded as not in any
way to injure the sale, and yet to embody stipulations without which the contract could not be enforced, or at best could not be enforced without a
heavy expence.

157. The importance of attentively wording the
conditions, whether by auction or on a private sale,
is but rarely considered till the vendor finds himself
disappointed in his sale, or put to great expence in
performing his contract.

158. Carefully drawn forms of agreement and conditions are given, Nos. 271 & 2, 314 & 315, and
with the following observations will guard the vendor's solicitor against many difficulties which would
otherwise arise.

159. In preparing purchase agreements, attention
35

should be turned to all the points mentioned in the headings of forms 271 & 272.

160. As very strict conditions of sale frequently impede the contract, or induce a lower offer, the best way in many cases is to provide that the expence of steward's certifying, of copies, affidavits, and other certificates, shall be equally borne between the parties. This stipulation will guard against the purchaser making unreasonable requisitions, and at the same time not make him feel an objection to the contract, and would be advantageous both on sales by private contract and by auction.

161. The terms of contract being arranged, the agreement will be engrossed on paper, and usually without a stamp, as it can be stamped within twenty-one days without any penalty. It is better to have two parts; and on signature the vendor's solicitor retains one, writing on it the name and address of the purchaser's solicitor, and delivers the other to the purchaser.

162. The vendor's solicitor should, on his client entering into a contract for sale, shortly explain to him the effect on any will he made, and that the party to whom he gave the estate will not be entitled to the produce.

Abstract.

163. The vendor's solicitor next proceeds to draw the abstract, or obtains it from the steward, and in some cases where the equitable title is special, he obtains a steward's abstract of the legal title, and makes an abstract of the equitable title from the documents in his possession.

164. In cases where the abstract is prepared in the solicitor's office. the following hints may be useful, especially to clerks, in preparing them.

165. State in the margin the date of the act of court, or document abstracted; and in stating the court, add whether a general or special court; the date of any surrender, &c. presented; the recital of any surrender or document, if not before abstracted,

36

or a reference to it, if previously abstracted; the act of court fully, as to the person, the parcels, and the habendum; and it would be right to add whether the vendor has a copy, an original document, &c.

166. In abstracting the proceedings under a will, it is generally right to state the recital or statement of the will very fully, and to add in what court proved, by whom, and when.

167. In abstracting a recovery, the different steps should be given, so as to shew the regularity of the proceedings, avoiding prolixity as far as can be done consistently with accuracy.

168. In the case of a bargain and sale not with the writings, the statement on the court rolls should be abstracted fully; but where the deed is elsewhere abstracted, a reference will be sufficient.

169. The mode of abstracting a discharge on a conditional surrender will be, to give the court, the date of the warrant, by whom signed, and its effect, with tolerable fulness.

170. When a clerk draws an abstract, he should always err on the side of fulness rather than of brevity, as his principal can with much more readiness settle the draft abstract.

171. The abstract will, when settled, be engrossed in the usual manner, and for facility of future reference, it will be of advantage that the clerk who copies it should mark the draft where each sheet ends.

172. Should the abstract be obtained from the steward, a draft copy will be made for reference, and a supplemental abstract will, when it does not embody all the title, be made to accompany it. In the margin of the steward's abstract, it would be advisable for the vendor's solicitor to note what documents can be delivered to the purchaser.

173. Having completed the abstracts, they will be sent to the purchaser's solicitor for his requisitions, and should he omit to send them in proper time, of course application must be made to him to furnish them.

174. On receipt of the requisitions, the vendor's solicitor will peruse them, and if he feels difficulty as to the compliance or refusal to comply with them, he will lay them with the abstract before counsel for his advice.

175. On doing so, he will send a copy of the purchase agreement with the abstract and requisitions; and in all cases where he peruses an abstract, he will not fail to give the most careful attention to the agreement.

176. Attention to the previous suggestions with regard to contracts and conditions of sale, will prevent much difficulty from arising as to the examination of the abstract, and the delivery of copies, which too frequently occasion difficulty in copyhold sales. Should the suggestions have been neglected, the observations on the duty of purchaser's solicitor will be a guide as to the points likely to arise. See s. 77, &c.

177. It may happen that the property to which title is shewn differs from that sold, either in quantity or in some quality, or that there exists a charge on the property not mentioned in the particulars or contract; and when any such case arises, either the purchaser objects to complete, or requires a compensation.

178. The question as to quantity generally arises on sale of an estate, when the property sold is stated to contain the quantity at which it is generally estimated, but on survey appears not to contain that quantity. In such case a purchaser would be bound to complete, receiving a compensation. See *Sir C. Shovel* v. *Bogan*, 2 Eq. Ca Abr. 688, pl. 1; *Hill* v. *Buckley*, 17 Ves 394; and even if the contract contained the words " more or less," it would seem from the latter case that the purchaser would be entitled to compensation, unless the difference were very trifling.

179. If differing in tenure, as if property sold as freehold, and appearing to be copyhold, the purchaser cannot be compelled to complete, unless the vendor obtains enfranchisement; *Twining* v. *Morrice*, 2 Bro.

C. C. 326, and *Sir Harry Hicks* v. *Phillips*, Prec. Cha. 575; and see 10 Mod. 504; and then of course he would have to go into the lord's title. See Enfranchisement, 259, &c.

180. The same principle would, it should seem, prevent a purchaser of copyhold at fines certain from being compelled to take copyhold subject to fines arbitrary, as the charge is uncertain, and not like a quit' rent, of a fixed annual amount; for if the rule depended on the mere possibility of fixing a value, it could be done as easily between freehold and copyhold as between copyhold on fines certain and fines arbitrary.

181. If the interest be different, as if entirety sold, and title only shewn to undivided part, the purchaser cannot be compelled to complete. See *Roffry* v. *Shallcross*, 4 Madd. 227; *Dalby* v. *Pullen*, 3 Simon 29; and *Wheatly* v. *Slade*, 4 Sim. 126.

182. Should the estate appear charged with a fixed annual amount, as a quit rent, the purchaser would be compelled to complete the purchase on a compensation. See *Esdaile* v. *Stevenson*, 1 Sim. & Stu. 122.

Compelling Purchaser to proceed.

183. It may happen that the purchaser refuses to either accept title which vendor can make, or relinquish the purchase: in which case the vendor's solicitor will, if he conceives he can make a good title, proceed to enforce specific performance, or proceed on agreement at law; but if he feels doubtful as to the title, he should give notice to the purchaser's solicitor, or perhaps it might be better to serve the notice on the purchaser, requiring him to elect whether to take such title as the vendor can give, or to relinquish the purchase within a limited time, and apprizing him that a bill will be filed to compel such election at the expiration of that time.

184. Should the purchaser be in possession, and refuse to complete or give up possession, a bill should be filed to compel him to complete or deliver up agree-

ment and possession of premises and account for rent. See *King* v. *King*, 1 Mylne & Keene, 442; and see *Tindal* v. *Colham*, 2 M. & K. 385.

185. Should the purchaser's solicitor neglect to send requisitions, or to proceed in the purchase on compliance with such requisitions as the vendor's solicitor thinks can be sustained, the vendor's solicitor must either proceed to enforce the contract by action, or which is better, by bill for specific performance. There is an important point too often omitted in copyhold sales, by which danger is very likely to arise, and which is the allowing the time appointed for completion to pass over without making the purchaser complete, by which delay *the vendor may die before a surrender is passed, and the expence of an admission by his heir will have to be incurred*; and it would be very desirable to be in such a position as to throw such expence on the purchaser. The best way to do this would be to serve him with a notice as in Appendix, No. 316, or a similar form, apprizing him of the vendor's readiness to complete, and that if he neglects completion, he will be held liable for all loss and expence in case of death. Should proceedings become requisite to enforce the contract, Sugden's Vendors & Purchasers will give the information requisite, and which could not, without too great an enlargement of the contents, be here inserted.

Perusing Drafts, &c.

186. On receiving the draft conveyance from the purchaser's solicitor, the vendor's solicitor will make a copy to keep and peruse, and settle the drafts. The forms in the Appendix will be a guide as to the usual contents, and will draw the attention to any parts inserted out of the ordinary course.

187. The vendor's solicitor will then prepare such warrants to enter satisfaction, covenants for production, releases or bonds of indemnity, as his client is to pay for—copies of which he will send the purchaser's solicitor for perusal on returning his drafts. Forms will

be found in the Appendix. Some correspondence may take place on the drafts, but on their being finally settled, it will remain to arrange for completion.

Arrangements for Completion.

188. The vendor's solicitor will learn at what time the steward can take the surrender from the vendor; or should it be more convenient to the vendor's solicitor to take the surrender himself as deputy, or to have it taken by other persons residing near the parties, he will apply to the steward, and request that he or those persons may take such surrender, and which it is the general practice for stewards to agree to on payment of a fee of one guinea on each surrender, or for each deputy, where there is more than one.

189. Having made the arrangement for taking the surrender, and learning what time will suit the executing parties, the vendor's solicitor will make an appointment with the purchaser's solicitor for completion.

190. It will frequently save much trouble, and in some cases (as where the parties are at a distance) it will be necessary to get the execution of the documents and passing the surrender before the completion, as in the obtaining the execution of freehold deeds, holding them till completion.

191. Before the day fixed for completion, it will be desirable to arrange with the purchaser's solicitor as to the amount to be paid for interest, the apportionment for rent, the costs to be paid by either side under the conditions or agreement, valuation monies, and any other questions of amount; and in cases where some of the documents cannot be obtained by the day appointed for completion, but can be afterwards obtained, it will be of advantage, in order to prevent delaying the sale, to offer the purchaser's solicitor an undertaking to deliver such documents within a specified time.

192. Before or by the time fixed for completion, the vendor's solicitor will take care that all the docu-

41

ments of conveyance are properly executed and completed, so as to give no ground to the purchaser's solicitor to delay the completion; and on the day of completion, the vendor's solicitor will have nothing further to do than to deliver up the papers and receive the purchase-money, less deposit; the interest, and any apportionment of rent, and to balance the costs either way.

193. On completion, the vendor's solicitor should point out to his client the consequences of the sale in the disposition of his property by will, by depriving the devisee of any benefit arising from the estate, and vesting the amount in his personal representatives with the remainder of his personal property.

PRACTICE ON MORTGAGES AND ASSIGNMENTS OF MORTGAGES.

Common Mortgages.

194. On application for a loan on mortgage, the usual practice is, to first shew a sufficient value in the proposed security, and for the mortgagor on the agreement to advance the money, to deposit the writings with the mortgagor's solicitor, or to have his own solicitor prepare an abstract, in order that the title may be inspected; and on its being approved of, the mortgage is prepared by the mortgagee's solicitor, and of course if required by the mortgagor, perused by his solicitor; but from the comparative simplicity of copyhold titles and securities, the more general course is to allow the solicitor through whom the money is borrowed, to transact all the business.

195. It would be prudent on the application for a loan, to have a memorandum similar to that in the Appendix, No. 317, signed by both parties, in order

42

to provide against the refusal by the intended mortgagee to complete the advance after a good title is shewn, and to provide for payment by the borrower of the expence of surveying the premises and investigating the title, in case there should appear an insufficient value, or the title prove defective.

196. The mortgagee's solicitor should carefully avoid taking upon himself any responsibility in advising on the sufficiency of the value, by requiring the survey and valuation to be made; or he should obtain from the mortgagee a memorandum that from his own knowledge he is satisfied with the value. This would be better obtained by a reply to a written communication on the subject, than by requesting a statement in writing from the client, who might be offended at the request of such a document.

197. On being satisfied as to the value, the mortgagee's solicitor will next, if the amount be small, inspect the writings and decide on the title, without putting the party to the expence of an abstract; but it would be advisable to write to the steward and obtain from him a certificate that there were no incumbrances affecting the property within such a period as would carry the title back to a clear state in the documents of title.

198. Differences sometimes arise as to this certificate, but in general if not extending over a very long space of time, the steward will furnish the certificate for 10*s.* or 13*s.* 4*d.*

199. Should the amount of the sum warrant the preparing an abstract, or should it appear requisite from the state of the title or want of documents, the mortgagee's solicitor will obtain the abstract from the steward; or when the documents are sufficient, prepare it himself and get it certified by the steward, or obtain a certificate of no incumbrances.

200. Should the abstract be furnished by another solicitor, the mortgagee's solicitor will compare it with the writings, and make requisitions as on a purchase. See section 45, &c.

43

201. On being satisfied as to the title, the mortgagee's solicitor will prepare the draft mortgage, (see forms, Appendix, Nos. 318, &c.) ; and when another solicitor acts for mortgagor, send the drafts for perusal. When the drafts are settled, the engrossments are to be made, the surrenders and bonds being usually on foolscap paper, bookways, and deeds of covenant on parchment. Duplicate copies of surrenders will be made as in purchases. The stamps will be found in the Appendix. On the engrossments being completed and examined, arrangements will be made for taking the surrender, &c. (See 138, &c. as to taking by deputation.) The bill for preparing the security will also in general be made out previously to completion, and is usually paid on completion of the security. The surrender will be handed to the steward as soon as possible after completion, if taken before deputy, and his receipt taken on the duplicate as on a purchase ; but admission is not taken on a conditional surrender, except when the mortgagee enters into possession as owner ; but as the mortgagee cannot enforce possession by any legal measures without admission, it will be in many cases prudent to take a warrant of attorney to confess judgment in ejectment ; a form of which is given in the Appendix, 321.

202. A schedule of writings will be delivered to the mortgagor, as in freehold mortgages ; and in some cases an appointment of receiver should be obtained, the form of which will be similar to that in freehold cases.

203. The steward's fees on a common surrender will be 1*l.* 6*s.* 8*d.* for taking, presenting, entering, and examining feme covert ; and 1*l.* if the wife is not a party to the surrender : when the surrender is very long, it will be rather more.

Where previous Mortgage to be paid off.

204. It will be advisable in the first place, after being satisfied as to value for amount required, to

44

ascertain from the present mortgagee the amount due on his security, and whether he has notice of any further security; apprizing him of the application to the intended mortgagee for advance; also to learn that the present mortgagee has had proper notice, or agrees to be paid off; at the same time an appointment will be made for comparison of the abstract when obtained, with the writings.

205. The next step will be to obtain the abstract either from the present mortgagee's solicitor or the steward, and a certificate from the latter that no incumbrances exist beyond the mortgage.

206. The abstract will then be compared with the writings in the hands of the mortgagee, perused, and the sufficiency of the title ascertained as in other cases.

207. The security should then be prepared (see Appendix 306, &c. and 318, &c.); and the draft warrant to enter satisfaction sent to the mortgagee's solicitor for perusal. On the return of the draft perused, the security and discharge on existing mortgage must be engrossed, appointments made with the mortgagee and mortgagor for completion, and arrangements made for passing the surrender, the engrossments requiring the signature of the purchaser's mortgagee being sent to his solicitor for examination and signature.

208. The bill of the mortgagee's solicitor should be obtained, and the items settled before the day fixed for completion, to prevent difficulty on that day. On the day fixed for completion, the writings will be received with the discharge properly signed. The new security will be passed and executed, and the principal and interest due to mortgagee, his costs, and the costs of the new mortgage, paid, and the balance handed over to the mortgagor. The surrender and satisfaction on previous surrender will afterwards be delivered to the steward for presentment, and his receipt obtained, as in other cases. His fee on surrender by man and wife will be 1*l.* 6*s.* 8*d.*, on warrant 13*s.* 4*d.*, total 2*l.*

45

Further Mortgage.

209. In this case, on receiving instructions from his client to prepare a further mortgage, the mortgagee's solicitor will only have occasion to obtain a certificate of no incumbrances subsequent to the previous surrender; and to prepare a further conditional surrender and bond or note, according to the amount required. (See Forms, Appendix, Nos. 323, 319.) These are to be engrossed, passed, and executed or signed, and the original surrender delivered to the steward, and his receipt obtained in the usual way.

Second Mortgage.

210. The solicitor of the intended second mortgagee will, on his client being satisfied as to the value of the property, obtain a statement from the first mortgagee of his claim, and whether he has notice of any further incumbrances. He will then obtain an abstract and certificate as to subsequent incumbrances, or otherwise satisfy himself as to the title, and as he will hold no writings, an abstract can hardly be dispensed with. The title being deemed good, the security will be prepared (see forms, 324, 319), engrossed, passed, and completed, and steward's receipts obtained in the usual manner, and notice is to be given to the first mortgagee of the second mortgage. (See form, 325.)

Assignment of Mortgage.

211. Having adopted the preliminary steps as to amount, title, &c. pointed out on a mortgage where another is to be discharged, the intended mortgagee's solicitor will prepare the security (form, 327) which he will get executed as any other deed, and have presented and enrolled by the steward; but as stewards frequently refuse to enrol any such deeds, and in scarcely any case can the assignment be of more benefit than a discharge of the previous surrender and passing a new one, except as affects the Stamp Act,

46

it will in most cases be better to adopt the more usual course, and to discharge the old surrender and prepare a new one.

212. The point as regards the Stamp Acts is this: An assignment of a mortgage is only liable to a 35*s.* stamp, and 25*s.* progressive duty, whilst a new surrender is considered to be liable to the *ad valorem* stamp; but it is conceived that the following plan might be adopted. Insert in the new surrender a recital that it is made on a transfer of the mortgage sum previously secured; and for further securing the same to the new mortgagee, have the previous mortgagee sign a warrant to enter satisfaction on the first mortgage, which the new mortgagee might hold till it became requisite on a future mortgage or a sale to present it. Such warrant might either be in the common form, or might authorize the entry of satisfaction on a direction to that effect by the new mortgagee. (See forms, 328, 306, &c.)

213. The steward's fee, should the assignment be presented and enrolled, would be 6*s.* 8*d.* for presenting, and 8*d.* (or some charge 1*s.*) per folio for enrolling, and as a draft court is made, the latter charge appears reasonable. Should the course here pointed out be adopted, the usual fees on surrender, and warrant, if entered should be paid, or in the event of the surrender being much increased in length, the steward might perhaps require an additional fee of a few shillings in proportion to the increased length.

Freehold and Copyhold Mortgages.

214. Where the property is part freehold and part copyhold, the freehold mortgage will be prepared in the form requisite according to the particular title, and will contain covenants for title, &c. (See form, 330.)

215. The only difference in the copyhold security will be the reference to the freehold security, and the statement of the *ad valorem* stamp being impressed on such security, and the surrender will then be on a 20*s.* stamp. (See form, 329.)

47

ANNUITIES.

Annuities in General.

216. The preliminary steps as to the value and title will be the same as on a mortgage. The security will be found in Appendix 332, as to ordinary cases; and in more special cases a reference to Bythewood's Conveyancing will give the required information. The security being drawn, the other steps will be the same as in a mortgage, with the addition of the memorial, full information as to which will be obtained in Bythewood's work, and which, from the infrequency of copyhold annuities, added to its great speciality, cannot be added here.

Annuities when Mortgage to be paid off.

217. The practice in these cases will be in the preliminary steps the same as in the case of a mortgage, where previous one to be paid off. The only difference between the security in this case and in the last will be the special statement of the mode in which the consideration is paid, and the preparing a common warrant to enter satisfaction on the mortgage. (See 306, &c.)

DISCHARGE OF MORTGAGES OR ANNUITIES.

218. Unless the parties will waive notice, a six months' notice must be given in the case of a mortgage, and the notice required by the security in the case of an annuity. A warrant to enter satisfaction should then be prepared (see forms 306, &c.) and sent for perusal by the solicitor of the party ; on its return engrossed in duplicate, on plain paper, and an appointment made for signature and delivery of writings ; and on attending the appointment to pay off the money, a receipt should be given on the deed of covenant or mortgage bond for the amount paid. The writings should be taken with the warrant properly signed, and which should be delivered to the steward for presentment, and his receipt obtained in the usual way. His fee will be 13s. 4d. The costs of mortgagee's solicitor for perusal, attendance, &c. must be also paid.

Partial discharge of a Mortgage.

219. This must of course take place by consent of the mortgagee, who retains the writings till an entire discharge, giving a receipt for the part paid on the bond or collateral security, and signing a warrant to enter satisfaction as to the amount paid (see form Appendix 307); and which is to be presented as in other cases.

Discharge of a Mortgage as to certain parts of Property.

220. It frequently happens on a sale of part of property in mortgage, that the mortgagee agrees to ac-

cept part of the purchase money, and discharge the part of the premises agreed to be sold, from his mortgage: in such case form No. 308 in Appendix should be followed, and a memorandum endorsed on the copy surrender and bond, as to such discharge of part of the premises.

Notice to pay off Mortgage.

221. A form is given in Appendix 333; but in strictness, unless the mortgage contains a stipulation that the mortgagee shall give notice, he is not bound to do so.

Proceedings to enforce payment on Copyhold Mortgages or Annuities.

222. Should the interest not be duly paid up, the party will, in the case of an annuity, or in the event of his not requiring payment of the principal on a mortgage, give the tenants notice to pay their rents to him in discharge of interest, or to pay as much as the interest amounts to (see Form 334); and in default of payment under such notice, the mortgagee will, under the authority of a recent case, be able to distrain, whether the tenancy commenced previous or subsequent to the mortgage.

223. Should the premises be in the occupation of the mortgagor, the mortgagee will not be able to distrain, unless he has inserted in his security an agreement by the mortgagor to be tenant of the mortgagee at a rent equal to the interest; and though the attornment might be deemed to operate as a lease, the writer has seen the opinion of an experienced counsel, that no stamp beyond that for a mortgage would be required.

224. The expediency of having a warrant of attorney to confess judgment in ejectment has been before adverted to; and if the mortgagee has attended to it, he will be able without difficulty to obtain possession of the premises, and by letting them can insure payment of the interest, and retain the control

over the possession till the principal is paid off or the mortgage foreclosed.

225. It may happen that a mortgagee, who has not obtained the warrant of attorney, has a power of sale; and if desirous to avail himself of it, he must give the notice to the mortgagor required under the power, and on the expiration of that period he will proceed to a sale agreeably to the power.

226. It would frequently be of advantage, with a view to save ultimate expence, that with a power of sale should be given a power of attorney to surrender on behalf of the mortgagee, by obtaining which and framing the conditions of sale similarly to those under a Dr. and Cr. deed, the sale might be more readily effected, and the necessity for admission by the mortgagee guarded against.

227. Should no power of sale have been given, the mortgagee must of course resort to the common remedies, and obtain payment by proceeding on the mortgage bond or other collateral security and bill of foreclosure in equity.

228. The proceeding by ejectment has the disadvantage that the mortgagee cannot recover in ejectment till after admittance, which is attended with very considerable expence, and a question might afterwards arise as to the liability of the mortgagee to pay it under the security.

229. It should seem that where it is deemed requisite to proceed for recovery of possession, the better way would be to give the mortgagor notice that the mortgagee requires possession under the security, and that unless given by a fixed time, he shall be obliged to obtain possession by ejectment, and for that purpose to take admission; and that in the event of his so doing, the mortgagor will be held liable for all consequent expences. This course might obviate the difficulty on the subsequent proceedings to a foreclosure.

230. In cases where no power of sale exists, but the mortgagee can obtain possession, and it is not expected that the mortgagor will attempt to redeem,

and it is important to guard against the expence of a suit for foreclosure, the mortgagee will obtain admission on the forfeited conditional surrender, and retain the possession as owner.   In this case it might be as well to give the mortgagor or his representative notice of the intention to take admission, for the reason before stated, in connexion with the costs, in the event of a subsequent suit to redeem.

231. The mode of obtaining admission will be similar to that on a purchase, merely apprizing the steward that the principal and an arrear of interest is due, and that the mortgagee intends to take admission.

232. After an admission under a forfeited conditional surrender, the mortgagee will take care that no accounts of subsequent interest appear on any of the documents of title, as such accounts would throw difficulties in the way on a future sale.

233. The steps to be taken on annuity surrenders will be similar to those on mortgages, depending in like manner upon the nature of the particular security taken, and in the case of annuities it would be always prudent to put the grantee in such a position that he can always have the power of distraining. This will be effected by the appointment of a receiver or the attornment of the grantor.

LEASES.

234. Without a licence, a copyholder cannot grant a lease for more than one year; but the usual way is to grant such lease for one year, and so on from year to year, for the specified number of years, provided the same can be done without fine or forfeiture; and in form No. 335, Appendix, will be found the words usually adopted in such leases.

235. When it is deemed advisable to obtain a licence, the terms on which it is granted are previously arranged with the lord or steward; it is entered on the court rolls, and a copy on parchment made by the steward, in form No. 533; the lease will then be as 336. Such lease, it should be remarked, is a common law interest, and subject to be taken in execution.

Settlements.

236. The points to be attended to by the solicitor will be the carefully noting down the instructions as to the particular mode in which the parties wish the property settled. He will then peruse the writings, or such of them as will shew how the legal and equitable ownership stands, and in the next place prepare the settlement. A form of surrender in the most usual form is given in Appendix 337; but in general settlements being drawn by counsel, it is deemed needless to give other forms.

237. It should, however, be observed, that the practice recommended in other parts of this work relative to the obtaining a power of attorney to surrender, would be frequently found attended with more convenience than resting satisfied with the mere

53

covenant from the intended husband, when the surrender is to be passed to trustees, as frequently the
having such power will prevent the necessity of proceedings to enforce performance of the covenant,

238. The draft, when completed and settled, will
be engrossed on the proper stamps and executed;
and subsequently, if not at the same time, any surrender which may be requisite under the settlement,
must be prepared and passed in the usual way, and
admission taken by the trustees.

239. As it may be sometimes requisite to discharge
the estate from existing entails, the form of Assurance substituted by the Fines and Recoveries
Abolition Act, is given in Appendix, No. 294.

240. Attention to the following points will be useful in taking instructions for marriage settlements:
the taking correctly the parties' names and descriptions; the particulars of the property to be settled,
and by whom; in whom the legal estate now vested;
whether subject to incumbrances; whether any pin-
money is to be secured to wife; whether powers of
sale and exchange are to be inserted; and as to the
provisions for children; the wishes of the parties
should of course be ascertained with regard to the
continuance in the male branch of the family, or
otherwise; and it should be suggested when long
trusts are created, that it would be of advantage to
insert a power to insure the lives of the trustees, so
as to provide for fresh admissions by a small annual
payment, instead of a large payment at death of the
trustees.

Assignments for benefit of Creditors.

241. It is too often that a very negligent mode is
adopted in these deeds, as respects copyhold property.
A covenant to surrender is generally inserted, which
with a troublesome debtor is of very little use.

242. The best way is to convey the freehold, leasehold, and personalty, and insert a power of attorney
to sell and convey the copyhold, and to pass a sur-

render and execute any deed of covenant for title or otherwise as may be requisite.

243. A precedent in the Appendix, 338, adopts this plan, and by providing in the conditions of sale for the acceptance by the purchaser of the surrender under the power, (Appendix 315,) no difficulty will be experienced on the sale.

244. The instructions, drawing, and engrossing deeds, and obtaining the execution, will of course all follow in the usual manner, except that the deed must, under the Bankrupt Act, be executed by the trustees within fifteen days, and attested by an attorney, and must be advertized in the Gazette and two other papers. See Bankruptcy Act, 6 G. 4. The attention to these points in execution and advertizing will limit the time within which a fiat could be obtained under the deed to six months; and it would be of service to obtain an affidavit by the insolvent, shewing all his debts on which a fiat could be supported, as such affidavit might satisfy a willing purchaser, and enable the completion of the sale before the six months, within which period a fiat might be obtained under the Bankruptcy Act.

Insolvency and Discharge under Act.

245. By 7 G. 4, c. 57, s. 11, it is provided, that on subscribing petition for discharge under the act, an assignment of all real and personal estate shall be made to the provisional assignee; and by s. 13, it is provided, that the assignment shall operate as an act of bankruptcy for two calendar months, and be avoided by fiat within that period, but shall be valid at expiration of that period, and not subsequently operate as an act of bankruptcy. By s. 16, the provisional assignee is entitled to take possession, and on order of the court, to sell either real or personal property. By s. 19, the court is authorized to appoint any creditor or creditors, assignee or assignees, at any time after petition being filed, and that provisional assignee shall then convey to such assignees. (The conveyance

is in a printed form, and generally prepared at the office of the court). The original assignment to provisional assignee, and counterpart of conveyance by him are to be filed; and an office copy, sealed by the court, is to be received as evidence. By s. 20, the assignees are to make sale of the insolvent's estate by auction within six months, or such other time as court may direct, and in such manner, and at such place as may, thirty days before sale, be approved in writing by major part in value of creditors meeting, on notice published fourteen days previously in London Gazette; and also if prisoner resided within bills of mortality, in some London daily newspaper; and in case he resided elsewhere, then in some newspaper generally circulated in or near the place where he resided. And where the prisoner is entitled to copyhold or customary estate, it is provided, that the conveyance from the provisional assignee shall be entered on the court rolls; and thereupon it shall be lawful for the assignee or assignees to surrender or convey to any purchaser or purchasers from such assignee or assignees as the court may direct; and the rents and profits shall in the mean time be received by the assignees for benefit of the creditors, without prejudice to the lord of the manor. Under this act the steps to be taken on sale of the insolvent's copyhold property, will be the obtaining the usual conveyance from the provisional assignee, with a counterpart. The filing the counterpart; the calling a meeting of the creditors for the purpose of approving of the sale, and advertizing such notice fourteen days before the meeting in the Gazette and newspapers, of which copies must be obtained; the resolution of the meeting,—the application to the court, and order thereupon,—the auction conditions and auction,—the abstract and title, and the conveyance to the purchaser, which might be by surrender from the assignees under sec. 20, or by a surrender from them and the insolvent and his wife, which would be more satisfactory to the purchaser. Of course the

56

assignees will not enter into any covenants, and it will rest with the purchaser to determine whether he will deem it advisable to have covenants from the insolvent, assuming that the conditions have not guarded against the purchaser requiring the concurrence of the insolvent. It should seem very doubtful whether, even without any stipulations on the sale, the commissioners would compel the insolvent to enter into covenants to the purchaser, or at least whether he would not be ordered to bear the expence of the application and order. See form of surrender, 289.

BANKRUPTCY.

246. It was formerly requisite to except the copyholds of the bankrupt in the bargain and sale from the commissioners to the assignees; but now no bargain and sale is made, and the appointment vests all the bankrupt's property, except the copyholds, in the assignees.

247. On sales by assignees, it would be prudent to stipulate that the expence of enrolling the proceedings, and of the copies, should be paid by the purchaser; or it would perhaps be more equitable to stipulate that each party should pay half the expence.

248. The form of conveyance in Appendix 302, will suggest the other points requiring attention on the part of the assignees.

249. When premises in mortgage, the mortgagee will be entitled to notice as in other cases, and will be made a party to the conveyance. The opinion and outline conveyance in Appendix 305, will shew the mode of conveying property mortgaged for more than its value.

250. It will be noticed that the conveyance under a bankruptcy, is different since the last Bankrupt Act from what it was previously ; a simple bargain and sale having been formerly taken as on a sale under executors, but under 6 G. 4, it is provided, that in the bargain and sale, the commissioners shall authorize some party to surrender to the purchaser. The form of surrender will be found in 288.

WILLS.

251. The solicitor should be particularly careful in obtaining the instructions, and he should give such suggestions as appear to him requisite, to prevent the testator from making such dispositions as may incur a heavy expence for admission ; as for instance, in devising to executors, upon trust to sell, instead of simply giving them a power, &c.

252. It would also be of great advantage when a testator gives his property upon long trusts, to provide for insuring his trustees' lives, so as to provide a fund to meet the fine and expences on a re-admission.

253. The Appendix will give the forms, enabling a practitioner to draw any general wills of copyholds.

254. The solicitor should obtain his client's signature to the instructions for his will, till a regular will is completed ; and though a will of copyholds does not require three witnesses, as that of freeholds, (see Scriven on Copyholds, 301, &c.,) yet it is always prudent to have the will attested by three witnesses, that if any part of the estate should turn out to be freehold, the will may not be questioned.

255. The necessity of a re-publication on a fresh purchase, has been before adverted to.

256. Where it is intended that a married woman should dispose of copyholds by will, she must, with her husband, surrender to the use of her will, and in such surrender be separately examined as in other cases. A surrender made by her previous to her marriage would not be operative. In other cases since 55 G. 3, c. 192, no surrender to will is requisite.

PARTITION.

257. Copyholds do not appear to be within the Act of 31 H. 8, c. 1, or the common law writ of partition, (see Scriven on Copyholds, 104; 2 Coventry on Copyholds, 152.) Nor do courts of equity appear to have entertained a suit to compel the partition of copyholds, (see Scriven on Copyholds, 609,) and therefore the partition of copyholds, when it takes place, is by the voluntary acts of the parties.

258. In the Appendix will be found forms of partition, and as in cases of joint property, the danger arising from the want of an actual surrender would not be likely to arise as in cases of simple ownership, when a subsequent mortgage or conveyance might be made, it will most frequently be better to effect an equitable partition, without necessity for an immediate re-admittance, and thereby avoid the heavy expence of the fine. See Appendix, No. 343, &c. Of course if an actual surrender is made, admittance must be taken, and a fine paid.

ENFRANCHISEMENT.

---

259. In the Appendix is given a rule, shewing the value of enfranchisement, so simplified as to be readily understood, and which, it might be remarked, has never before been published.

260. On a treaty for an enfranchisement, it would be prudent on the part of the tenant to stipulate for a deduction of the lord's title to the manor, though it would most brobably be held on a contract for the enfranchisement, that the shewing such title would be a necessary incident of the contract without express stipulation, as the lord could not enfranchise unless he was enabled to convey the fee simple of the freehold. On the other hand, the solicitor of the lord should stipulate, either that the expence of deducing such title should be borne by the tenant, or he should provide in the contract for limiting the enquiries to the conveyance or will under which the lord claims; or within such period as he may deem unobjectionable.

261. A copyholder having a limited estate may obtain an enfranchisement, but it will operate for the benefit of those in remainder to the copyhold.

262. The lord cannot, it seems, on an enfranchisement, reserve any services to himself, for though a yearly payment might be reserved, it would be as a rent-charge, or rent-seek, or obligatory on the tenant on his special covenants; but not as services in consequence of tenure.

263. The enfranchisement will destroy the cus-

tomary descent, and also all rights and privileges annexed to the copyholder's estate, a right of common will cease to exist, and such commonage will not pass by the word "appurtenances," in the enfranchisement, but must be expressly conveyed as a new grant. There might however be cases in which equity would interfere on this point. See *Styant* v. *Staker*, 2 Vern. 250.

264. The enfranchisement should always be taken in the name of the copyholder, and not to a trustee, as otherwise the copyhold interest would still continue, leaving the vendor entitled to her customary dower, and the customary heir to recover the possession in ejectment. See 1 Scriv. 617; and see *Howard* v. *Bartlett*, Hob. 181; *Walker* v. *Bartlett*, 2 Roll. Rep. 178; *Waldoe* v. *Bartlett*, Cro. Jac. 573; S. C. Palm. 111; *Lashmer* v. *Avery*, Cro. Jac. 176; *Murrell* v. *Smythe*, 4 Co. 24 b; 1 Vern. 392; and *Croft* v. *Lister*, cited 2 Vern. 164.

265. To guard against the inconvenience which might arise from the acceleration of right under the freehold tenure with its incumbrances, conveyancers frequently advise the creation of a term of years out of the copyhold tenure prior to enfranchisement, that, if requisite, the title to possession may depend on that tenure. See form 368.

266. See generally as to enfranchisement, Scriven on Copyholds, 616, &c., and 1 Coventry on Copyholds, 435, &c.

267. The form of agreements to enfranchise, and of an enfranchisement, will be found in No. 347, &c.

268. The deed will be prepared by the copyholder's solicitor in general, or by the steward, as may be agreed on; and perused, engrossed, and executed, as in other cases.

269. The requisitions on title, will be similar to those on a sale, qualified of course, by the contract; and the expences of each party will, in the absence of stipulations in the contract, be subject to the same rules as on a sale; but most frequently the lord sti-

pulates that he shall be put to no expence in the matter: this however must be matter of contract.

270. On a future sale the owner should stipulate that no enquiry should be made into the lord's title, as to the parts enfranchised, or should at least provide for his not being required to adduce a further title than that he has obtained from the lord. See 314.

APPENDIX

TO COPYHOLD PRACTICE.

PURCHASE AGREEMENTS.

(271.) *Copyhold Estate.*

Clause (*a*) Parties and date.
    (*b*) Contract and purchase money.
    (*c*) Description.
    (*d*) Time of giving possession or rents.
    (*e*) Payment of interest, &c.
    (*f*) Delivery of abstract.
    (*g*) Execution of conveyance.
    (*h*) Expence of copies, affidavits, &c.
    (*i*) Recitals in old documents to be proof.
    (*j*) Limit of title as so time, and identity of descriptions.

Clause (*k*) Title to waste.
    (*l*) Vendor to retain deeds, and as to copies, &c.
    (*m*) Purchasers to pay for timber by valuation.
    (*n*) —— Valuation between incoming and outgoing tenant.
    (*o*) —— for fixtures.
    (*p*) Mode of taking valuations.
    (*q*) Errors to be matters of compensation.
    (*r*) Conclusion.
    (*s*) Receipt for deposit.
    (*t*) Stamps.

(*a*) Memorandum of agreement made this   day of, &c., between, &c., as follows.

(*b*) The said A. B. agrees to sell to the said C. D., and the said C. D. agrees to purchase of him, at the sum of £ payable as follows, (*vis.*) £   on the signature hereof, (the receipt whereof is acknowledged,) and the remainder to be paid on the   day of   next.

(*c*) All that copyhold farm, called, &c., situate at, &c. and comprising, &c., free from all incumbrances, the land tax now £   per annum, and the fines and services to the manor of , of which the said premises are holden, only excepted.

(*d*) The said A. B. and his heirs, to pay all outgoings [*and keep the premises insured,*] and to be entitled to the rents and profits up to the said   day of   next; and on and from that day, on payment of the remainder of the purchase money as aforesaid, [*and of the valuation money after mentioned,*] the said C. D., his heirs or assigns, shall have possession [*or the rents and profits.*]

(*e*) And in default of payment as aforesaid, [*from whatever cause arising*] the said C. D. shall pay interest at the rate

63.

of 5*l.* per cent. per annum on the remainder of the purchase money unpaid [*and on any valuation of crops or produce increasing in value,*] [or, instead of interest, " *shall pay to the said A. B. a proportionate part of the rent,*] *up to the day of completion.*"

(**f**) And it is agreed between the said parties hereto, that the said A. B., shall, within fourteen days from the date hereof, deliver to the said C. D., or his solicitor, an abstract of the title to the said premises, (certified by the steward of the said manor,) and subject to the stipulations herein contained, make a good and marketable title to the same.

(**g**) And that the said A. B., and all other requisite parties, shall, on or before the said   day of   next, on payment of the remainder of the purchase money and completion of the purchase, on the part of the said C. D., pass and execute a proper surrender and assurance to the said C. D., his heirs and assigns, or as he or they shall direct, the same to be prepared by and at the expence of the said C. D.

(**h**) Who shall also bear (half) the expence of all copies, extracts, affidavits, and certificates, and searches for, or production of court rolls, or documents, or evidences of title not in the possession of the said A. B.

(**i**) And no proof shall be required of any facts stated or implied in any deeds, wills, court rolls, or documents above 30 years old.

(**j**) That the said A. B. shall not be called on to shew any earlier title than the year 17   , nor to identify the old with the present descriptions.

(**k**) Neither shall the said A. B. be required to shew any other title to the small pieces of land formerly waste, than the grant of the lord of the said manor of   .

(**l**) And that, the title deeds relating to other property of greater value, the vendor shall be entitled to retain the same on endorsing a memorandum of this sale on the copy of his admission, and delivering to the said C. D. attested or examined copies thereof, and a deed of covenant for production, (the expence of such deed and covenants to be borne by the said A. B. and C. D. equally.)

(**m**) It is further agreed that the said purchaser shall pay, in addition to, and with the remainder of the said purchase money, for the timber and other trees, down to those of the value of 1*s*, the same to be valued as hereinafter mentioned. [See s. 22, as to this stipulation.]

(**n**) And the purchaser shall also pay the usual valuation as between incoming and outgoing tenant, in respect of the said farm and lands; and also cart all the outgoing tenants' corn and grain to any place, not exceeding the distance of ten miles, having the straw, chaff, and calder in the usual manner.

(**o**) And the purchaser shall also pay by valuation for the fixtures in and about the said dwelling house.

(**p**) And it is further agreed, that all valuations shall be·

64

made by two referees, one to be chosen by each party, or by the umpire of such two referees, in case of their disagreement; and on neglect of either party to nominate a referee within ten days, after notice in writing, the decision of the referee first appointed, to be binding; and in case of the referees not agreeing on an umpire, the same to be appointed by Mr. A., Mr. B., or Mr. C., in the order in which named, on the request of either party. The valuations aforesaid to be made by the   day of   next; and if the amount be not paid by the day before fixed for completion, to bear interest at the rate aforesaid until payment, except on such part of the valuation as shall relate to fixtures.

(q) And it is lastly agreed, that any error in the above description shall not vitiate this contract, but (except as to the quantity of land, which being taken from an actual survey, shall be deemed conclusive) a compensation shall be paid or allowed, as the case may require, the same to be settled by referee or umpire, to be appointed as aforesaid.

(r) Witness the hands of the said parties, the day and year first above written.

(s) Receipt for deposit to be written at foot or annexed.

(t) Stamp 20s. if not under seal, and not above 15 folios.
　　,,　　35s. if under seal, or above 15 folios.
　　,,　　25s. progressive duty, each 15 folios additional.

In preparing purchase agreements, a reference to the conditions of sale Nos. 331, &c. may be useful.

(272.) *Freehold, Copyhold, and Leasehold.*

Clause (a) Parties and date.
(b) Contract and purchase money.
(c) Parcels.
(d) Time of giving possession or rents.
(e) Payment of interest, &c.
(f) Delivery of abstracts.
(g) Execution of conveyances
(h) Expence of copies, &c.
(i) Recitals in old documents to be proof.
(j) Limitation of title as to time.
(k) Title to waste.
(l)　,,　glebe
(m)　,,　enfranchized parts.

Clause (n) Vendor to retain deeds, delivering copies, &c.
(o) Purchaser to pay for timber by valuation.
(p) Purchaser to pay for farming valuation.
(q) Purchaser to pay for fixtures.
(r) Mode of taking valuations.
(s) Errors to be matters of compensation.
(t) Purchaser to indemnify against covenants in leases.
(u) Conclusion.
(v) Receipt for Deposit.
(w) Stamps.

(a and b) As in last precedent.

(c) All that farm called, &c. situate, &c. containing, &c. the farm-house and buildings, and 84 acres being freehold, 37 acres being copyhold of the manor of H.; a field called　　, containing 8 acres, being held by the said A. B. for the resi-

65

due of a term of 90 years, created by an indenture bearing date, &c. and made between, &c. and determinable on the decease of F.. F., G. H., and I K. ; and the field called   , containing 6 acres, held by the said A. B. for a term expiring on, &c. and created by an indenture bearing date, &c. and made between, &c. Free, &c. [271 *c*, *adding amount of rents.*]

(𝕯 and *ℓ*) These can be drawn from the last precedent.

(f) That the said A. B., his heirs, executors, or administrators shall, within twenty-one days from the date hereof, deliver to the said C. D. or his solicitor, proper abstracts of title to the said freehold, copyhold, and leasehold premises, and subject to the stipulations herein contained, make good titles thereto respectively ; but no abstract or evidence of title to the said leasehold premises respectively shall be required beyond the said original leases, and the consequent deeds and evidences.

(g) That the said A. B. and all other requisite parties shall and will on or before the said day of   next, on receiving the residue of the said purchase money and valuation money aftermentioned, execute and pass proper conveyances, surrenders, assignments, and assurances of the said freehold, copyhold, and leasehold premises respectively to the said C. D., his heirs, executors, administrators, and assigns, or as he or they shall direct, free from incumbrances, the said land tax, the fines, rents, and services in respect of the said copyhold hereditaments, and the rents and covenants in respect of the said leasehold premises only excepted; such conveyances, surrenders, assignments, and assurances to be prepared by and at the expence of the said C. D., his heirs, executors, administrators, and assigns, and to contain the usual and other proper covenants for title, quiet enjoyment, and further assurance.

(𝕳) That the purchaser shall bear [*half*] the expence of all copies, extracts, affidavits, and certificates, and searches for and production of deeds, wills, court rolls, surrenders, assignments, documents, or evidences of title not in the vendor's possession ; and also of or in relation to the preparing, perusing, and executing any assignment of outstanding terms to attend the inheritance, and the searching for and enabling any party to make such assignment.

(*i*, *j*, *k*) Can be taken from last precedent.

(*l*) That no further title than the conveyance in the usual form shall be required as to any parts of the estate formerly glebe, and sold to redeem land tax ; nor shall the vendor be called on to distinguish the freehold from the copyhold parts of the estate, or identify the old with the modern descriptions.

(m) Nor shall the lord's title be enquired into as to any parts formerly copyhold, and enfranchized.

(n) The clause authorizing vendor to retain the writings, can readily be drawn from 271, cl. *l*.

(*o*, *p*, & *q*) These valuation clauses can also be obtained from 271, cl. *m*, *n*, and *o*.

(*r*) The valuation arrangement clause. See 271 *p*.

(*s*) Errors to be matters of compensation. See 271, *q*.

(*t*) And, lastly, it is agreed that the said C. D., his executors or administrators shall, if required by the said A. B., his heirs, executors, or administrators, execute to him and them a proper bond or deed of covenant to indemnify him and them from payment of rent, or observance of covenant in respect of the said leasehold premises respectively, and against any loss, costs, or expence to arise from the said rent being unpaid, or the said covenants not being performed.

(*u*) Conclusion. (*v*) Receipt. (*w*) Stamps. See last precedent, *r*, *s*, and *t*.

---

273. *Notice to Vendor, requiring Inspection of Court Rolls.*

Sir,

I beg to apprize you that I have applied to Mr. C. D., steward of the manor of G., to allow the examination of the abstract of title to the premises copyhold of that manor, purchased by my client Mr. W. B. of you, with the court rolls of the above manor, and that the steward refuses to allow such examination.

I therefore give you notice that my client cannot proceed to the completion of the purchase without such examination being obtained, and that I am ready to attend and make such examination whenever an opportunity is afforded me of so doing; and I require you to obtain for me the opportunity of such examination.

Dated, &c.

---

274. *Undertaking to pay Steward's Fees on Inspection of Court Rolls.*

In order to prevent delay in completion of Mr. A. B.'s purchase of my client Mr. W. H., I hereby undertake to repay to Mr. A. B, all reasonable fees which he may pay to the steward of the manor of G. on inspecting the court rolls of that manor, and examining the abstract of title delivered by me with such court rolls.—Dated, &c.

---

275. *Notice of Appropriation of Purchase Money.*

I hereby give you notice that the sum of   *l.*, the unpaid purchase money for the estate purchased of you by Mr. A. B., was this day deposited at the bank of Messrs. C. & Co., at G., appropriated to the said purchase; and that the same may be invested in the purchase of Exchequer Bills, until completion of the purchase, if desired by you. And I further give you notice that the said A. B. is ready to proceed to a completion of the purchase agreeably to his contract; and on his behalf I require you to comply with the provisions of the contract on your part. Dated, &c.

---

276 A. *Absolute Surrenders.*

Vendor and Wife to Purchaser.

1. Manor of } The   day of   in the year of our
{ Lord, 183 .

2. Be it remembered, that on the day and year above written (Vendor), of, &c., and   his wife, copyhold tenants, or one of them a copyhold tenant of the said manor, came before me [*C. D. gentleman, deputy steward for this purpose only of*], R. G., gentleman [*chief*], steward of the said manor and the courts thereof.

3. And (she the said [*wife*], having been by me the said [*deputy*] steward first examined, separate and apart from her said husband, touching her free and voluntary consent to the making and passing the surrender hereinafter mentioned, and freely and voluntarily consenting thereto, as by law required).

4. Did out of Court, in consideration of the sum of £ of lawful money of Great Britain, to them or one of them in hand well and truly paid by [*purchaser*] of, &c. at or immediately before the passing the surrender hereinafter mentioned, the receipt of which sum, and that the same is in full for all consideration money on sale of the hereditaments hereinafter mentioned to be surrendered, is hereby, and by the receipt for the same sum hereunder written, acknowledged.

5. Surrender out of their and each of their hands into the hands of the lord [*s and lady*] of the said manor, by the hands and acceptance of me, the said [*deputy*] steward, by the rod, according to the custom of the said manor.

6. All that, &c. (*add description,* or *if general description is to be inserted*, say, "All and singular the messuages or tenements, lands, hereditaments, and premises whatsoever, of them the said [*vendor*] and   his wife, or either of them holden of the said manor by copy of court roll, with their and every of their rights, members, and appurtenances).

7. And the reversion and reversions, remainder and remainders, yearly and other rents, issues and profits thereof.

8. And also all the estate, right, title, interest, inheritance, use, trust, benefit, property, possession, power, claim, and demand whatsoever, both at law and in equity of them the said [*vendor*], and   his wife, or either of them, of in, to, or out

68

of the said hereditaments and premises, hereby surrendered or mentioned so to be, with the appurtenances.

9. To the use and behoof of the said [*purchaser*], his heirs, and assigns, for ever absolutely, according to the custom of the said manor.

10. Taken (together with the private ⎫
 examination of the said (wife),   ⎬ {[*Vendor's Signature*]
 the day and year first above   ⎬ [*Wife's Signature.*]}
 written   by me. ⎭

C. D.

The said [Deputy] *Steward.*

" Received the day and year first above ⎫
 written, of and from the above   ⎪
 named [*purchaser*] the sum of £   ⎪
 the consideration money above   ⎬ £
 mentioned, to be paid by him to us ⎪
 [*or me.*] As Witness our [*or my*] ⎪
 hands [*or hand.*]   ⎭

Witness,   _____

[*Signatures, or that of husband alone.*]

277, B.—*Vendor to Purchaser.*

The same form will readily serve for drawing this surrender, as the only alteration will be to omit the parts relating to the wife, and substitute the word " his," for " their and each of their," and " him," for " them or one of them," or, " them or either of them," and making a trifling alteration in the receipt.

278, C.—*Vendor to Purchaser, when Mortgage of even date.*

As in common surrender as far as " Use," *and then add*, subject nevertheless to a certain conditional surrender, this day made and passed by the said [*vendor*] and [*wife*] by direction of the said [*purchaser.*] To the use of, &c. Upon condition to be void, &c.; and to the principal money and interest thereby secured. See No. 343.

279, D.—*Surrender to two or more Purchasers as Joint Tenants.*

1, 2, and 3, as in precedent A.

4. Did out of court in consideration of the sum of £ of lawful money of Great Britain, to them or one of them in hand well and truly paid by [*purchaser*] of, &c. (2*d purchaser*) of, &c. [*adding names and descriptions,*] at or immediately before, &c. as in A. 4.

5 to 8. as in A.

9. To the use and behoof of the said [*purchasers,*] their heirs, and assigns for ever absolutely, as joint tenants, according to the custom of the said manor.

10. as in A.

11. The only alteration in this clause, will be to add the names of the purchasers, and substitute " them " for " him."

280, E.—*To Two or more, as Tenants in Common.*

The only difference between this and D., will be in clause 9, which will be as follows :

" To the use and behoof of the said [*purchasers*], their heirs and assigns for ever absolutely, as tenants in common, and not as joint tenants."

281, F.—*To Three, as Joint Tenants for Life, with remainder to Heirs of One.*

1, 2, and 3, as in A.

4. Did out of court, in pursuance of a covenant for that purpose contained in a certain indenture, bearing date on or about, &c., and made between, &c. and in consideration of the sum of £   of lawful money of Great Britain, to them or one of them in hand well and truly paid by A. B., of, &c. at or before the passing the surrender hereinafter mentioned, the receipt whereof is hereby, and by the receipt for the same sum endorsed on the said indenture, acknowledged ; and of 10s. in like manner paid by C. D., of, &c., and E. F., of, &c., the receipt whereof is also acknowledged; and at the request, and by the direction of the said A. B., testified by his signing his name at the foot hereof.

5 to 8, as in A.

9. To the use and behoof of the said A. B., C. D., and E. F., and their assigns for and during the term of their natural lives, and the natural lives of the survivors and survivor, and from and immediately after the decease of the survivor, to the use and behoof of the heirs and assigns of the said A. B. absolutely, according to the custom of the manor.

10, as in A.

11. Omitted, at the foot is the following memorandum, signed by directing party :—

" I consent to and direct the passing the above surrender." Dated, &c.

---

282 G.—*To a Purchaser, for his own life.*

1, 2, 3, as in A.

4. Will be altered by stating the consideration money to be in full, on sale of the " estate " instead of " hereditaments."

5, 6, 7. as in A.

8. Must have the following words added at the end of it, " during the natural life of the said " [*purchaser.*]

9. " To the use and behoof of the said [*purchaser*], and his assigns, for and during the term of his natural life."

10 and 11. as in A.

---

283 H.—*Of Vendor's Life Estate.*

1, 2, 3, as in B.

4. Will be altered by stating the consideration money to be for sale of the " life estate of the said [*vendor*], in the hereditaments hereinafter described or mentioned, is hereby, &c.

5, 6. as in B.

7. With the yearly and other rents, issues, and profits thereof.

8. Omit " inheritance," and after the words " of him the said " [*vendor,*] *add* " during the term of his natural life."

9. To the use and behoof of the said [*purchaser*], his heirs and assigns during the natural life of the said [*vendor*], according to custom of the said manor.

10, 11. as in B.

---

284 I.—*By Copyholder for Lives.*

Be it remembered, that on the day and year above written, [*vendor*] of &c., who at a court held &c., was admitted to the after described hereditaments, to hold to him and his heirs during the lives of [*nominees*], and the life of the longest liver of them, came before &c., (*then proceed as in A., omitting the parts relating to wife, substituting the words* " life interest " *for* " hereditaments" *in clause* 4, *and in clause* 9, *after* " heirs and assigns," *omit* " for ever absolutely," *and insert* " during the lives of the said [*nominees*] and the longest liver of them.")

---

285 J.—*Of a Reversion.*

1, 2, 3. As in B.

4. *Substitute the words* " reversion or remainder expectant on the decease of J. R., of and in the hereditaments herein after mentioned or described," *between the words* " on sale of the," *and* " is hereby."

5. as in B.

6. All that the reversion or remainder expectant on the decease of J. R., of and in all &c. [as in A.]

7. With the yearly and other rents, &c.

8 to 11. as in B.

71

286 K.—*Of a Moiety or other Share.*

1, 2, 3, as in A. or B.

4. Add the word "moiety" or other apt words before "hereditaments" and after "sale of the   ."*

5, as in A.

6. All that one undivided moiety or half part, the whole into two equal parts to be divided, [*or* all that one undivided sixth part of a moiety, and also all that one undivided fifth part of another sixth part of the said moiety &c. [*as the case may require*)] of and in all, &c.

7 to 11, as [in A., limiting clause 8 to the parts sold, if the vendor retains any part.

----

287 L.—*Of Premises subject to a Mortgage.*

1, 2, 3, as in precedent A. or B.

4. Vary this from A. by adding "subject to a certain conditional surrender passed &c., [*stating when surrender passed, by whom, and amount secured*], and to the said principal sum of £   and interest thereon as aforesaid, from the day of   last, is hereby and by," &c.

8. Add the words "equity of redemption" after "trust."

9. *Add*, subject 'nevertheless to the aforesaid conditional surrender, to the use of the said C. D., and his heirs, and to the principal sum of £   thereby secured, and all interest thereon from the   day of   last.—

10 and 11. as in A.

----

288 M.—*Under a Bankruptcy.*

It is as well to have the commissioners authorize the bankrupt and his wife to surrender, as it obviates all question under the bankruptcy, as they also surrender their own interest; but any other person could surrender, see p. 57.

1. *By bankrupt and wife.*

Clause 1, 2, and 3. as in A.

4. Did out of Court, in pursuance of a power to them given in and by a certain indenture of bargain and sale bearing date &c., and made between &c., in the names and on behalf of the said [*commissioners*], and also in consideration of 10*s* to them in hand paid by the said [*purchaser*], the receipt &c., for themselves and on their own behalf.

5, 6, and 7. as in A.—In clause 8, *after* "of them the said [*commissioners,*] *add* "and of them the said [*bankrupt and wife,*"] any or either of them respectively, of, into, &c.

9 and 10. as in A.

Omit the parts applying personally to the bankrupt and wife.

----

289 N.—*In pursuance of a Deed, and by direction.*

The above form and F. will give the surrender in this case, and the directing party should sign a memorandum at the foot, as follows :—

" I consent to and direct the passing the above surrender." Dated, &c.

---

290 O.— *Under Act for Relief of Insolvent Debtors.*

By Assignees and Insolvent and Wife.

Be it remembered &c. [*stating the parties as in R., if passed before different stewards, otherwise*] that on &c. A. B. of &c., and C. D. of &c., assignees of the estate and effects of E. F. of &c., an insolvent debtor, duly appointed by the Court for the Relief of Insolvent Debtors in England, and to whom the usual conveyance of the real and personal estate was duly made by I. K. of &c., provisional assignee of the said Court, by indenture bearing date &c., and that on &c., the said E. F., the insolvent, and A. his wife, came before me L. M., gentleman, steward of the said manor, and of the courts thereof. And (she the said A., *see* A 3,) did out of Court, in consideration of &c. [*state consideration paid to assignees, from A.* 4,] and in consideration [*nominal consideration to insolvent and wife*] surrender out of their and each and every of their hands, &c., [A 5 *to end.*]

The surrender from the assignees alone can readily be drawn from this form.

The conveyance to the assignees is to be enrolled, see 245.

---

291 P.—*On a Sale under a Court of Equity.*

Be it remembered, that on the day and year above written, A. B., of &c., a copyhold tenant of the said manor, came before me C. D., steward of the said manor and the courts thereof, and did, out of court, in consideration of the sum of £   , the apportioned consideration money for the hereditaments hereinafter described, and part of the sum of £   , the purchase money paid into the Bank England by C. D., of &c., with the privity of the Accountant General of the High Court of Chancery, to the credit of the cause, " B. v. G. and others," as appears by the receipt of the Accountant General, dated, &c ; and in pursuance of an order of the said Court, bearing date &c., whereby a report by A. B. Esq., one of the masters of the said Court, made on &c., and declaring the said C. D. the purchaser of certain estates therein mentioned, and comprising the copyhold hereditaments hereinafter mentioned, was ordered to be confirmed ; and that all requisite parties should make, pass, and execute proper conveyances, insurances, and assurances, to the said C. D., his heirs and assigns. Surrender &c., (*as in B.*)

292 Q.—*Under a Power of Attorney.*

Be it remembered, that on the day and year above written, [*vendor*] of, &c.,[a copyhold tenant of this manor, by [*attorney*] of, &c., his lawful attorney, for that purpose duly authorised in and by a certain power of attorney, bearing date, &c., under the hand and seal of the said [*vendor*], came before &c., (as in A)., [*omit clause* 2,] and did out of court in consideration of [*purchase money*] to him in hand &c., the receipt &c., [*A. clause* 4,] surrender out of his hands into the hands of the lord, [*lords or ladies, as the case may be*] of the said manor, by the hands and acceptance &c., (A. clause 5, add clause 6, 7, 8, and 9. In 10, omit the examination part, and the attorney will sign the vendor's name to the receipt, *adding,* " by A. B., his attorney, by virtue of the aforesaid power of attorney.")

---

293 R.—*Where passed before several Deputy Stewards.*

The date in clause 1, must be omitted, and the surrender commence as follows. Manor of W. H. Be it remembered, that on the   day of   , [*first vendor*] of, &c., a copyhold tenant of the said manor, and G. his wife, came before the undersigned [*first deputy*] of &c., deputy steward for that purpose of [*steward*], chief steward of the said manor and the court thereof ; and that on the   day of   , [*second vendor*] of, &c., a copyhold tenant[&c., 'came before the undersigned [*second deputy*] of, &c., (deputy steward for that purpose of the said steward), and she the said G., having been by the said [*first deputy*], first examined &c., (see clause 3 A,) the said [*first vendor*] and G. his wife, and [*second vendor,*] did out of court [*proceed with remaining clauses of A., adding the words* " and every" *after* "each."]

The surrender from the said [*first vendor*] and G. his wife, was with the private examination of the said G., taken the   day of   , by me,   .

The said Deputy Steward, *pro. hac. vince.*

The surrender by the said [*second vendor*] was on the   day of   , taken by me,

The said Deputy Steward, *pro. hac. vince.*

Separate receipts to be signed by the parties, and the consideration clause altered in that respect, if separate sums paid.

74

294 S.—*Under Fines and Recoveries Act.*

By 3 & 4 W. 4, c. 74, s. 50, a disposition by legal tenant in tail shall be made by surrender, and the consent of protector may be by deed or on the memorandum of surrender, ss. 51, 52.

When no Protector.

Be it remembered, that on &c., A. B., of, &c., a copyhold tenant of the said manor, came before me, C. D., &c., and did out of court, in consideration of, &c., (as in form A.) surrender &c., all &c. To which said hereditaments and premises the said A. B. was admitted tenant at a general court baron, or customary court, held for the said manor, on &c. to hold to him and the heirs of his body, according to the form and effect of a certain will therein mentioned or referred to. And the [reversion &c., and all the estate &c., To the use &c. (As in A).

---

295 T.—*Where a Protector consents.*

Be it remembered, that on &c., A. B. of, &c., a copyhold tenant &c., came before &c., and did out of court, by and with the consent of C. D., of &c., protector of the settlement under the will hereinafter mentioned, in pursuance of the power in that behalf contained in an act passed in the 3d and 4th years of the reign of his late Majesty, King William the Fourth, intituled, "An Act for the Abolition of Fines and Recoveries, and the substitution of more simple modes of assurance," testified by his signing his name at the foot of this surrender, and in consideration &c. (As in last Form).

---

296. *Deed of Covenant on Absolute Surrender.*

1. Commencement and parties.	7. Lawfully seised.
2, 3, & 4. Recital of surrender, parcels, and uses.	8. Good right to convey.
	9. For quiet enjoyment.
5. Recital of agreements to enter into covenants.	10. Free from incumbrances.
	11. For further assurance.
6. Testatum and covenant.	12. Stamps.

1. This indenture, made, &c. between [*vendor*] of, &c. of the one part, and [*purchaser*] of, &c. of the other part.

2. Whereas the said [*vendor*] has, with E. his wife, on the day of the date of these presents, for valuable considerations surrendered into the hands of the lord of the manor of W., in the said county of S., according to the custom of the said manor, [*where the surrender is of all and singular, &c. add* "by a general description of all and singular," &c.

3. All those, &c. [*description*.]

4. To the use of the said [*purchaser*], his heirs and assigns.

5. And whereas, previous to the passing the said surrender, it was agreed by and between the parties hereto, that the said [*vendor*] should enter into the covenants hereinafter contained for the estate, title, possession, and assurance of the said hereditaments and premises.

6. Now this indenture witnesseth, that in pursuance of the said agreement, and for the considerations before mentioned, and in consideration of 10s. to him in hand paid at the execution hereof by the said [*purchaser*], the receipt whereof is hereby acknowledged, he, the said [*vendor*], doth hereby for himself, his heirs, executors, and administrators, covenant, promise, and agree with and to the said [*purchaser*] his heirs and assigns, in manner following. (viz.)—

7. That for and notwithstanding any act, deed, matter, or thing whatsoever by him the said [*vendor*] and E. his wife, or either of them, at any time heretofore made, done, committed, occasioned, executed, or willingly suffered to the contrary, he the said [*vendor*] at the time of passing the said surrender of even date herewith, was and stood lawfully seised of the said hereditaments and premises hereinbefore mentioned to have been surrendered, with their appurtenances, for a good, sure, perfect, absolute, and indefeasible estate of inheritance, in fee simple in possession, according to the custom of the manor of W. aforesaid, without any manner of condition, trust, or other restraint, cause, matter, or thing whatsoever, to alter, change, defeat, revoke, impeach, make void, charge or determine the same.

8. And also that for and notwithstanding any such act, deed, matter or thing as aforesaid, he the said [*vendor*] then had good right, full power, and lawful and absolute authority, with the said E. his wife, to surrender all and singular the said hereditaments and premises hereinbefore mentioned to have been surrendered, with their appurtenances, in manner expressed in and according to the true intent and meaning of the surrender of the said hereditaments and premises hereinbefore mentioned.

9. And moreover, that it shall and may be lawful to and for the said [*purchaser*], his heirs and assigns, from time to time, and at all times for ever hereafter, peaceably and quietly to enter into and upon, have, hold, use, occupy, possess, and enjoy, all and singular the same hereditaments and premises, with their appurtenances, and to receive and take the rents, issues, and profits thereof, to and for his and their own use and benefit, without any lawful let, suit, trouble, molestation, eviction, ejection, interruption, or disturbance whatsoever of, from, or by the said [*vendor*] and E. his wife, or his heirs, or of, from, or by any other person or persons whomsoever lawfully or

equitably claiming or to claim by, from, under, or in trust for him, her, them, or any of them.

10. And that free and clear, and freely, clearly, and absolutely acquitted, exonerated, and discharged or otherwise, by the said [*vendor*], his heirs, executors, and administrators, well and sufficiently saved, defended, kept harmless, and indemnified of, from, and against all and all manner of former and other surrenders, gifts, bargains, sales, leases, mortgages, jointures, settlements, dowers, freebench, annuities, trusts, wills, entails, forfeitures, escheats, and all and singular other estates, titles, troubles, charges, and incumbrances whatsoever, had made, done, committed, executed, occasioned, or suffered by him the said [*vendor*] and E. his wife, or either of them ; or by any person or persons whomsoever lawfully or equitably claiming or to claim by, from, through, under, or in trust for him, her, or them, or by or through his, her, or their acts, means, default, privity, consent, or procurement.

11. And further, that he the said [*vendor*] and E. his wife, and his heirs, and all and every other person or persons having, or lawfully or equitably claiming or to claim any estate, right, title, or interest into or out of the said hereditaments and premises, or any part thereof, by, from, under, or in trust for him, her, or them, shall and will from time to time, and at all times hereafter, at the reasonable request, costs, and charges of the said [*purchaser*] his heirs or assigns, make, do, pass, execute, and perfect, or cause and procure to be made, done, passed, executed, and perfected, all and every such further and other acts, deeds, surrenders, conveyances, and assurances in the law whatsoever, for the further, better, more perfectly and absolutely surrendering, conveying, assuring, and confirming all and singular the said hereditaments and premises hereinbefore mentioned to have been surrendered, with the appurtenances, to the use of the said [*purchaser*], his heirs and assigns for ever, according to the true intent and meaning of the said surrender, and according to the custom of the said manor of W., as by the said [*purchaser*] his heirs or assigns, or his or their counsel in the law, shall be lawfully and reasonably devised or advised and required; but so as the said [*vendor*] or the said E. his wife, or his heirs, be not required to go or travel from his or their usual and respective places of abode or dwelling for the doing thereof. In witness, &c.

12 Stamp 35*s*.

25*s*. progressive, if 30 folios, for each entire 15 beyond first.

77

(297.)   *Bond for Covenants, instead of Deed of Covenant.*

1. Obligation.	9. Free from incumbrances.
2 to 5. Recitals of Contract, &c.	10. Further assurance.
6. Condition, lawfully seised.	11. Termination.
7. Right to convey.	12. Stamps.
8. Quiet enjoyment.	

1. Know all men that I [*vendor*] of, &c., am held and firmly bound to [*purchaser*] of, &c., in the penal sum of £ [*double purchase money,*] of lawful money of Great Britain, to be paid to the said [*purchaser*] or his certain attorney, executors, administrators or assigns, for which payment to be well and truly made, I bind myself, my heirs, executors and administrators, and every of them, for ever firmly by these presents, sealed with my seal. Dated this   day of   , in the   year of the reign of our Sovereign Lady Queen Victoria, and in the year of our Lord 183 .

2. Whereas the above bounded [*vendor*] has with [*Mary*] his wife on, &c. [*See* No. 2, last form.]

3. As No 3, last form.

4. To the use of the above named [*purchaser*], his heirs and assigns.

5. And whereas previous to the passing the said surrender, it was agreed that the above bounden [*vendor*] should enter into the bond or obligation above written, with the condition hereinafter contained.

6. Now the condition of the above written obligation is such, that if notwithstanding any act, &c., by the said [*vendor*] and his   wife, or either of them, at any time, &c. they the said [*vendor*] and   his wife, at the time, &c., were, &c. [296, cl. 7.]

7. And also for and notwithstanding, &c., they the said [*vendor*] and   his wife, then had, &c. [296, cl. 8.]

8. And if the said [*purchaser*], his heirs and assigns, from time to time, &c., do and shall peaceably, &c., without any lawful, &c., by the said [*vendor*] and   his wife or either of them, their, or either of their heirs, &c. [296, cl. 9.]

9. And that free, &c., suffered by the said [*vendor*] and   his wife, or either of them, &c., in trust for him, her, them, or by or through his, her, or their acts, &c. [296, cl. 10.]

10. And further, if he the said [*vendor*] and   his wife, and his [or her] heirs, and all, &c., in trust for him, her, them, &c. [296, cl. 11.]

11. Then the above written obligation to be void, or else to be and remain in full force and virtue.

12. 35*s.* stamp.

(298.) *Release of Right, under the Direction of a Court of Equity, from Infant Heir, equitably interested.*

To all to whom these presents shall come : J. C. of, &c., now an infant of the age of eighteen years or thereabouts, youngest son and customary heir of E., formerly the wife of W. C., late of, &c., deceased, sendeth greeting : Whereas J. L., formerly of, &c., deceased, in and by his last will and testament bearing date, &c., gave and devised unto A. B. and C. D., and to the survivor of them, and the heirs of such survivor, all his messuages, &c., upon certain trusts therein expressed, and ultimately for the benefit of the children of the said J. L., of whom there were five, (vis.) Priscilla, then the wife of R. B., and now Priscilla the wife of T. S., the said E. C. and Maria L., Sarah L., and Penelope L. : And whereas in or about the year 1813, certain parts of the estates comprised in the said devise, were, with the concurrence of all the parties interested, sold to J. P., then of, &c., since deceased; and on such sale thereof, the freehold parts of the said estates were duly conveyed, and the copyhold parts thereof were covenanted to be surrendered, to the said J. P. on the various manors by the parties respectively then standing admitted and entitled thereto : And whereas the said C. D., the surviving trustee, at the time of such sale stood admitted tenant to the parts of the said estate hereinafter described and mentioned to be released, and holden of the manor of, &c.; and in pursuance of the said covenant, the said copyhold hereditaments were surrendered, or intended to be surrendered to the use of the said J. P. and his heirs by the said C. D., and the said J. P. was admitted tenant thereto : And whereas on the death of the said J. P., which happened on or about, &c., his youngest son and customary heir, J. R. P., was admitted tenant to the said copyhold hereditaments : And whereas the said J. R. P. on or about, &c., departed this life, having by his last will and testament, bearing date on, &c., devised his real estate, including the said copyhold hereditaments to [*trustee*] upon certain trusts in the said will mentioned ; and the said [*trustee*] hath been lately admitted tenant to the said copyhold hereditaments : And whereas by a decree of the High Court of Chancery, made in a cause wherein W. B. on behalf of himself, and all other the creditors of the said J. R. P., but since deceased, was plaintiff, and M. P. and others are defendants, it was ordered that the real estate of the said J. R. P., including the said copyhold hereditaments, should be sold, and that all proper parties should join in conveying and assuring the same to the purchaser : And whereas the said after-described hereditaments, together with certain other hereditaments of the said J. R. P., have been accordingly sold pursuant to the said decree : And whereas the said E. C. departed this life on or about, &c., and the said J. C., party hereto, is the youngest son and heir according to the custom

of the several manors hereinafter mentioned, of the said E. C. :
And whereas the [*purchaser*] hath required, in order to perfect
the equitable title to one-fifth part of the hereditaments hereinafter described, that the same should be released and discharged from all estate claim or demand of the customary
heir of the said E. C. : And whereas by an order of the High
Court of Chancery, bearing date, &c., and made in the said
cause, *B. v. P. and others*, it was ordered that it should be referred to W. B., Esquire, one of the Masters of the said Court,
to examine and certify whether the said J. C. was an infant
trustee within the meaning of the act of parliament of the
first year of the reign of his late Majesty King William the
Fourth, entitled " An Act for amending the Laws respecting Conveyances and Transfers of Estates and Funds vested
in Trustees and Mortgagees, and for enabling Courts of
Equity to give effect to their decrees and orders in certain cases, and for whom :" And whereas the said Master
by his report in the said matter, bearing date, &c., certified that the said J. C. was a trustee within the intent and
meaning of the said act of parliament, and that he was such
trustee for W. H., trustee under the will of the said J. R. P.,
and for the several persons interested in the said copyhold
estates : And whereas by another order of the said Court of
Chancery, made in the said cause and bearing date, &c., it
was ordered that the said master's report should be confirmed,
and that the said J. C. the infant, should make and execute to
W. H., or to such person as he should direct, a proper release,
surrender and conveyance of the said copyhold hereditaments and premises, so far as regards the one-fifth share to
which the said E. C. was entitled as hereinbefore mentioned.
Now KNOW YE, that in pursuance of and in obedience to the
said lastly hereinbefore recited order, he the said J. C in consideration of 10*s.* of lawful money of Great Britain, to him
in hand paid by the said [*trustee*] at or before the execution
hereof, (the receipt whereof is hereby acknowledged,) hath
remised, released, and for ever quitted claim, and by these
presents doth remise, release, and for ever quit claim unto
the said [*trustee*] and his heirs, according to the customs of
the respective manors whereof the same are holden, *All*
the estate, right, title, interest, trust, power, property, benefit, claim and demand whatsoever (if any) of him the said
J. C., as customary heir as aforesaid, of and in all that, &c.,
which premises are holden by copy of court roll of the manor
of G. B. in the county of S. And also of and in, &c., which
premises are holden by copy of court roll of the manor of
G. H. in the county of S. ; and also of and in, &c., which
said last described premises are holden by copy of court roll
of the manor of K. in the county of S., and are the same premises as are mentioned or referred to in and by the said
master's report hereinbefore recited : To the only and absolute

use and behoof of the said [*trustee*], his heirs and assigns for
ever, according to the custom of the said several manors respectively, freed and absolutely discharged of and from all the
estate, right, title, claim and demand whatsoever, both at law
and in equity, of him the said J. C., of, in, to, or out of the
said several and respective hereditaments and premises, and
every part and parcel thereof respectively, with the appurtenances, so that neither he the said J. C., nor his heirs may
have, claim, challenge or demand therein or thereto, any
estate, right, title or interest whatsoever; but shall for ever
hereafter be therefrom by this release precluded and barred.
In witness, &c.

(299.) *Surrender and Release of Equitable Right of Married
         Woman, under Direction of Court of Chancery.*

Manor of   , the   day of   A. D. 18 .
Whereas John Leach, formerly of, &c. [*recite as in release
from John C. to sale under decree.*]   And whereas, R. B. the
husband of the said Priscella B., died some years since, and the
said E. B. subsequently intermarried with and is now the wife
of Thos. Searle, of &c.

And whereas the said [*purchaser*] having required, that in
order to perfect the equitable title to one-fifth part of the
hereditaments hereinafter described, the same should be surrendered and released by the said P. Searle and the said Thos.
Searle, her husband.

Now be it remembered, that on the day and year above
written, the said Thos. S. and P. his wife, came before me,
G. B., gent., deputy steward for that purpose of A. B.,
gent., chief steward of the said manor, and (she the said P.
having been by me the said deputy steward first examined,
separate and apart from her said husband, touching and concerning her free and voluntary consent to the making and
passing the surrender hereinafter contained, &c. (A)) did out
of court, in pursuance of the said order, and in consideration
of 10s. to them or one of them in hand paid by the said [*tenant*], the receipt whereof they do hereby acknowledge,

Surrender, &c. (A. 5); and also remise, release, and for
ever quit claim unto the said [*tenant,*] tenant by virtue of the
aforesaid admission, and to his heirs and assigns,

All the estate, right, title, interest, trust, power, property,
benefit, claim, and demand whatsoever (if any) both at law
and in equity, of them the said Thos. S. and P. his wife, or
either of them, of, in, to, or out of   . All, &c. and
the reversion, &c.

To the only and absolute use and behoof of the said [*tenant*],
his heirs and assigns for ever, according to the custom of
the said manor, freed and absolutely discharged from all
estate, right, title, claim and demand whatsoever, both at law

and in equity, of them the said T. S. and P. his wife, of, in, to, or out of the said hereditaments and premises, with the appurtenances, so that neither the said T. S. and P. his wife, or either of them, or his or her heirs, may have, claim, challenge, or demand therein or thereto, any estate, right, title, or interest whatsoever, but shall for ever hereafter be therefrom by this surrender and release precluded and barred.

Taken (together with the private examination of the said Priscella,) the day and year first above written, by me,

> The said Deputy Steward.

———

Stamp, 35s.
To be presented and entered at next Court.

———

(300.) *Release of Husband's Courtesy.—(Dower will be similar.)*

To all to whom, &c.

Whereas, [*recite admission of wife,—her death, seised,—admission of younger son as customary heir, and agreement to re-courtesy.*]

Now these presents witness, that in pursuance of the said consent and agreement, and in consideration of the natural love and affection which the said J. B. hath and beareth towards the said B. B. his son, and also in consideration of 10s. to him at the execution hereof paid by the said B. B., the receipt whereof is hereby acknowledged,

He the said J. B. hath remised, released, and for ever quitted claim, and by these presents, doth remise, &c. unto the said B. B., his heirs and assigns,

All the customary [*courtesy, husband's estate,*] claim, right, title, interest, and demand whatsoever, of him the said J. B. of, in, to, or out of

All those, &c. And the reversion, &c.

To the use and behoof of the said B. B., his heirs and assigns for ever absolutely, according to the custom of the said manor of   ; to the end and intent that the said B. B. his heirs and assigns may henceforth have, hold, possess and enjoy all and singular the hereditaments and premises hereinbefore described, freed and discharged from the customary, [*courtesy*] and all other estate, right, title, interest, claim, or demand, of him the said J. B., of, in, to, or out of the said hereditaments and premises, or any part thereof; and of and from all actions, suits, claims, and demands in respect thereof, or in anywise in relation thereto. In witness, &c.

35s. Stamp.

Common surrenders and releases of right, are generally made in Court. See Court Keeping Forms, 528, &c.; and if advisable, a power of attorney to surrender and release can be prepared from No. 329.

---

301. *Bargain and Sale from Executors.*

1. Commencement.
2. Parties.
3. Recital of Admission.
4. ————— Will.
5. ————— Death and proof of will.
6. ————— Death of Tenant for life.
7. ————— Contract for sale.
8 Testatum, consideration, and receipt.
9. Reference to power.
10. Bargain and Sale.
11 Description.
12. Reversion and Estate.
13. Habendum.
14. Covenant from Executors.

1. This indenture, made, &c.

2. Between [*executors, describing them*] of the one part, and [*purchaser*] of, &c. of the other part.

3. Whereas, at a general court baron, or customary court, held for the manor of, &c. on, &c. the [*testator*] of, &c. was duly admitted to the after-described hereditaments, to hold to him and his heirs, according to the custom of the said manor.

4. And whereas the said [*testator*] in and by his last will and testament, bearing date, &c., after giving the said hereditaments to C. D. for life, directed, authorised, and empowered the said [*executors*], or the survivor, his executors or administrators, to make sale and dispose thereof [*stating the power as in the will, and stating fully the declaration that the receipts by executors should be discharges*].

5. And whereas the said [*testator*] departed this life on or about, &c. without having altered or revoked his said will, and the same was, on or about, &c. duly proved in, &c. by the said executors.

6. And whereas the said C. D. died on or about, &c.

7. And whereas the said [*executors*] by virtue of the said power in the will of the said [*testator*] contained, lately contracted with the said [*purchaser*] for the sale to him of the hereditaments after described, free from incumbrances, at the sum of £　.

8. Now this indenture witnesseth, that in pursuance of the said contract, and in consideration of the said sum of £ of lawful money of Great Britain to the said [*executors*] in hand well and truly paid by the said [*purchaser*] at or immediately before the execution of these presents, the receipt whereof and that the same is in full for the absolute purchase of the customary fee simple and inheritance of the said hereditaments, the said [*executors*] do hereby acknowledge, and of and from the same and every part thereof, do hereby, and by the receipt

hereupon endorsed, acquit, release, and for ever discharge the said [*purchaser*] and his heirs, and also the said hereditaments.

9. They the said [*executors*] in further pursuance and exercise of the said power or authority in this behalf given to them in and by the said recited will, and of all and every other power and powers, authority and authorities, them enabling hereunto.

10. Have, and each of them hath, bargained and sold, limited, appointed, conveyed, and assured, and by these presents do, and each of them doth, bargain, &c. unto the said [*purchaser*] his heirs and assigns.

11. All, &c. [*description*] together with all houses, outhouses, &c. [*general words applicable*].

12. And the reversion, &c. And all the estate, &c. [*see absolute surrender*].

13. To have and to hold all and singular the said [*messuage or tenement*] hereditaments and premises mentioned, or intended to be hereby bargained and sold, or otherwise assured, with the appurtenances, unto and to the use of the said [*purchaser*] his heirs and assigns, for ever, according to the custom of the said manor.

14. And the said [*executors*] do hereby for themselves severally, and for their several and respective heirs, executors, and administrators, covenant and declare with and to the said [*purchaser*] his heirs and assigns, that they the said [*executors*] have not nor hath either of them, at any time heretofore, made, done, committed, executed, or suffered, or been party or privy to any act, deed, matter or thing whatsoever, whereby or by means whereof the said hereditaments hereby mentioned to be bargained and sold, or otherwise assured, with the appurtenances, are, is, can, shall, or may be impeached, charged, affected, or incumbered in title, estate, or otherwise howsoever. In witness, &c

Conveyance stamp.

302.—*Bargain and Sale under a Bankruptcy, where Premises mortgaged.*

1. Commencement.	9. Bargain and Sale.
2. Parties.	10. Description.
3. Recital of Admission.	11. Reversion and Estate, &c.
4. —————— Conditional Surrender.	12. Habendum.
5. —————— Fiat and Proceedings.	13. Authority to Surrender.
6. —————— Contract for Sale.	14. Covenant from Assignees and Mortgagee.
7. —————— Agreement by Bankrupt and Wife to join.	15. Covenant by Bankrupt for further Assurance.
8. Testatum, Consideration and Receipts.	

1. This indenture made, &c.

2. Between [*A. B., C. D., and E. F.*] esqrs., the major part of the commissioners named and appointed in and by a

84

fiat in bankruptcy, awarded and issued, and now in prosecu-
tion against [*bankrupt*,] of, &c. [*wine and brandy merchant*,]
dealer and chapman, of the first part; G. H. of, &c. and I. K.
of, &c., assignees of the estate and effects of the said bankrupt
of the second part; C. K. of, &c. [*bankrupt*] and E. his wife,
of the third part; [*mortgagee*] of, &c. of the fourth part;
and [*purchaser*] of, &c. of fifth part.

3. Whereas, &c. [*recite admission of bankrupt. See last
form.*]

4. And whereas, on or about, &c. the said [*bankrupt*] and
his wife, out of court, duly surrendered all and singular,
&c., to the use of the said [*mortgagee*], his heirs and assigns,
upon condition to be void on payment to him, his executors,
administrators, or assigns, of £   , and lawful interest on,
&c., but which was not paid, and with an arrear of interest
still remains due and payable to him.

5. And whereas a fiat in bankruptcy, bearing date, &c.,
and directed to, &c. duly issued against the said [*bankrupt*],
by the direction of, &c. and the said [*bankrupt*] was, on or
about, &c. duly adjudged a bankrupt, and on or about, &c.
the said [*assignees*] were duly chosen, nominated, and appointed assignees of the estate and effects of the said [*bankrupt*,] and the certificate of such appointment was duly signed
by the said [*commissioners.*]

6. And whereas the said [*assignees*] lately contracted with
the said [*purchaser*] for the absolute sale to him of the
after-described hereditaments, at the sum of £   , out of
which sum it is agreed that the principal and interest monies
due to the said [*mortgagee*,] being the sum of £   as the
said [*assignees*] and [*mortgagor*] do hereby respectively acknowledge, shall be paid and satisfied.

7. And whereas, the said [*bankrupt*] and   his wife have
agreed to join in conveying and assuring the said hereditaments.

8. Now this indenture witnesseth, that in pursuance of
the premises, and in consideration of the sum of £   of
lawful money, &c. to the said [*mortgagee*,] and of £   of
like lawful money, remainder of the said sum of £   , to
the said [*assignees*], with the privity and approbation of the
said [*commissioners*], testified by their execution hereof, in
hand well and truly paid by the said [*purchaser*,] at or immediately before the execution hereof, the receipt of which
sums respectively, making together the said purchase money,
they the said [*mortgagee*] and [*assignees*] do hereby respectively admit and acknowledge, and thereof and therefrom,
and from every part thereof, do acquit, release, and for
ever discharge the said [*purchaser*], his heirs, executors, &c.
and also the said hereditaments by these presents, and in consideration of 10*s.* each to them the said [*commissioners*] [*and*

85

the said bankrupt and wife] in like manner paid, the receipt whereof is hereby acknowledged,

9. They the said [*commissioners*] have bargained, sold, assigned, conveyed, and assured, and by these presents do bargain, &c. and the said [*assignees*,] and the said [*bankrupt*] and wife have, and each and every of them hath bargained, sold, remised, released, and confirmed, and by these presents do bargain, &c. and the said [*mortgagee*] hath released and quitted claim, and by these presents doth release, &c. unto the said [*purchaser*], his heirs, and assigns.

10. All that, &c. [*Description and general words.*]

11. And the reversion, &c. and all the estate, &c. of all said parties [*in surrender A.*]

12. To have and to hold the said hereditaments and premises mentioned, or intended to be hereby bargained and sold, or otherwise assured, with the appertunances, unto and to the use of the said [*purchaser*], his heirs and assigns for ever, at the will of the lord, and according to the custom of the said manor of   by the rents and services therefore due, and of right accustomed.

13. And this indenture also witnesseth, that in pursuance of the said sale and purchase, and of the act or acts of parliament enabling them in that behalf, and for the considerations aforesaid, they the said [*commissioners*] do hereby authorize and entitle, and also nominate and appoint the said [*bankrupt*] their true and lawful attorney, for them the said [*commissioners*] and on their behalf, or in the name or stead of the survivors of them, to surrender into the hands of the lord or lords, lady or ladies for the time being, of the said manor of   , according to the custom thereof, all and singular the said hereditaments and premises hereinbefore described, and hereby bargained and sold, or intended so to be, and every part and parcel thereof, with the appurtenances, and all the estate, right, title and interest of them the said [*commissioners*,] and also of the said [*bankrupt*] of, in, and to the same, to the use of the said [*purchaser*,] his heirs and assigns for ever, at the will of the lord, and according to the custom of the said manor, and for them the said [*commissioners*], and the survivors of them, in their or his names or name to do and execute all and every act, matter, and thing that shall be required for making such surrender as aforesaid, and for procuring the said [*purchaser*], his heirs, and assigns, to be admitted to the said copyhold premises accordingly, as fully to all intents and purposes as if they were personally present and did the same themselves, and the said [*commissioners*] do hereby ratify and confirm all and whatsoever their said attorney shall lawfully do or cause to be done in and about the premises.

14. And the said [*assignees*] and [*mortgagee*] do hereby

86

severally, &c. [*add covenants from assignees and mortgagor that they have not encumbered. See last precedent.*]

·15. And the said [*bankrupt*] for himself, and the said
, his wife, and his [*and her, if wife's property*], heirs, executors and administrators, doth hereby covenant, promise and agree to and with the said [*purchaser*], his heirs, and assigns, that he the said [*bankrupt*], and the said
his wife, and his [*her*] heirs, shall and will at any time or times hereafter, at the request, costs, and charges of the said [*purchaser*], his heirs or assigns, make, pass, and execute, and join and concur in making, passing, and executing all such further acts, surrenders and deeds, whatsoever, for further, better, and more effectually conveying and assuring the aforesaid hereditaments, with the appurtenances, to the use of the said [*purchaser*], his heirs and assigns, or as he or they shall direct, according to the custom of the said manor, as by him or them, or his or their counsel in the law, shall be reasonably devised, advised, or required.

> This deed must be acknowledged and enrolled. See
> 6 G. 4, c. 16, s. 68, and the following will be the
> exhibit on the deed and affidavit of execution.
> The surrender passed under the power in this deed,
> will be found in form 288.
> A warrant to enter satisfaction must also be prepared.
> [*See form* 306.]

------

303. *Exhibit to be written on Deed.*

This is the indenture of bargain and sale referred to in the affidavit of D. C. M., gentleman, sworn before me this
day of   . [*To be signed by the master, or master extraordinary, before whom affidavit taken.*]

------

304. *Affidavit.—2s. 6d. Stamp.*

D. C. M., of &c., gentleman, maketh oath and saith, that he was present on, &c., and did see the indenture hereunto annexed, bearing date, &c., and made between, &c., signed, sealed, and delivered by the said [*one party, usually purchaser.*] And that the names " D. C. M." and " R. A." set or subscribed as witnesses to the due execution of the said indenture by the said [*purchaser*] are of the respective proper hands writing of the said R. A., and of this deponent.

D. C. M.   Sworn [*at W. in the county of S.*] the   day
         of   18   , before me,
                        C. D.
                  A master extraordinary in Chancery.
> The bargain and sale will be on conveyance stamp, and
> the surrender, on a 20s. stamp.

305.—*Opinion of an eminent Conveyancer, as to the mode of Conveyance, under the following circumstances.*

John T. being seised of certain copyhold hereditaments, passed a conditional surrender thereof to William G., for securing 1500*l.* and interest. The premises subsequently became of less value than the sum secured on them. T. became a bankrupt. An assignment was made of his personal estate, but no bargain and sale of his real estate. The assignee died having appointed executors. The mortgagee also died, and his executors contracted with H. E., for sale of the premises at 850*l.* One of the acting commissioners was dead, and another not to be found. No dividend was made under T.'s bankruptcy, and most of the creditors who had proved were dead.

" The proper mode of proceeding to make a title to the purchaser, is for the mortgagees to apply to the commissioners for a sale of his security, and then for the commissioners, by the direction of the personal representative of the assignee, to bargain and sell, and for a person appointed by them to surrender to the purchaser. I do not see that the title can be rendered unexceptionable, unless the course I have suggested is pursued, though as far as security goes, it will be safe and sufficient for all purposes of enjoyment, if either of the following plans be adopted, *vis.* that the customary heir of W. G. should be admitted, and by the direction of his executors, surrender to the purchaser; or that the bankrupt, in whom the legal estate still remains, and in whom it will remain till the admittance of the heir of the mortgagee, or a bargain and sale by the commissioners, should by the like direction, surrender to the use of the purchaser, and the assignee release to him ; and the consent of the creditors individually being obtained to either of these arrangments, I do not see who could question the purchaser's title ; but I do not think that the consent of creditors, present at a meeting convened for the purpose of acceding to the proposed sale, would be binding on those who are absent; at least it is inexpedient that such a consent should be relied on.

9th June, 1828.

(305.)   *Warrants to enter Satisfaction on Conditional Surrenders.*

(Common form.)

1. Manor of,   . To the steward of the said manor, or his lawful deputy for the time being.

2. I [*mortgagee*] of &c.

3. Do hereby authorize and require you, or one of you, to enter full satisfaction and discharge in the court books or on the court rolls of the said manor, of and for.

4. A certain conditional surrender, made and passed [*out of court*], by A. B., of &c., and C. his wife, copyhold tenants, or one of them, a copyhold tenant of the said manor, on, &c.

5. Of all and singular &c., [*or of certain hereditaments in the memo randum of surrender described.*]

6. To the use of me the said [*mortgagee*], and my heirs, for securing to me, my executors, administrators, and assigns, the sum of £.   , and interest, at the rate and manner in the said memorandum of surrender expressed.

7. And for your so doing this shall be to you and each of you a sufficient warrant and authority.

8. As witness my hand this   day of   , 18 .
   Witness.—

Two parts on plain paper; receipt for money to be given on mortgage bond.

(307.)   *Where Part of Mortgage Money paid off.*

I &c., do hereby authorize and require you or one of you, to enter satisfaction in the court books or on the court rolls of the said manor, of and for the sum of £   , part of the principal money, secured by a certain conditional surrender, [*proceed as in last form, clauses* 4, 5, 6, 7, and 8.]

(308.)   *Where part of Property discharged.*

2. Whereas on or about &c., A. B., of &c., and C. his wife, copyhold tenants, or one of them, a copyhold tenant of the said manor, [*out of court*] surrendered all &c., to the use of me, the undersigned [*mortgagee*] of &c., my heirs and assigns, subject to a condition for making the same void on payment to me, my executors, administrators, or assigns, of the sum of £   , and lawful interest, on &c., but which sum was not paid according to such proviso.

3. And whereas the said A. B., having lately contracted for the sale to E. F., of &c., of all &c., being part of the hereditaments comprised in the said recited surrender, hath applied to and requested me the undersigned [*mortgagee*], to discharge such hereditaments, so contracted to be sold, from the said recited conditional surrender, and to allow the said mortgage money to remain secured on the residue of the said hereditaments, which I have agreed to do.

4. Now I the said [*mortgagee*] do hereby authorize and require you, or one of you, to enter satisfaction and discharge in the court books or on the court rolls of the said manor, on the said surrender, so far only as respects the said hereditaments hereinbefore described and mentioned to have been sold to the said E. F. And for your so doing, &c., (clause 8.)

(309.)   *Where part of Property discharged, and part of Principal paid off.*

1. As in form 306 ; 2 and 3 as in 308, altering 3 as follows : *after* " conditional surrender," *add*, on receiving the sum of £   , part of the consideration money on such sale, and to allow the remainder of the said mortgage money to remain &c. And in pursuance whereof, the said sum of £   , hath this day been paid to me accordingly, and for which I have given my receipt on the mortgage bond from the said A. B., and which reduces the amount of principal money to remain secured on the said surrender to the sum of £   , with interest thereon, from, &c.

Now I the said [*mortgagee*], do hereby authorize and require you, or one of you, to enter satisfaction and discharge for the sum of £   , part of the said principal sum secured on the said surrender, and also to enter satisfaction and discharge on the said surrender, as far as respects the said hereditaments so contracted to be sold as aforesaid. And for your so doing, &c.

(310.)   *By Executor or Administrator, Assignees of Bankrupt, &c.*

I, [*executor*] of, &c., executors named and appointed in and by the last will and testament of [*mortgagee*], bearing date &c., [*assignees of the estate and effects, of, &c., a bankrupt.*] Do hereby &c., (to clause 5,) to the use of the said [*mortgagee*], his heirs and assigns, for securing to him, his executors, &c., [*as in form* 306, *clause* 6, 7.]   As witness our hands, &c.

(311.)   *Conveyance of Freehold and Copyhold.*

1. Commencement.	9. Reversion, &c. Estate, &c.
2. Parties.	10. Deeds.
3. Recital of Contract.	11. Habendum.
4. „ Apportionment.	12. Covenants : lawfully seised.
5. „ Surrender.	13. „ good right to convey.
6. Testatum, Consideration, and	14. „ for quiet enjoyment.
Receipt.	15. „ free from incumbrances.
7. Grant.	
8. Parcels.	16. „ Further Assurance.

1. This indenture made the   day of   A. D, 18

2. Between [*vendor*] of, &c. of the one part, and [*purchaser*] of, &c. of the other part.

90

3. Whereas the said [*vendor*] hath lately contracted and agreed with the said [*purchaser*] for the sale to him of the freehold hereditaments hereinafter described, and intended to be hereby granted and released, with the appurtenances, for an estate of inheritance in fee simple in possession, and also of the customary or copyhold hereditaments hereinafter also described and [*mentioned to have been*] surrendered, with their appurtenances, for a like estate of inheritance, according to the custom of the manor of W. in the county of S., and respectively free from incumbrances (the quit rent of, &c. and the rents and services in respect of the said copyhold hereditaments only excepted) at the price or sum of £   .

4. And whereas, for the purpose of complying with the provisions of the acts of parliament imposing duties *ad valorem* on conveyances, it has been agreed that the sum of £   shall be apportioned as the consideration money for the freehold hereditaments, and the sum of £   , as the consideration money for the copyhold hereditaments.

5. And whereas, in pursuance and towards performance of the said contract and agreement, the said [*vendor*] has, on the day of the date hereof, duly surrendered into the hands of the lord of the aforesaid manor, by the hands of A. B., gentleman, steward thereof, all, &c. being the aforesaid copyhold hereditaments, to the use of the said [*purchaser*] his heirs and assigns, according to the custom of the said manor ; and on the memorandum of such surrender, the *ad valorem* stamp in respect of the said apportioned consideration money is duly impressed.

6. Now this indenture witnesseth, that in further pursuance of the said recited contract and agreement, and in consideration of the sum of [*freehold consideration*] of lawful money, &c. to the [*vendor*] in hand well and truly paid by the said [*purchaser*] at or immediately before the execution of these presents, the receipt whereof the said [*vendor*] doth hereby and by the receipt hereupon written acknowledge, and of and from the same, and every part thereof, doth acquit, release, exonerate, and discharge the said [*purchaser*] his heirs, executors, administrators, and assigns, and every of them, for ever by these presents.

7. He the said [*vendor*] hath granted, bargained, sold, aliened, released and confirmed, and by these presents doth grant, &c. unto the said [*purchaser*] (in his actual possession, &c.) and to his heirs and assigns.

8. All, &c. [*if the freehold and copyhold cannot be separately described, say* " all such part and parts, and so much as be freehold or charterhold, and not of copyhold or customary tenure, of and in all," &c.] together with all houses, &c. to the said freehold parts, hereditaments and premises belonging, or in anywise appertaining, or therewith usually held, occupied,

or enjoyed, or accepted, reputed, deemed, taken, or known as part, parcel, or member thereof.

9. And the reversion, &c. and all the estate, &c.   (*See surrender.*)

10. And all deeds, evidences, and writings in anywise relating to the same hereditaments and premises, now in the custody or power of the said [*vendor*] or which he can procure without suit at law or in equity.

11. To have and to hold all and singular the said freehold parts, hereditaments, and premises hereinbefore granted and released, or mentioned or intended so to be, with their appurtenances, unto the said [*purchaser*], his heirs and assigns, to the only proper use and behoof of the said [*purchaser*], his heirs and assigns for ever, and to or for no other use, intent, or purpose whatsoever.

12. And the said [*vendor*] doth hereby for himself, his heirs, executors, and administrators, covenant, promise, and agree to and with the said [*purchaser*], his heirs and assigns, that for and notwithstanding any act, deed, matter, or thing by him the said [*vendor*] at any time heretofore made, done, commenced, or suffered to the contrary, he the said [*vendor*], at the time of executing these presents, is and standeth lawfully and rightfully seised of the said freehold messuages, hereditaments, and premises hereby granted and released, or intended so to be, and of every part thereof, with the appurtenances, for a good, sure, perfect, lawful, absolute, and indefeasible estate of inheritance in fee simple in possession, and at the time of passing the before-recited surrender of the said copyhold hereditaments and premises, was and stood in like manner seised of the said copyhold hereditaments of a like estate of inheritance, according to the custom of the manor of W. aforesaid, without any manner of condition, trust, power of revocation, limitation of use or uses, or any other restraint, cause, matter, or thing whatsoever, to alter, change, defeat, revoke, impeach, make void, or determine the same.

13. And also that he the said [*vendor*] now hath in himself as to the said freehold hereditaments, and at the time of passing the said surrender as to the said copyhold hereditaments, had in himself, good right, full power, and lawful and absolute authority to grant, bargain, sell, release, surrender, convey, and assure all and singular the said freehold and copyhold hereditaments, and premises hereinbefore granted, released, and mentioned to have been surrendered respectively, with their appurtenances to the use of the said [*purchaser*], his heirs and assigns, according to the true intent and meaning of these presents and of the said surrender.

14. And further, that it shall and may be lawful to and for the said [*purchaser*], his heirs and assigns, from time to time, and at all times hereafter, peaceably and quietly to enter into

92

and upon, have, hold, occupy, possess, and enjoy all and singular the said freehold and copyhold hereditaments and premises respectively, with their appurtenances, and to receive and take the rents, issues, and profits thereof, and of every part thereof respectively, to and for his and their own use and benefit, without any lawful let, suit, trouble, molestation, eviction, ejection, interruption, or disturbance whatsoever, of, from, or by the said A. B. or his heirs, or any other person or persons whomsoever, lawfully or equitably claiming, or to claim, any estate, right, title, trust, or interest in, to, or out of the same hereditaments and premises, or any part thereof respectively, by, through, under, or in trust for him, them, or any of them.

15. And that free and clear, and freely, clearly, and absolutely acquitted, exonerated, and released, and for ever discharged or otherwise, by him the said [*vendor*] his heirs, executors, and administrators, well and sufficiently protected, defended, saved harmless, and kept indemnified of, from, and against all and all manner of former and other estates, titles, charges, liens, claims, and incumbrances whatsoever, at any time, or from time to time hereafter, had, made, occasioned, permitted, or suffered by him the said [*vendor*] or his heirs, or any person claiming, or to claim by, from, through, under, or in trust for him, them, or any of them, or by his, their, or any of their acts, means, consent, default, privity, or procurement.

16. And moreover, that he the said [*vendor*], and his heirs, and all and every other person and persons having, or lawfully or equitably, or rightfully claiming, or to claim any estate, right, title, trust, charge, or interest at law or in equity, of, in, to, or out of the said freehold and copyhold hereditaments, hereby released and mentioned to be surrendered, or intended so to be, or any part thereof respectively, by, from, through, under or in trust for him or them, shall and will from time to time and at all times hereafter, upon every reasonable request, and at the costs and charges of the said [*purchaser*], his heirs or assigns, make, do, acknowledge, pass, execute, and perfect, or cause or procure to be made, &c., all such further and reasonable acts, deeds, conveyances, surrenders, and assurances in the law whatsoever, for the further, better, more perfectly, lawfully, and absolutely or satisfactorily conveying and confirming, or otherwise assuring the said freehold and copyhold hereditaments, and every part and part thereof respectively, with their respective appurtenances, unto and to the use of the said [*purchaser*], his heirs and assigns for ever as aforesaid, and according to the true intent and meaning of these presents, and of the said mentioned surrender, as by the said [*purchaser*], his heirs or assigns, or his or their counsel in the law, shall be reasonably devised, or advised

and required, and tendered to be made, done, passed, or executed. In witness, &c.

> Forms of conveyances with a covenant to surrender the
> copyhold, will be found in Serjeant Scriven's and Mr.
> Coventry's works, and in most books of Conveyancing
> Precedents; but it is really so imprudent to rest sa-
> tisfied with a covenant, when a surrender may so readily
> be obtained in all cases, that it is deemed useless to
> add any such forms here.

> The surrender can be drawn from No. 276, &c., adding
> at the statement of the consideration, money "being
> the apportioned consideration money on sale, &c."

---

312. *Power of Attorney to surrender Copyholds, where Purchase-
Money paid.*

Know all men by these presents, that I [*vendor*] of, &c.,
a copyhold tenant of the manor of   , in the county of
have made, ordained, constituted, and appointed and by these
presents do make, &c., [*attorney*] of, &c., my true and lawful
attorney for me and in my name, to appear at the next or
any subsequent general or special court baron to be holden
for the said manor, and then and there, or out of court, to
surrender into the hands of the lord, lords or ladies, of the
said manor, by the hands and acceptance of the steward or deputy steward for the time being, according to the custom of
the said manor, all, &c., with the rights, members, and appurtenances [*and all other the messuages, lands, tenements, and
hereditaments, copyhold of the said manor, whereto I stand admitted,*] and by such description as may be deemed advisable
or expedient; and the reversion, &c., and all my estate, &c.
[*see form of Surrender*] to the use and behoof of [*purchaser*]
of, &c., his heirs and assigns for ever, according to the custom of the said manor; and for me and in my name to do,
and execute all and every such acts, matters, and things as
may be needful or expedient for making such surrender as
aforesaid, and for procuring the said [*purchaser*], his heirs or
assigns to be admitted tenant to the said copyhold premises,
and as fully and effectually to all intents and purposes as I
myself might or could do, being personally present, hereby
agreeing to ratify and confirm all and whatsoever my said
attorney shall lawfully do or cause to be done by virtue of
these presents. In witness, &c.

> This form is slightly altered from one in Serjeant
> Scriven's work, but it would be better to recite the
> deed under which the power is made, as in the fol-
> lowing outline form.

To all to whom these presents shall come: [*vendor*] of, &c.,
sendeth greeting: Whereas, &c., [*recite covenant to surrender,*

94

payment of money, and that ad valorem *stamp was impressed.*]
Now I the said [*vendor*] do hereby nominate, constitute, and
appoint A. B. of, &c. and C. D. of, &c. jointly and severally
my true and lawful attorneys, &c. [*making the power to the
two, and slightly altering the form accordingly.*]

---

313. *Power of Attorney to receive Rents, Sell, and Convey.*

KNOW ALL MEN by these presents that I, Sir W. J. P.,
of, &c., bart. (heretofore called W. J. P., esq.) for divers
good causes and considerations me hereunto moving, have
made, ordained, constituted, and appointed, and by these presents do make, ordain, constitute, and appoint, and in my
place and stead put T. G. E., of the city of Norwich, gentleman, and G. C. of, &c. gentleman, my true and lawful attorneys irrevocable, for the intents and purposes following (that
is to say) either jointly or severally, for me and in my name
place, and stead, to ask, demand, and receive all rents and
arrears of rent now due, or which shall hereafter accrue or
become due from the former or present tenant or tenants of
all and every my messuages, lands, tenements, and hereditaments, situate, lying, and being in G. B. and L. B., or either
of them, or in any other town, parish, or place thereto adjoin-
ing, or adjacent, or elsewhere, in the county of S., late of Sir
C. P., Bart., my late brother, deceased, or from the representatives of such tenant or tenants, or any of them ; and on
non-payment thereof, to enter and distrain for the same in
due course of law, or to commence and prosecute any action
or actions at law or equity, for recovery of the same, every or
any part thereof, and on the receipt thereof for me, and in my
name and stead, to sign and give acquittances, receipts, and
other effectual discharges for the same. And I do also empower my said attorneys, either jointly or severally, for me
and in my name, place, and stead, to sell and dispose of all
and every my said messuages, lands, tenements, and hereditaments in G. B. and L. B. aforesaid, or elsewhere in the
said county of S., to any person or persons who shall be willing to become the purchaser or purchasers thereof, or of any
part thereof, for the best price and prices, and most money
that can or may be reasonably had or obtained for the same,
and to receive the consideration money and give receipts and
effectual discharges for the same. And I do also empower
my said attorneys, either jointly or severally, for me, and in
my name, place, and stead, to convey and assure such part or
parts of the said hereditaments and premises as shall appear
to be freehold, if any, unto and to the use of the purchaser
or purchasers thereof, his, her, or their heirs and assigns, or
otherwise, as he or they shall direct or appoint, and to sign,

95

seal, and deliver all such deed and deeds, instrument or instruments in writing, as shall be necessary in that behalf. And I do hereby further authorise and empower my said attorney, either jointly or severally, for me and in my name, place, and stead, at any general or special court or courts baron, to be held for the manor of S. H. in the said county of S., or for any other manor or manors, or out of court, by the rod according to the custom thereof, to surrender out of my hands into the hands of the lord or lords, lady or ladies, of the said manor or manors, all and every my said messuages, lands, tenements, and hereditaments, so hereby directed to be sold as aforesaid, held of the said manor or manors by copy of court roll, with their and every of their appurtenances, and the reversion and reversions, remainder and remainders thereof, and also all the estate, right, title, interest, use, trust, property, inheritance, claim, and demand whatsoever of me, the said Sir W. J. P. of, in, to, or out of the said hereditaments and premises, every or any part thereof, with their appurtenances, to the use and behoof of such person and persons who shall purchase the same, his, her, and their heirs and assigns, for ever absolutely, and without any manner of condition whatsoever, or otherwise, as such purchaser or purchasers shall direct or appoint. And also for me and in my name to execute any proper deed or deeds of covenant for estate, title, possession, and further assurance. And I do hereby empower and direct my said attorneys, either jointly or severally, for me and in my name, place, and stead, to do and transact all such other acts, matters, and things, as shall be proper and necessary for vesting a good and absolute estate in fee simple of and in the said hereditaments and premises in the purchaser or purchasers thereof, his, her, or their heirs or assigns, as fully and effectually to all intents and purposes whatsoever, as I, the said Sir W. J. P., might or could do if personally present. Hereby ratifying, confirming, and allowing all and whatsoever my said attorneys shall either jointly or severally lawfully do or cause to be done in the premises by virtue of these presents. In witness, &c.

314.—*Conditions of Sale.—Freehold and Copyhold, in Lots.*

1. The highest bidder [*for each lot*] to be the purchaser; and if any dispute arise, the [*lot in dispute*] to be put up again at a former bidding.

2. No person to advance less than   *l.* at each bidding [*for any lot*], and no bidding to be retracted.

3. The purchaser [*of each lot*] to give in his or her name and place of abode at the fall of the hammer, and pay to the auctioneer the auction duty, and a deposit of 10*l.* per cent on

the amount, and in part of the purchase money, and sign an agreement for payment of the remainder at [*the office of Messrs. C. M. & Co., at W.*] on or before the [11*th day of October next*], on which day the purchase is to be completed; but if [*from whatever cause arising*] the remainder of the purchase money should not be paid on that day, such purchaser shall pay to the vendor interest at the rate of 5*l.* per cent. on the amount unpaid from that day until payment, but without prejudice to the right of the vendor under the eleventh condition.

> [*Or,* the purchaser shall pay to the vendor a proportionate part of the rents and profits up to and on the day of the completion; and the vendor shall discharge the outgoings in like manner to that day, but without prejudice, &c.]

4. The vendor shall, within fourteen days from the day of sale, deliver to the purchaser [*of each lot*] or his or her solicitor, an abstract of title to the lot purchased by him or her, and subject to these conditions, deduce a good title; and on payment of the remainder of the purchase [*and valuation*] money agreeably to these conditions, proper conveyances, surrenders, and assurances, shall be made, passed, and executed to the said purchaser, the same to be prepared by, and passed and executed at the expence of the purchaser.

5. All attested, official, or other copies of, extracts from, or searches for, or production of deeds, wills, letters of administration, court rolls, or other documents, writings or assurances, and of and for all affidavits, certificates, or other evidence, whether for comparing or verifying the abstract, or for whatever purpose required, shall be made and obtained by and at the expence of the purchaser requiring the same. [*And who shall also bear the expence of, or in relation to the preparing, perusing, and executing the assignment of any outstanding term to attend the inheritance,* (*should any such term exist*) *and the searching for and enabling any party to make or join in such assignment.*]

6. The vendor shall not be called on to shew any further title to the small parts [*of any lot*] formerly glebe, and sold to redeem land tax, than the conveyance of such glebe, nor to any parts formerly waste, than the grant in court by the lord of the manor of W.; neither shall the vendor be called on to shew any earlier title to the premises [*comprised in lot* 3] than, &c., nor to distinguish the boundaries of the freehold or copyhold parts, or identify the present with the former description of any lot; and no proof shall be required of any facts stated, recited, notified, or implied in any deed, will, court roll, or document dated upwards of [*thirty*] years since, nor shall proof be required of the lord's title to any parts [*of any lot*] formerly copyhold and enfranchised.

7. The purchaser [*of each lot*] shall pay by valuation as after mentioned for the fixtures [*in and about such lot*], of which an inventory will be produced at the sale; also for the tillage of the summer lands, rents of lands, and charges on the same; for seed sowing and hoeing of turnips;, for all hay and straw left on the premises, which shall be stacked in the usual places; for all feed and after-grass on the pastures and stubbles; for all clover and other seeds, and for sowing, harrowing, and cultivating the same with the spring crops; for muck, mixtures and composts, and for labour in turning over such as shall not be carted on the land; and for the carting, when carted on the land; and for all such matters and things as are customary to be allowed and paid by an incoming to an outgoing tenant [*also for the brick kiln, and at the option of the purchaser, all bricks, tiles, ware and prepared earth; but if not taken, the vendor to have till, &c., to complete and dispose of the same, and use of the brick kiln and yards for that purpose.*] Also for all timber and timber-like trees, saplings, willows, pollards, and stands [*being upon each lot*] down to and including those of 1*s.* a stick; also for the young plantation and underwood, the whole to be valued as hereinafter mentioned. The present year's corn and crops are to be laid in the barns or stacked on the premises; the purchaser is to pay for threshing and dressing and getting in the stacks, and carrying the corn, when dressed, to market, not exceeding the distance of, &c., and to have the straw, chaff, and colder arising therefrom, the vendor appointing the threshers, and having the use of the barns and barn yards up to the day of   for that purpose.

8. That all valuations under these conditions shall be made by two referees, one to be chosen by each party, or by the umpire of such two referees; and on neglect of either party to nominate a referee within seven days after notice in writing, the decision of the referee first appointed to be binding; and in case of the referees not agreeing on an umpire, the same to be appointed by M. D., M. E., or M. F., in the order in which named, on request by either party, the valuation to be made on the   day of   , and if not paid on the day named for completion of the purchase, to bear interest as to the farming and timber valuation at the same rate, and payable in the like manner as the interest reserved on the purchase-money remaining unpaid.

9. The vendor shall have the right by himself or his agent of bidding once for each lot.

10. If there should be any error or omission in the aforegoing particulars, in tenure, outgoings, or otherwise (except as to the quantity of land, which shall be deemed satisfactory and conclusive) the same shall not vitiate the sale, but a compensation shall be made or taken as the case may require, and be settled agreeably to the 8th condition.

11. If the purchaser [*of any lot*] should neglect or fail to comply with any of these conditions, his or her deposit money shall be absolutely forfeited to the vendor, who shall be at liberty to resell [*such lot*], either by public auction or private contract, and the deficiency [*if any*] on such resale, together with the attendant expences, shall be made good by the defaulter at this sale, and in case of the non-payment thereof, the same shall be recoverable by the vendor as and for liquidated damages; and it shall not be necessary to tender a conveyance or surrender to the defaulter at this sale, and any increase on such resale, shall be retained by the vendor.

---

315. *Variations and Additions in Conditions as to Title and Writings.*—See No. 6 above.

TITLE.—The purchaser [*of each lot*] shall within fourteen days after delivery of the abstract, send to the vendor or his solicitor a statement in writing of the objections [*if any*] to the title, and all objections not then made, shall be deemed waived; and in case any objections shall be taken to the title [*of any lot*], it shall be in the power of the vendor to annul the sale [*thereof*] and to return the deposit money to the purchaser, in full satisfaction of all damages, costs, and charges which such purchaser may sustain.

VARIATION, 2.—In order to save useless expence to both parties, and the title having been inquired into on the estate having been purchased by the vendor [*and also on a subsequent mortgage for a considerable amount*] it is expressly stipulated, that the title shall be taken as it is, and without any requisitions thereon.

WRITINGS.—The writings in the vendor's custody, solely relating to any lot, shall, on completion of the purchase, be delivered to the purchaser of such lot; but as to those writings affecting more than one lot, the same shall be retained by the vendor until sale and conveyance of all the lots to which the same relate, subject to the right for each purchaser to have a memorandum of his conveyance endorsed on any such writings; and then delivered to the purchaser whose lot shall be sold for the largest sum; and such purchaser shall at the time of such delivery, execute proper deeds of covenants to any other purchaser to whose lots the deeds shall relate, such deeds to be prepared by and at the expence of the purchaser requiring the same.

[*Should difficulty be expected to arise by biddings from insolvent persons, it would be advisable to guard against the difficulty as well as circumstances will allow, by the following addition to the first condition.*]

No offer to be deemed a bidding until accepted as such by the auctioneer, and if required, the auction duty and deposit previously paid into his hands.

It would be expedient, when the necessity of any such altera-
tion is anticipated, to insert the following note at the
foot of the condition.

N.B. Should any alterations in or additions to these conditions be found necessary, they will be mentioned at the
time of sale.

Where the sale takes place under a trust deed for benefit
of creditors, with a power to sell and surrender copyholds,
condition 4, should be altered, by the insertion after the
words "passed and executed to the said purchaser," of the
words, "by the vendors, under the power given them in the
deed, under which they are trustees," the same to be, &c.

In condition 5, it would also be as well to insert after the
words "verifying the abstract," "proving that any party is
living, or the death of any party," or for whatever purpose, &c.

316.—*Notice to Purchaser to Proceed.*

I hereby, as solicitor for Mr. A. B., give you notice that he
is ready to perform on his part the contract entered into with
you for sale of, &c., and to surrender and assure the same to
the use of you and your heirs, or as you or they may direct,
according to such contract, on payment of the remainder of
the purchase money and interest, and performance on your
part of such contract.—[I further give you notice, that Mr.
A. B. is willing to have the title and contract submitted to
Mr. E., Mr. F., or any other barrister of   years standing,
who has not acted for either you or the said A. B., or your
respective solicitors, and to comply with any requisitions such
barrister may make on the title and contract.]   And I further
give you notice,, that Mr. A. B. stands admitted tenant of the
said estate and premises; and that in the event of your
neglecting to comply with the terms of your contract, you will
be held responsible for all costs and expences to arise in case
of his death, for admission to the said copyholds, or otherwise, in relation to the said contract. And 1 lastly require
you to return the draft surrender and deed of covenant herewith sent, approved by you or your solicitor, that the same
may, at your expence, be completed by the day fixed by the
contract for completion of the purchase. Dated, &c.

MORTGAGES.

317.—*Agreement on Treaty for a Loan.*

Mr. A. B. having applied to Mr. C. D., to advance him the
sum of 2000*l.* on mortgage of the estate, called, &c., situate,
&c., containing, &c., and being freehold, with the exception
of   acres, or thereabouts, copyhold, on the security and

100

title being approved, and proper securities entered into; it is mutually agreed between the said parties that the estate shall be forthwith surveyed by Mr. E., at the expence of the said A. B., and on his approving of the security, the said A. B. shall make out and deduce a good title to the estate, to the satisfaction of the counsel of the said C. D., and execute such proper mortgage and other securities as such counsel shall deem proper, [*including, should he deem the same requisite, a power of sale, a warrant of attorney to confess judgment in eject-ment, and an appointment of receiver,*] and that the expence of investigating the title and of the securities shall be borne by the said A. B.

The said C. D. agrees to make the advance, on the security and title being approved, and securities completed as above, and to pay the intended mortgage money into the bank of G. & Co., on or before, &c. appropriated to such intended mort-gage; and it is further agreed, that in the event of the re-port of the surveyor being against the security, or the counsel being of opinion that a good title is not made, or should the said A. B. fail to comply with the requisitions of such counsel on the title, or to execute and complete the securities settled by him; the expence of the survey, investigating the title, and preparing the securities, shall be borne by the said A. B., who shall also pay to the said C. D. interest, at the rate of 5*l.* per cent. per annum, from the day of appropriation of the said sum to the date of the contract being rescinded by either party, or removal of the said sum by the said C. D. from the appropriated account, receiving the interest allowed by Messrs. G. & Co.

Witness the hands of the said parties, the   day of 1837.

318.—*Common Conditional Surrender.*

Manor of   { The   day of   , in the
                 { year of our Lord, 18

2. Be it remembered, that on the day and year above written, A. B. of, &c., and E. his wife, copyhold tenants, or one of them, a copyhold tenant of the said manor, came before me, [*C. D., gent., deputy steward for this purpose only of E. F., Esq.,*] chief steward of the said manor, and the courts thereof.

3. And she the said E. having been by me the said [*deputy*] steward first examined separate and apart from her said husband, touching and concerning her free and voluntary consent to the making and passing the surrender hereinafter mentioned, and freely and voluntary consenting thereto, as by law required,

4. Did out of court, in consideration of the sum of £ of lawful money of Great Britain, to them or one of them, in

101

hand well and truly paid, lent and advanced by [*mortgagee*] of, &c., at or immediately before the passing the said surrender, the receipt whereof is hereby and by the receipt for the same sum hereunder written, acknowledged,

5. Surrender out of their and each of their hands into the hands of the lord of the said manor, by the hands and acceptance of me the said [*deputy*] steward, by the rod, according to the custom of the said manor,

6. All, &c., [or, *all and every their and either of their messuages and tenements, lands, hereditaments, and premises, holden by copy of court roll of the said manor, with their and every of their rights, members, and appurtenances,*

7. And the reversion and reversions, remainder and remainders, yearly and other rents, issues and profits thereof, and of every part thereof, with appurtenances ;

8. And all the estate, right, title, interest, inheritance, use, trust, benefit, property, possession, power, claim and demand whatsoever, both at law and in equity, of them the said and A. B., and E. his wife, or either of them, of, in, to, from, or out of the said hereditaments and premises, and every part thereof, with the rights, members, privileges, appendages, and appurtenances,

9. *To the use* and behoof of the said [*mortgagee*,] his heirs and assigns for ever, according to the custom of the said manor,

10. *Subject* nevertheless to and upon this express condition, that if the said A. B., his heirs, executors, or administrators, do and shall, well, and truly pay, or cause to be paid unto the said [*mortgagee*,] his executors, administrators, or assigns, the sum of £ of lawful money of Great Britain, on the   day of, &c. [*usually six months,*] together with interest for the same at and after the rate of 5*l.* for 100*l.* by the year, to be computed from the date of this surrender, without any deduction or abatement whatsoever,

11. Then this surrender to be void and of no effect, otherwise to remain in full force and virtue.

Taken (together with the private examina-⎫
tion of the said E.,) the day and year⎰ A. B.
first above written, by me, C. D.,⎰ E. B.
deputy steward, *p. h. v.* ⎭

Receipt to be written at foot, see No. 276.

All the special varieties in surrenders, will be found in forms 276 to 295, the conditional surrenders having the same form as absolute surrenders, except as to the condition being inserted in the former.

319.—*Mortgage Bond.*

1. Obligation.	7. For seisin.
2. Recital of passing surrender.	8. For power to surrender.
3. ————— parcels surrendered.	9. Free from incumbrances.
4. ————— use.	10. For further assurances.
5. Condition of bond.	11. To insure.
6. ————— for payment.	12. Conclusion.

1. Bond from A. B. [*mortgagor*] of, &c.   in the county of   , to [*mortgagee*] of, &c.   , in the penal sum of £ [*double amount secured*].
To bear date with surrender.—(*See* Form of Obligation, 297.)

2. Whereas the above-bounden A. B. and E. his wife, copyhold tenants, or one of them, a copyhold tenant of the manor of   , in the county of   , have on the day of the date of the above written bond or obligation, in consideration of the sum of £   , of lawful money of Great Britain, to them or one of them paid by the above-named [*mortgagee*], surrendered into the hands of the lord of the said manor, by the hands and acceptance of   , gentleman, steward of the said manor and the courts thereof, all, &c. [*or if not described in surrender, say, by a general description thereof*, all, &c. *and then add the full description*].

4. To the use and behoof of the said [*mortgagee*], his heirs and assigns for ever, according to the custom of the said manor,

5. Subject nevertheless to a proviso or condition for making void the said surrender, on payment by the said A, B., his heirs, executors, or administrators, unto the said [*mortgagee*], his executors, administrators, or assigns, of the sum of £   , and interest for the same at the rate of £5 for £100 by the year, on, &c.

6. *Now the condition* of the above obligation is such, that if the said A. B. his heirs, executors, or administrators, do and shall well and truly pay or cause to be paid unto the said [*mortgagee*], his executors, administrators, or assigns, the sum of £   of lawful money of Great Britain, on the   day of   now next ensuing, and which will be in the year of our Lord 18   , together with interest for the same, at and after the rate of £5 for £100 by the year, to be computed from the date of the above-written obligation, without any deduction or abatement whatsoever, being the same principal money and interest above mentioned to be secured by the said recited conditional surrender of even date herewith, on which the *ad valorem* stamp of £——— is impressed;

103

7. *And also* if the said A. B. was, or the said A. B. and E. his wife were, at the time of making the said surrender, rightfully and absolutely seised of and in the said copyhold hereditaments and premises, with the appurtenances, for an estate of inheritance therein according to the custom of the said manor;

8. *And also* if they then had good right, full power, and lawful and absolute authority to surrender the same to the use of the said [*mortgagee*] and his heirs, in manner and form aforesaid;

9. *And that* free and clear of and from all liens, charges, and incumbrances whatsoever (save and except the rents, suits, and services therefore due, and of right accustomed);

10. *And moreover*, if he the said A. B., and the said E. his wife, and his heirs, and all persons claiming or to claim any estate or interest in, to, or out of the said hereditaments and premises by, from, through, under, or in trust for him, her, and them, or any of them, do and shall from time to time, and at all times hereafter during the continuance of the said principal sum and interest, or any part thereof, on this security, at the request of the said [*mortgagee*] his executors, administrators and assigns, but at the costs and charges in all things of the said A. B., his heirs, executors, and administrators, make, pass, execute, and perfect, or cause to be made, passed, executed, and perfected, all such further and other surrenders and assurances, for better conveying and confirming the said copyhold hereditaments and premises, with the appurtenances, unto the said [*mortgagee*], his heirs and assigns, as he or they or his or their counsel in the law shall reasonably advise and require;

11. *And also* if he the said A. B., his heirs, executors or administrators, do and shall, at his and their expence, forthwith insure, and, during the continuance of the said principal and interest on the said security, keep insured the aforesaid messuage or tenements, hereditaments and premises, in some responsible Fire Insurance Office, to be approved of by the said [*mortgagee*], in the sum of £ at least, and shall and do deliver all policies and receipts for premium and duty to the said [*mortgagee*], his executors, administrators, or assigns, and shall and do pay or apply all monies to be received by virtue of any such insurance, either in or towards payment of the principal money and interest hereby secured, or in reinstating and rebuilding the said buildings and premises, as the said [*mortgagee*], his executors, administrators or assigns, shall direct;

12. Then the above written obligation to be void and of no effect, or else to be and remain in full force and virtue.

Sealed and delivered ⎱
in the presence of ⎰

A deed of covenant in lieu of this bond can readily be framed from this precedent, and that of deed of covenant on sale : see 296.

Clause 9 in 296, might be inserted after cl. 9 in 319, *adding* "after default," &c ; but a warrant of attorney (321, would be preferable.

320.— *Note of Hand as Collateral Security, to be given instead of Bond in small Mortgages.*

[*place and date*]

£   Six months after date, I promise to pay Mr. [*mortgagee*] or order, the sum of   with lawful interest, value received, being the same sum as is mentioned in a certain conditional surrender of even date, passed by me and F. my wife, of certain hereditaments, copyhold of the manor of   , To the use of the said [*mortgagee*] and his heirs.

                                             A. B.

321.— *Warrant of Attorney to confess Judgment in Ejectment.*

To A. B. & C. D., gentlemen, attorneys of her Majesty's Court of Queen's Bench (*or Common Pleas*) at Westminster, jointly and severally, or to any other attorney of the same Court.

These are to desire and authorize you, the attorneys above named, or any one of you, or any other attorney of the Court of Queen's Bench (*or Common Pleas*) aforesaid, to appear for me [*mortgagor*] of &c. in the said court, as of this present term, or of any other subsequent term, and then and there to receive a declaration for me in an action of trespass and ejectment of farm, at the suit of John Doe, on the demise of [*mortgagee*] for   messuages,   curtilages, yards,   barns,   stables,   orchards,   gardens, acres of land,   acres of pasture,   acres of meadow, and   acres of arable, and   acres of wood, with common of pasture for all manner of cattle, with the appurtenances, situate at   , in the county of   , which the said [*mortgagee*] on the   day of   last, had demised to the said John Doe for the term of 21 years, from the said day of   last ; and thereupon to confess the same action, or else to suffer judgment by *nil dicit* or otherwise to pass against me in the same action ; and to be thereupon forthwith entered up against me of record in the said court, for the recovery of the said term yet to come of and in the said lands and tenements, with the appurtenances, and also for recovery of 40*s.* damages, besides costs of suit. And I the said [*mortgagor*] do hereby further authorize and empower you the said attorneys, or any one of you, after the said judgment shall be entered up as aforesaid, for me and in my name, and as my act and deed, to sign, seal, and execute a good and sufficient release in the law to the said [*mortgagee*], his heirs, executors, and administrators, of all and all manner of error and errors, writ and writs of error, and all benefit and advantage thereof, and all misprisions of error and errors, defects, and imperfections whatsoever, had, made, committed, done, or suffered in, about touching or concerning any writ, warrant, process, declaration, plea, entry, or other proceedings whatsoever, of or any way concerning the same. And for what you, the said attorneys, or any one of you, shall do or cause to be done in the premises, or any of them, this shall be to you and every of you a sufficient warrant and authority. In witness whereof I have hereto set my hand and seal the   day of   in the   year of the reign of our Sovereign Lady Victoria, by the Grace of God Queen of the United Kingdom of Great Britain and Ireland, Defender of the Faith, and in the year of our Lord 18 .

Signed, sealed, and delivered, ⎫
  in the presence of A. B.   ⎬   [*Mortgagor.*]
                              ⎭

Defeasance.—Memorandum.—That the within written warrant of attorney is given to secure the repayment of the sum of (£5000) and interest, from the within named [*mortgagor*], his heirs, executors, and administrators, to the within named [*mortgagee*], his executors, administrators, and assigns, collaterally with a certain mortgage of the within-mentioned messuages, lands, and premises, bearing even date with these presents, and made and passed, or expressed to be made and passed, by the within named and undersigned [*mortgagor*], to the use of the within named and undersigned [*mortgagee*] ; and it is hereby declared and agreed by and between the said undersigned parties hereto, that judgment shall not be entered up in pursuance of the said warrant of attorney, until after the   day of   next, and that no execution shall be thereafter issued or taken out thereupon, unless and until default shall be made in payment by the said [*mortgagor*], his heirs or assigns, of the said sum of (£5000) and interest, after the said [*mortgagee*], his heirs, executors, administrators, or assigns, shall have given unto the said [*mortgagor*], his heirs, executors, or administrators, or left at his or their last or most usual place of abode in England,   calendar months' notice in writing, requiring payment of the same. And it is also declared, that it shall not be necessary for the said [*mortgagee*], his heirs, executors, administrators, or assigns, to revive, or cause to be revived, the said judgment, or do any act, matter, or thing to keep the same on foot, although the same shall not have been entered of record for the space of one year or upwards. And that the said [*mortgagor*], his heirs, executors, and administrators, shall not nor will have, receive or take any plea, exception, proceeding, or other benefit, from the omission of the said [*mortgagee*], his heirs, executors, administrators, or assigns, to revive the said judgment, although the same shall not have been entered for the space of one year or upwards; and that if the said [*mortgagor*], his heirs, executors, or administrators, shall attempt so to do by action or other legal proceeding or proceedings whatsoever, this present agreement shall and may be pleaded or shewn in bar thereto, any rule or practice of the courts, or any of them, to the contrary thereof in anywise notwithstanding. In witness whereof, the said parties hereto have hereunto set their hands and seals the   day   , 183 .

Witness to the signing,}   [*Mortgagor.*]   (L. S.)
            W. Y.}   [*Mortgagee.*]   (L. S.)
                    20s. stamp.

----

322. *Conditional Surrender, with Power of Sale.*

This will be the same as a common conditional surrender, as far as the words, " full force and virtue," at the end; then add as follows :

And it shall and may be lawful to and for the said [*mortgagee*,] his heirs or assigns, immediately after default, without any further consent or concurrence of the said [*mortgagor*,] his heirs or assigns, to make sale and absolutely dispose of the whole of the hereditaments and premises comprised in this surrender, with the appurtenances, or any part or parts thereof, either together or in parcels, and by public auction or private contract, at discretion, with liberty to buy in and resell the same, and after admittance thereto, to surrender, convey and assure the same, when so sold, unto the purchaser or purchasers thereof, his, her or their heirs and assigns, or as he, she or they shall direct or appoint, and shall stand possessed of the proceeds of such sale or sales, and the rents and profits of the said hereditaments and premises until sale, in trust to pay and discharge, as far as such proceeds shall extend, the monies due to the said [*mortgagee*], his executors, administrators or assigns, and all other incumbrances affecting the same hereditaments and premises, together with the costs attending such sale or sales, and the necessary proceedings to enable the making and completing such sale or sales, and the surrenders and assurances of the said hereditaments and premises on sale thereof, and all other costs, charges and expences in respect thereof or arising therefrom, and in trust to pay the remainder of such proceeds, if any, after full payment and satisfaction of such monies, incumbrances, costs, charges and expences, unto the said [*mortgagor*], his executors, administrators or assigns, and to re-surrender, reconvey, and assure such parts of the said hereditaments and premises, if any, as shall remain unsold, for any of the purposes afore-said, unto the said [*mortgagor*], his heirs and assigns, or as he or they shall direct or appoint, and the receipts of the said [*mortgagee*] his heirs, executors, administrators or assigns, shall be good and sufficient discharges for all purchase or other monies therein expressed to be received; and the pur-chaser or purchasers, or other person or persons, paying him, her or them any monies, and taking such receipts, shall not afterwards be required to see to the application thereof, nor be answerable or accountable for the misapplication or non-application thereof.

Taken, together with the private examina- ⎫
tion of the said [*wife*], the day and year ⎬   [*Mortgagor.*]
first above written be me,   ⎭   [*Wife.*]
                            W. B.

The said [*deputy*] steward, *pro. hac. vice.*

Received the day and year first above ⎫
written, of and from the above named   ⎪
[*mortgagee*] the sum of   pounds, ⎬ £   :   :   .
being the consideration money above   ⎪
mentioned to be paid by him to me, as ⎪
witness my hand,   ⎭
Witness,   [*Mortgagor.*]
    W. B.

N. B. A power of attorney to surrender in the name of the mortgagor, would be of advantage in preventing the necessity of the mortgagee taking admission.

---

323. *Further Mortgage, with Security for future Advances.*

This will be in the same form as a common surrender, as far as the use to the mortgagee. The condition will then be as follows :

Subject nevertheless to a certain conditional surrender, made and passed by the said A. B. and E. his wife, on or about, &c. to the use of the said [*mortgagee*] and his heirs, for securing to him, his executors, &c. the sum of £   , and lawful interest.

And subject also to and upon this express condition, that if the said A. B., his heirs, executors, or administrators, do and shall well and truly pay, or cause to be paid, unto the said [*mortgagee*], his executors, administrators or assigns, on the   day of   next ensuing the date hereof, the said sum of 300*l.* now advanced, with interest for the same at and after the rate of 5*l.* for 100*l.* by the year, to be computed

108

from the day of the date hereof, and also do and shall pay, or cause to be paid unto the said [*mortgagee*] his executors, administrators or assigns upon demand, all and every such further sum and sums of money, as he the said [*mortgagee*] shall from time to time advance to the said A. B. on this security, not exceeding in the whole, with the sum of 300*l.* now advanced, the sum of 500*l.* (the stamp duty in respect of which latter sum is hereupon impressed) with interest for the same, at the rate of 5*l.* for 100*l.* by the year, to be computed from the time of advancing the said sums respectively, and to be paid half-yearly, on &c. during the continuance of this security, and do and shall make such respective payments without any deduction or abatement whatsoever, then, &c. [*as in common surrender.*]

Receipt for the present advance to be written at foot.

On the further advances being made, an acknowledgment of each advance should be written on the copy surrender, and on the collateral security; and it might also be as well, where the amount is at all considerable, to have the mortgagor sign a memorandum to the following effect, and to have the same presented and entered on the court rolls.

Mannor of, &c. To the steward of the said manor, or his lawful deputy, for the time being.

I, A. B. of, &c. do hereby authorise and require you, or one of you, to enter on the court rolls or in the court books of the said manor, this my acknowledgment, that on this day of, &c. [*mortgagee*] of, &c. has advanced to me the further sum of £ on the security of the conditional surrender passed by me and E. my wife, on or about, &c. to the use of the said [*mortgagee*], his heirs and assigns, for securing the sum of 300*l.* then advanced, and of further advances to be made, not exceeding 500*l.*, and that the sum of £ and interest now remains due on such surrender. Witness my hand, &c.

———

324. *Second Mortgage.*

This will be in the same form as an ordinary conditional surrender, as far as the use to the mortgagee. The condition will then be as follows :—

Subject nevertheless to a certain conditional surrender, made and passed of the said hereditaments by the said A. B. and E. his wife, on or about, &c., to the use of E. F., of, &c., and his heirs, with a condition for making the same void on payment to him, his executors, administrators, or assigns, of the sum of £ , with lawful interest, at the time and in manner in the memorandum of such surrender mentioned.

And subject also to and upon this express condition, that, if, &c. [*as in common conditional surrender.*]

325. *Notice to first Mortgagee.*

Sir,

I hereby give you notice that on this   day of, &c., I, A. B., of, &c., and E. my wife, have, out of court, according to the custom of the manor of, &c., duly surrendered all and singular the hereditaments comprized in my conditional surrender, bearing date, &c., and passed to your use for securing to you, your executors, &c., the sum of, &c., To the use of C. D. of, &c., his heirs and assigns, subject to the aforesaid conditional surrender to your use, and upon condition to be void on payment by me, my heirs, &c., to the said C. D., his executors, &c., of the sum of £   , with lawful interest as in the memorandum of surrender delivered to the steward of the said manor is expressed. Dated, &c.

> A notice from the mortgagee can readily be drawn from this form.

---

326. *Conditional Surrender, by Direction of Purchaser.*

The same as 318, to end of clause 3.

4. Did out of court (at the request and by the direction of [*purchaser*], of, &c, the purchaser of the copyhold hereditaments hereinafter mentioned or described, testified by his signing his name at the foot hereof, and in consideration of the sum of £   of lawful money, &c., lent and advanced to the said [*purchaser*] by E. J. of, &c., the payment whereof is acknowledged by the said [*purchaser*] at the foot hereof.

Surrender, &c.   Clauses 5 to 9, as in 318.

Subject nevertheless to and upon this express condition, That if the said [*purchaser*], (to the use of whom and his heirs the said hereditaments are intended immediately after the passing this surrender to be by the said A. B. and E. his wife surrendered absolutely) his heirs, executors, or administrators, do and shall, &c., [*as in common condition,* 318.]

Receipt by purchaser for consideration money, to be written at foot, and also the following consent :—

" I consent to and approve of this surrender."

A mortgage of even date with a sale is thus prepared, as otherwise no conditional surrender could be obtained till admission of the purchaser. The absolute surrender will be found in 278 C.

327. *Assignment of Mortgage.*

1. Commencement.
2. Parties.
3. Recital of surrender and bond.
4.   ,,   default.
5.   ,,   payment being required, &c.
6. Testatum and consideration.
7. Grant.
8. Of surrender.
9. Of bond and other securities.
10. Of principal money, &c.
11. Right, &c.
12. Habendum of surrender.
13.   ,,   principal, &c.
14. Power of attorney.
15. Covenant from mortgagee.
16.   ,,   mortgagor.

1. This indenture made, &c.

2. Between C. D. [*mortgagee*] of first part, A. B. [*mortgagor*] of second part, and J. K. [*assignee*] of third part.

3. Whereas, &c. Recite conditional surrender and bond.

4. And whereas default was made in payment of the said sum of £   at the time in condition of the said surrender mentioned, and still remains due upon the said surrender, as the said A. B. doth hereby acknowledge; but all interest thereon hath been paid up to the date hereof, as the said C. D. doth acknowledge;

5. And whereas the said C. D. having required payment of the said sum of £   , the said J. K., upon the application of the said A. B., hath agreed to pay off the same on having the assignment hereinafter contained;

6. Now this indenture witnesseth, that in pursuance of the said agreement, and in consideration of £   of lawful money, &c. to the said C. D. paid by the said I. K., at or before the execution hereof, the receipt whereof in full of [*all principal money*] as aforesaid the said C. D. doth hereby, and by the receipt hereupon endorsed, acknowledge, and of and from the same and the interest paid up as aforesaid, doth hereby acquit and release the said I. K., his heirs, executors, and administrators, and also the said A. B., his heirs, executors, and administrators, and in consideration of 10*s*. of lawful money, &c. in like manner paid to the said A. B. (the receipt whereof is hereby acknowledged)

7. He, the said C D., hath bargained, sold, assigned, transferred and set over, and by these presents doth bargain, &c.; and the said A. B. hath granted, ratified, and confirmed, and by these presents doth, &c. unto the said J. K., his heirs, executors, and administrators,

8. All that the said recited conditional surrender on the aforesaid manor of, &c.

9. And also the said in part recited bond, and all other deeds, securities, and writings, given or obtained for better securing the said sum of £   and interest, and all benefit and advantage to arise or be had, received, or taken from the same respectively.

111

10. And also all that the said principal sum of £   , secured by the said recited conditional surrender and bond respectively, and all interest henceforth to accrue and grow due in respect thereof, together with all powers and remedies, both at law and in equity, now vested in the said C. D. for recovering and compelling payment thereof;

11. And all the estate, right, title, interest, benefit, power, claim, and demand whatsoever, both at law and in equity, of him the said C. D., in, to, and out of the said surrender, and the hereditaments therein comprized by virtue thereof, as well as the said principal sum, interest, securities, and premises hereby assigned, or intended so to be, and every of them respectively;

12. To have and to hold the said surrender, and all benefit and advantage thereof, unto the said I. K., his heirs and assigns for ever, To the intent that the said I. K., or his heirs, may at any time hereafter have and claim admission and be admitted tenant or tenants of the said copyhold hereditaments and premises, with their appurtenances, at the will of the lord or lords, lady or ladies, of the said manor of, &c. by and under the rents, suits, and services therefore due and of right accustomed, subject nevertheless to such equity of redemption as the said copyhold hereditaments and premises are subject and liable to by virtue of the same surrender respectively. [*This clause, though taken from a draft settled by counsel, might be deemed objectionable by many stewards.*]

13. And to have and to hold, receive, take, and enjoy the said principal sum of £   and interest, and all and singular other the monies, securities, and premises hereby assigned, or intended so to be, unto and by him the said I. K., his executors, administrators, and assigns, as and for his and their own absolute use and benefit, in as full, ample, and beneficial a manner to all intents and purposes whatsoever, as he the said C. D. might have held, received, or enjoyed the same if these presents had not been made.

14. And for the considerations aforesaid, he the said C. D., doth hereby irrevocably nominate, constitute, and appoint the said I. K., his executors, administrators, and assigns, the true and lawful attorney and attorneys of him the said C. D., his executors or administrators, for the purpose of using his, their, or either of their names, in demanding, suing for, recovering, and receiving of and from the said A. B., his heirs, executors, administrators, and assigns, and all and every or any other person or persons whomsoever, liable to or who ought to pay the same, or whom else it may concern, the said sum of £   and interest hereby assigned, or intended so to be, and also in giving effectual receipts and discharges for the same, he the said I. K., his executors, administratois, and assigns, saving harmless the said C. D., his executors and

112

administrators, from all costs, charges, damages, and expences incident or relating thereto.

15. And the said C D. doth hereby for himself, his heirs, executors, and administrators, covenant and declare with and to the said J. K., his executors, administrators, and assigns, That he the said C. D. hath not at any time heretofore done, committed, or suffered, or been party or privy to any act, deed, matter, or thing whatsoever, whereby or by means whereof the said surrender, or the said sum of £   , or the interest thereof, or the securities for the same respectively, are, is, can, shall, or may be in anywise assigned, impeached, charged, incumbered, or prejudicially affected in title, estate, or otherwise howsoever.

16. A covenant for further assurance by mortgagee must be added. See form in bond, No. 319.

---

328. *Surrender in lieu of this Assignment.*

Be it remembered, &c., as in No. 318, 1, 2, and 3.

Did out of court, at the request and by the direction of C. D., of, &c., testified by his signature at the foot hereof, and as an additional and further security to J. K., of, &c., who has on the day of the date hereof paid to the said C. D. the principal money, or sum of £   , secured by a conditional surrender made and passed, &c. [*state surrender*], and has become entitled to such sum, and the benefit of such surrender, and in consideration of the sum of 10*s.* of lawful money of Great Britain to the said A. B., paid by the said J. K. at or immediately before the passing the surrender hereinafter contained, the receipt whereof is hereby acknowledged,

Surrender, &c. [*As in Conditional Surrender,* 318.]

Which said principal money is the same sum as was mentioned to be secured by the aforesaid conditional surrender, passed to the use of the said C. D., and his heirs, &c. Then the said above written surrender to be void, or else to remain in full force and virtue.

I direct and approve of the passing this surrender.

                                        C. D.

The original mortgagee will sign a receipt for the money as paid by the new mortgagee, on the mortgage bond or deed of covenant; and will also sign a warrant to enter satisfaction on the first conditional surrender, which the new mortgagee will hold and have presented when he deems it advisable.

A reference to the Stamp Act, under the head "mortgage," will show the law on the subject of these stamps.

MORTGAGE OF FREEHOLD AND COPYHOLD.

329. *Conditional Surrender.*

This will be in the same form as 318, with the following addition at the end of the words, " abatement whatsoever:" which said sum of £   and the interest thereof, are the same principal money and interest as are mentioned to be secured in a certain indenture of release, bearing even date herewith, and made or expressed to be made between, &c., and whereon the *ad valorum* duty payable by law in respect whereof is duly impressed.

Then the above surrender to be void, &c.

———

330. *Mortgage of Freehold.*

1. Commencement.	10. Habendum.
2. Parties.	11. Proviso.
3. Recital of Contract.	12. Covenant for Payment.
4. ——— Surrender.	13. ——— ——— Title.
5. Testatum and Consideration.	14. ——————— Right to Convey.
6. Release.	15. ———————Quiet enjoyment
7. Parcels.	after default.
8. Reversion, &c.	16. Free from Incumbrances.
9. Deeds.	17. For further Assurances.

1. This indenture, made, &c.

2. Between A. B. of &c. of the one part, and C. D. [*mortgagee*] of, &c. of the other part.

3. Whereas the said A. B. having occasion for the loan of £   , hath applied to and prevailed on the said C. D. to advance and lend him the same on security of the freehold and copyhold hereditaments hereinafter described, and intended to be hereby released, and mentioned to have been surrendered as hereinafter contained and recited;

4. And whereas, in pursuance and part performance of such agreement, the said A. B. hath, with E. his wife, on the day of the date hereof, duly surrendered into the hands of the lord of the manor of W., whereof the said copyhold hereditaments are holden, by the hands and acceptance of N. M., the steward of the said manor, All, &c. being the said copyhold hereditaments, To the use of the said C. D., his heirs, and assigns, according to the custom of the said manor, upon condition, nevertheless that if, &c. [*stating condition.*]

5. Testatum and Consideration.

114

6. Grant.

7. Parcels.

8. Reversion.

9. Deeds, as in No. 311.

10. To have and to hold all and singular the said freehold parts, hereditaments, and premises, unto the said C. D., his heirs and assigns, To the use and behoof of the said C. D., his heirs and assigns for ever, subject nevertheless to the proviso or condition for redemption of the said premises hereinafter contained, (that is to say.)

11. Provided always, and these presents are upon this express condition, and it is the true intent and meaning of these presents, and of the said parties hereto, that if the said A. B., his heirs, executors, administrators, or assigns, do and shall, &c. [*as in copyhold surrender*, to " absolute whatever"] for or by reason of any taxes, charges, assessments, payments or impositions whatsoever, already or at any time hereafter to be taxed, charged, assessed or imposed upon, or in respect of the said hereditaments and premises, or any part thereof, or the said principal sum, or the interest thereof, by authority of parliament or otherwise howsoever; then and in such case these presents, and every clause, matter, and thing herein contained shall cease, determine, and be utterly void to all intents and purposes whatsoever, any thing herein contained to the contrary in anywise notwithstanding.

12. And the said A. B. for himself, his heirs, executors, and administrators, doth hereby covenant, promise and agree to and with the said C. D., his executors, administrators and assigns, that he the said A. B., his heirs, executors, or administrators, shall and will, well and truly pay, or cause to be paid unto the said C. D., his executors, administrators, or assigns, the said sum of £   with interest for the same, after the rate, at the day, and in manner hereinbefore appointed for payment thereof, without any deduction or abatement whatsoever, according to the true intent and meaning of these presents, and of the condition in the said recited conditional surrender contained.

13 & 14. And the said A. B. doth hereby for himself, his heirs, executors and administrators, covenant, promise and agree to and with the said C. D., his heirs and assigns, in manner following ; (that is to say), that he the said A. B. at the time of executing, &c. [*add absolute covenants for title and right to convey. See* 311, 12 & 13.]

15 & 16. And further, that it shall and may be lawful to and for the said C. D., his heirs, and assigns, from time to time and at all times after default in payment as aforesaid, and [*as in* 311. cl. 14, *adding* cl. 15.]

17. The covenant for further assurance can be drawn from 311, 16, providing for further assurance being at the expence of the mortgagor, adding before the words " as by the said

C. D., &c." at the latter part : and also after default in payment of the said principal money and interest, or any part
thereof, agreeably to these presents and the said conditional
surrender, for further, better, more perfectly, lawfully, and
absolutely or satisfactorily conveying, surrendering, and
assuring the said freehold and copyhold hereditaments, and
every part and parts thereof respectively, with the respective
appurtenances, unto and to the use of the said C. D., his
heirs and assigns for ever, or as he or they may direct, freed
and absolutely discharged from the proviso or condition for
redemption hereinbefore and in the said surrender contained,
and of and from all right, power and equity or benefit of
redemption whatsoever, as by the said, &c. In witness, &c.

331.—*Certificate of Consideration on Surrender in Court.*
Manor of   . The   day of, &c.

I, A. B. of, &c. a copyhold tenant of this manor, do propose
with M. my wife, to surrender this day in open court, All
and singular, &c. [*Or*, All that my copyhold house, called, &c.
and more fully described in the court rolls of this manor.]
To the use of C. D. of, &c. his heirs and assigns for ever
absolutely, according to the custom of this manor : And pursuant to the act or acts of parliament requiring the same,
I do certify that such proposed surrender is upon a sale, and
that the whole consideration is the sum of £   pounds [*or*,
that such proposed surrender is not upon a sale, and that
there is no pecuniary consideration in respect thereof]. As
witness my hand, the day and year above written.
   Witness.——

> To be written on plain paper, and delivered to the
> steward before passing a surrender in court. See
> Stamp Act, 55 Geo. 3. The steward charges a small
> fee, varying from 3s. 6d. to 7s., for the certificate; and if
> not prepared previously, will prepare it at the court.

332.—*Annuity Surrender.*

Manor of }   The   day of   , in the year of our
         }   Lord, 18   .

Be it remembered, that on the day and year above written,
A. B., of &c. and E. his wife, copyhold tenants, or one of
them, a copyhold tenant of the said manner, came before
me, &c., [see 318, cl. 2 & 3.]
   Did out of court, in consideration of the sum of £
of lawful money of Great Britain, by C. D., of &c. to the
said A. B. in hand well and truly paid, at or before the passing this surrender, in manner following ; that is to say, by a

draft or cheque, bearing even date with these presents, drawn
by the said C. D., on Messrs.   & Co. bankers, in
aforesaid, for the said sum of £   , payable to the said A. B.,
or bearer, on demand, being the consideration money on the
purchase by the said C. D., of the said A. B., of an annuity
or yearly sum of £   of lawful money of Great Britain,
free from taxes, and clear of all other deductions whatsoever,
for and during the natural lives of him the said C. D., of [*two
nominees*] of &c., and the lives and life of the survivors and
survivor of them ; and to be secured by the bond or obligation of the said A. B., and a warrant of attorney for entering
up judgment thereon, by the surrender hereinafter contained,
and by a deed of covenant on such surrender, already prepared, and intended to bear date herewith.

Surrender, &c. 318, cl. 5 to 9.

Subject nevertheless to and upon this express condition,
that if the said A. B., his heirs, executors, administrators, or
assigns, do and shall well and truly pay, or cause to be paid,
unto the said C. D., his executors, administrators, and assigns, for and during the natural lives of him the said C. D.,
and of the said [*nominees*], and the lives and life of the survivors and survivor of them, one annuity or yearly sum of
£   of lawful money of Great Britain, free from taxes,
and clear of all other deductions whatsoever, on the following
four days in each year; that is to say, &c. by even and equal
portions, the first payment to begin and be made on &c. And
also if the said A. B., his heirs, executors, or administrators,
do and shall well and truly pay or cause to be paid, unto the
executors, administrators or assigns of the said C. D., in case
the survivor of them the said C. D. and [*nominees*] should
die on any day on which any quarterly payment of the said
annuity or yearly sum of £   shall become due, the
whole of such quarterly payment; and if on any other day,
a proportional part of such annuity from the last day of payment up to the day of such death ; or if the said A. B., his
heirs, executors, administrators, or assigns, do and shall give
to the said C. D., his executors, administrators, or assigns,
seven days notice of such intention, and do and shall at any
time hereafter well and truly pay or cause to be paid unto
the said C. D., his executors, administrators, or assigns, the
full sum of £   , of lawful money of Great Britain,
being the original purchase money, and two quarterly payments of the said annuity of £   , as and for the consideration money for such repurchase, together with all
arrears that shall be due on the same, and a proportionate
part thereof from the last day of payment preceding such
repurchase (and also any costs, charges, and expences then
incurred in or about any of the trusts hereinafter contained, or
relating to the recovery of arrears on the said annuity) Then,

117

and in either of the said cases the above-written surrender
to be void and of no effect; otherwise to remain in full force
and virtue. And it shall and may be lawful to and for the
said C. D., his heirs, executors, administrators, or assigns,
in case the said annuity or yearly sum of £   , or any
part thereof, shall be behind and unpaid for the space of
forty days next over or after any of the said days or times
whereon the same is limited and appointed to be paid as aforesaid, to make sale, &c. (see *Power of Sale*, No. 322.) And to
stand possessed of and interested in all and every the sum
and sums of money to arise from any such sale or sales, and
of the rents and profits of the said hereditaments, after the
same shall become saleable, upon trust thereout, in the first
place, to retain and reimburse himself and themselves all such
costs, charges, and expenses as he or they shall or may sustain, expend, or be put unto in or about the making and
completing such sale or sales, or otherwise in the execution of
the trusts hereby in him and them reposed; and after payment thereof, as to the surplus of the money arising from
such sale or sales as aforesaid, upon trust thereout to retain
and pay so much of the said annuity or yearly sum of £
as at the time of completing such sale or sales shall be in
arrear and unpaid; and also all such sum and sums of money,
losses, costs, charges, damages, and expenses (if any) as the
said C. D., his executors, administrators, or assigns, or any
of them, shall pay, sustain, or be put unto by reason or
means of the non-payment of the said annuity or yearly sum
of £   , or any part thereof, in the manner hereinbefore
mentioned, or appointed for payment thereof, or in anywise in
relation thereto. And upon further trust, to place out and
invest the residue of the money to arise by such sale or sales,
and of the mesne rents and profits, upon government securities at interest, in the name of the said C. D., his executors,
administrators and assigns. And shall stand possessed of
and interested in the money so to be placed out and invested
upon trust, by and out of the interest, dividends, and annual
proceeds thereof, and if the same shall be insufficient, then in
addition thereto, by calling in, selling, and disposing from
time to time, of a sufficient part of the principal money, so
to be invested, or the stocks, funds, and securities for the
same, to retain and pay to himself and themselves the said
annuity or yearly sum of £   , as and when the same
shall become due and payable: and upon trust also, by and
out of the money to be placed out and invested, and the dividends, interest, and proceeds thereof, to retain to him the
said C. D., his executors, administrators, and assigns, all
such costs, charges, and expences as he or they may sustain
or be put unto in the execution of trusts hereby reposed in
him and them respecting the money hereinbefore directed to

be invested or placed out at interest; and subject to the aforesaid trusts, in trust for the said A. B., his executors, administrators, and assigns, to and for his and their own absolute use and benefit; and the receipt and receipts of the said C. D., his executors, administrators or assigns, shall from time to time well and effectually discharge any tenant, purchaser, or other person paying money to him or them in or in relation to the premises, for the money therein expressed to be received, and from subsequent liability to see to the application, or be answerable for the misapplication or nonapplication thereof.

Taken, &c.   A. B.

This surrender will be accompanied with a bond, in a penalty of double the purchase money, having a condition for payment of annuity or amount of repurchase; a warrant of attorney, having a defeazance similar to the condition in the bond.

The deed of covenant will recite the contract, the nature of the security intended to be given, the execution of the bond, and warrant, and passing the surrender. The grantor will then covenant that he is seised; has right to convey; that premises shall remain to uses of the surrender after default, free from incumbrances, and for further assurances; and it would be attended with advantage to add a further testatum, giving the grantee a power of attorney to surrender the copyholds, and execute proper deeds of covenant in the name of the grantor, as a mode of avoiding the necessity for admission. (See Debtor and Creditor Deed, form 338.)

By 55 Geo. 3, c. 141, a memorial of an annuity must be enrolled in Chancery within 30 days after date of security, and which must state the date of each security, the nature, the names of parties; names of witnesses; parties beneficially interested; for whose lives granted; consideration how paid, and amount of annuity.

This does not, however, extend to annuities granted by will or settlement, or secured on freehold or copyhold or customary lands, of equal or greater annual value than the annuity, over and above any other annuity, and the interest of any principal sum charged or secured thereon, of which the grantee had notice at the time of the grant, s. 10.

333.—Notice to pay off Mortgage.

Sir,

I hereby give you notice that at the end of six calendar months from the date hereof, I shall require payment of all principal and interest monies due on your mortgage to

119

me, of the estate called, &c., bearing date, &c.; and that in default of payment agreeably to this notice, I shall proceed to such remedies for enforcing payment as I may be advised to adopt.   Dated, &c.

334.—*Notice to Tenant to pay Rent to Mortgagee.*

Sir,

Take notice, that on the   day of, &c., the premises now in your occupation, and held as tenant under Mr. A. G., of, &c., were duly conveyed and mortgaged to me for securing the repayment of £   , and lawful interest, at a certain day now past, and that such principal sum, and an arrear of interest, is still due and unpaid from the said A. G. to me; I do therefore give you notice not to pay any rent now due, or hereafter to become due for the said premises to the said A. G., or to any other person than to me, or to whom I shall appoint; and to pay the same to me or such person accordingly.   Dated, &c.

LEASES.

355.—*Lease without Licence.*

The only difference between this and a common lease will be in the habendum, which will be as follows :—

To have and to hold all such part and parts, and so much of the said demised premises as are or be freehold or charterhold, and not copyhold or customary hold, unto the said [*lessee*] his executors, &c. [*common form*]. And to have and to hold all such part and parts, and so much of the said demised premises as are copyhold or customary hold, unto the said [*lessee*], his executors and administrators, from the day of   instant, for the term of one whole year from thence next ensuing, and so on from year to year, for years longer, provided the same can be done without fine or forfeiture, yielding and paying, &c. (*in usual terms*).

336.—*Lease with Licence.*

The only difference between this and a common lease will be after the consideration the using the following words:—He the said [*lessor*], by and with the licence and consent of the lord of the manor of W., obtained as to the copyhold parts of the said hereditaments, hath demised and leased, &c.

(337.) *Surrender on Marriage.*

Manor of } The   day of   , in the year of our
———— } Lord 1837.

BE IT REMEMBERED, that on the day and year above written,
J. W., of, &c., a copyhold tenant of the said manor, came
before me [C. D., *deputy steward for that purpose only of,*]
A. B., chief steward of the said manor, and the courts thereof,
and did out of court, (in consideration of a marriage about to
be had and solemnized between him the said J. W., and E. J.,
of, &c., surrender out of his hands into the hands of the lord of
the said manor, by the hands and acceptance of me the said
deputy steward, by the rod, according to the custom of the
said manor, *All*, &c., *And* the reversion &c., *And* all the
estate &c., To the use of the said J. W. and his heirs, until
the solemnization of the said intended marriage; and from
and after the solemnization thereof, To the use of the said
J. W., and his assigns for and during the term of his natural
life, and from and after his decease, To the use of the said E.
his intended wife and her assigns, for and during her natural
life; and from and after the decease of the survivor of them
the said J. W. and E. his intended wife, To the use of the
first son of the body of the said J. W. by the said E. his intended wife, and the heirs of the body of such first son lawfully issuing; and in default of such issue, To the use of the
second, and all and every other son and sons of the body of the
said J. W. by the said E. his intended wife, severally, successively, and in remainder, one after another as they and
every of them shall be in seniority of age and priority of
birth, and of the several and respective heirs of the body of
all and every such son and sons lawfully issuing; the eldest
of such sons, and the heirs of his body, to take and be pre-
ferred before the younger of such sons and the heirs of his
body; and for default of such issue, To the use of all and
every the daughter and daughters of the body of the said
J. W. by the said E. his wife, equally to be divided between
or amongst them, share and share alike, as tenants in common,
and not as joint tenants, and of the several and respective
heirs of the body and bodies of all and every such daughter
and daughters, lawfully issuing; and on failure of the issue
of any one or more of the said daughters of the intended marriage, (in case there shall be more than one such
daughter), then as to or concerning the original part or share
of the same daughter or daughters, and also as to the part or
parts which shall belong to the same daughter or daughters,
or her or their issue, by virtue of the present provision of
cross limitation, To the use of the other or others of the said

daughter or daughters of the said intended marriage, to be equally divided between or amongst them, if more than one, share and share alike, as tenants in common and not as joint tenants, and the heirs of the body, or several and respective bodies, of the same daughter or daughters respectively lawfully issuing; and on failure of the issue of all the said daughters, to the use of the said J. W., his heirs and assigns for ever.

(338.)   *Trust Deed for the Benefit of Creditors.*

This indenture, made &c.   Between [*debtor*] of first part, [*trustees*] of second part, and the several other persons whose names are hereunto set and seals affixed, creditors of the said [*debtor*], of the third part.

Whereas the said [*debtor*] is seised of or well entitled for an estate of inheritance in fee simple in possession, according to the custom of the manor of W., in the county of S., to the messuage and hereditaments hereinafter mentioned, with the appurtenances, and is also possessed of certain stock in trade and personal estate and effects.

And whereas &c., [*recite being indebted and inability to pay, with proposal to make assignment.*]

Now this indenture witnesseth &c., [*insert the usual assignment of personalty, upon trust to sell, with the common power of attorney.*]

And this indenture further witnesseth, that in further pursuance and part performance of the said proposal and agreement, and for the considerations aforesaid, he the said [*debtor*] with the like consent, privity, and approbation of his said several creditors, testified as aforesaid, hath made, ordained, constituted, and appointed, and by these presents doth make &c., the said [*trustees*] jointly and severally, and the survivor of them, his true and lawful attorneys and attorney, for him and in his name to sell and dispose of, either by public auction or private contract, and for the best price or prices that can in their or his judgment be had or gotten for the same, All that &c.   And also to make and enter into any contract or contracts in writing, with any person or persons whomsoever, in relation to such sale or sales, at discretion and in the name and stead of the said [*debtor*] either at some general or special court baron, to be holden for the said manor of W., or out of court, at any time or times after such sale or sales, to surrender into the hands of the lord or lords, lady or ladies of the said manor, according to the custom thereof, the said hereditaments so to be sold by the description thereof contained in the court rolls of the said manor, or such other description as may be deemed advisable or proper.   And the reversion &c.   And all the estate &c., (see

122

surrenders,) To the use and behoof of the purchaser or purchasers of the said hereditaments, and his, her, or their heirs or assigns, or as he, she, or they may direct or require, and according to the custom of the said manor of W. And moreover for the said [*debtor*] and in his name, and as his act and deed, to sign, seal, execute and deliver any deed or deeds, to be prepared by and on the part of such purchaser or purchasers, pursuant to any such contract for sale, containing all reasonable and proper covenants on the part of the said [*debtor*,] his heirs, executors, and administrators, for the estate, title, possession, and assurance of the said hereditaments, so to be sold as aforesaid, and to receive and take the rents, issues, and profits of the said hereditaments until sale and conveyance thereof, and to give discharges for the same from time to time ; and generally for the said [*debtor*], and on his behalf, to do, perform and execute, any such other acts, deeds and assurances, matters and things, as shall be necessary or expedient in or about the premises, and as fully and effectually to all intents and purposes, as the said [*debtor*] himself could lawfully do being personally present, he hereby ratifying and confirming, and agreeing to ratify all and whatsoever his said attorneys or attorney shall lawfully do or cause to be done in the premises.

A declaration that receipts shall be discharges is then to be added, with the usual trusts for application and division of the money, and the usual covenants from the debtor, and a covenant from the debtor that he and all other parties whose concurrence may be reasonably required, will join and concur in any sale, surrender, deeds or assurance, adding the usual declaration that such concurrence shall not be essential to validity, but merely for satisfaction of a purchaser. In the trustees' provision, will be inserted a power to buy in and resell, without being liable for loss, and the usual creditors' release, and covenant by trustees, will complete the deed.

> Under the Bankrupt Act, 6 Geo. 4, this deed will not operate as an act of bankruptcy to support a fiat, unless the fiat be issued within six months, provided it be executed by the trustees within fourteen days of the date, and such execution, attested by an attorney or solicitor, and notice advertized in gazette and papers as mentioned in the act.
>
> It would be prudent on a sale under this deed, to avoid fixing a date within six months for completion, as by giving the six months, a purchaser can feel safe if the deed was properly executed and advertized.
>
> In form 315, will be found the points to be attended to in framing conditions of sale under a trust deed.

WILLS.

[As to wills made after 1837, see abstract of 1st Vic. c. 26, at end of Court-Keeping Forms.]

339.—*Simple Devise.*

1. This is the last will and testament of me, A. B. of &c. made this   day of   , in the year of our Lord, 18

2. I nominate and appoint [*add appointment of executors, and bequests of personalties.*—See "Practical Man," *Wills*, 1 to 16.]

3. I give and devise my copyhold dwelling house, with the lands, grounds, and premises belonging, situate, &c. unto and to the use of Mr. G., his heirs and assigns, for ever.

4. And as to all and every of the freehold, copyhold, customary and leasehold manor, messuages, lands, tenements, hereditaments and real estate, whereof or whereto I or any persons or person in trust for me, am, are, or is seised or entitled, or which I have power to dispose of by this my will, and all other my real estate whatsoever and wheresoever, in possession, reversion, remainder, or expectancy, with the appurtenances, I give, devise, and dispose thereof unto and to the use of I. G. of, &c. his heirs, executors, administrators, and assigns for ever, according to the nature of the said estates respectively.

5. [*Add declaration that executors shall only be answerable for wilful defaults, and that they may repay themselves disbursements.*]

6. And lastly, revoking all former wills, I declare this to be my last will and testament, In witness whereof, I have to this my last will and testament, written on [*three*] sheets of paper, set my hand and seal; that is to say, my hand to the first two sheets thereof, and my hand and seal to this third and last sheet, the day and year first above written.

7. Signed, sealed, published, and declared by the said A. B. the testator, as and for his last will and testament, in the presence of us, who in his presence, at his request, and in the presence of each other, subscribe our names as witnesses hereto.   A. B.   (L. S.)

340.—*For Life, and afterwards in Tail.*

This is the last will and testament, &c.

I give and devise all that my copyhold estate, called, &c. situate, &c. unto my eldest son [*name*], for and during his natural life, without impeachment of waste; and after his decease to the use of his sons successively, according to their respective seniorities, in tail male; and for default of such issue, to the use of my son [*second son*] for his natural life, without impeachment of waste; and after his decease, to the use of his sons successively, according to their respective seniorities, in tail male. And for default of such issue, to the use of my daughters [*names*], during their respective lives in equal shares as tenants in common, without impeachment of waste; and as to the respective shares therein of each of them my said daughters, after her decease, to the use of her sons successively, according to their respective seniorities, in tail male, and on the failure of the issue male of any one or more of my said daughters, then and so often as the same shall happen, as to as well the share or respective shares originally limited to the daughter or daughters whose issue shall so fail as the share or respective shares which by virtue of this present clause shall have become vested in her or them, or her or their issue male, to the use of the daughter or daughters of my said daughters during her or their life or respective lives, in equal shares as tenants in common, without impeachment of waste, and after the decease of any such last mentioned daughter, then, as to the share or shares lastly limited to her, to the use of her sons successively, according to their respective seniorities, in tail male; and if there shall be a failure of such issue male of all my said daughters but one, then as to the entirety of the said estate, to the use of such only daughter for her life, without impeachment of waste; and after her decease, to the use of her sons successively, according to their respective seniorities, in tail male; and for default of such issue, to the use of my said several sons and daughters, as tenants in common in tail general, with cross remainders between and amongst them in tail general; and if all my said children but one shall die without issue, to the use of such only remaining child in tail general; and for default of such issue, to the use of my own right heirs for ever.

341—*To secure Annuity to Wife, and subject thereto to Son.*

1. This is the last will and testament, &c.
2. [*Appointment of executors, bequests of personalty, &c.*]
3. I give unto M. my wife, an annuity of £   during her natural life, (provided she shall so long continue my widow), charged and chargeable upon my estate, at &c. with powers of distress and entry for the recovery thereof, as if the same had been secured by a lease for years; the same annuity to be paid half yearly, on, &c. with a proportionate part up to the day of the decease of my said wife, and the first payment to be made on the first of such days happening after my decease; the same to be in lieu of dower and free bench, but in addition

125

to the jointure settled upon her by our marriage setlement, and which I hereby confirm.

4. I give and devise unto [*trustees*], their heirs and assigns, all that my copyhold estate, situate, &c. upon trust that they or the survivors, or the heirs of such survivor, or other the trustee to be appointed as hereinafter mentioned, do and shall, by and out of the rents and profits thereof, or by mortgage or otherwise as they shall think fit from time to time, to raise and pay the costs, charges and expenses of or attending their admission to the said estate and otherwise in the trusts herein contained in relation thereto, and also do and shall from time to time in like manner, raise, levy, and pay to my said wife, for and during the term of her natural life, (provided she shall so long continue my widow and during her widowhood) one clear annuity of £   , by equal half yearly payments, on, &c. with a proportionate part thereof up to the decease of my said wife to her executor or administrator, together with all costs and expenses attending the non payment thereof, and subject thereto and to the trusts aforesaid, upon trust for W. my son, his heirs and assigns for ever. And upon trust from and after the decease or marriage of my said wife, whichever shall first happen, to surrender and assure the said estate whenever requested by my said son, his heirs or assigns, and at his or their expense, to his and their use absolutely, or as he or they may direct or appoint, subject nevertheless to all mortgages or other incumbrances created under the trusts hereinbefore contained.

5. And I declare that it shall and may be lawful for my said trustees to insure their lives in a responsible insurance office, in such sum as they may reasonably estimate the amount of fine and expenses of admission of other trustees on their deaths would amount to, with a view to provide for the expense of any such admission by an annual payment in lieu of a large single payment; and I declare that my trustees shall and may retain and pay the expense of such insurance out of the annual rents and profits of the said estate or otherwise, as before provided with respect to the costs of their own admittance in the trusts hereby reposed in them. [*The usual trustee powers will then be added, with the conclusion.*—See "Practical Man," *Wills*, 1 to 16.]

342.—*Freehold and Copyhold; part to be sold immediately, and part on death of wife.*

1. This is the last will and testament of me, E. C., of &c.

2. I give and devise unto [*trustees*], their heirs and assigns, all and singular my freehold messuages or tenements, lands, and hereditaments (and parts thereof) situate in H. aforesaid,

or elsewhere in England, to hold the same unto the said [*trustees*], their heirs and assigns, to the uses, upon the trusts, and to the intents and purposes following (that is to say) :

3. As to the freehold messuage or dwelling-house in H. aforesaid, in the occupation of M. B., with the yards and gardens thereunto belonging, to the use of my wife, H. C., and her assigns, for and during the term of her natural life;

4. And as to the same premises, from and after the decease of my said wife, and as to all other the said freehold hereditaments, from and immediately after my decease, to the use of the said [*trustees*], their heirs and assigns, upon the trusts following.

5. And I do hereby empower and direct the said [*trustees*], and the survivor of them, and the heirs and assigns of such survivor, with all convenient speed after my decease, to make sale and dispose of my said freehold estates (except the messuage or tenement so given to my said wife for her life as aforesaid, which is not to be sold during her life without her concurrence) ; and also of all the customary or copy-hold messuages, lands, tenements, and hereditaments [*or parts thereof*] of or to which I may be seised or entitled at the time of my decease, either together or in parcels, and either by public auction or private contract, for the most money and best prices that can be reasonably had or gotten for the same.

6. And I do hereby declare and direct that the receipts in writing of the said [*trustees*], or the survivor of them, or the heirs or assigns of such survivor, shall be good and effectual discharges to the purchaser or purchasers of all or any part of the said freehold and copyhold or customary hereditaments, and that such purchaser or purchasers shall not afterwards be bound to see to the application of, or be answerable or accountable for, any loss, misapplication, or non-application of his, her, or their purchase money, expressed or acknowledged in such receipt or receipts to have been received.

7. And I do hereby direct that the monies arising by sale of my said freehold and copyhold estates, shall sink into and become part of my personal estate, and that the rents, issues, and profits thereof, till sold, shall be paid and applied in such manner as is hereinafter directed with respect to the dividends, interest, and annual proceeds of the funds and securities in or upon which the monies to arise by such sale or sales are here-inafter directed to be invested ;

8. Provided always, and I do hereby direct, that in case the said messuage and premises hereinbefore devised to my said wife for her life as aforesaid, shall be sold with her concurrence during her life, then and in such case the purchase or consideration money for the same shall be invested, during her life, in or upon government or real securities, in the names or name of the said [*trustees*], or the survivor of them, or the

127

executors of such survivor; and that during the life of my
said wife, the dividends, interest, and annual proceeds thereof
shall be paid to her my said wife in lieu of her life estate or
life interest in the said premises, and that the principal after
her death shall be considered as part of my personal estate.

[Then follow the usual trusts for investment and division
of the proceeds of the sale.—See " Practical Man,"
Wills, 31 to 38.]

In the " Practical Man" many other forms of wills will be
found.

PARTITION.

343.—*Between Joint Tenants.*

This indenture, made, &c., between A. B. of, &c. of the
one part, and C. D., of, &c. of the other part.

Whereas at a court, &c. [*recite admission.*]

And whereas the said A. B., and C. D., have mutually agreed
to divide and make partition between themselves of the said
hereditaments, and that the said A. B. shall have and be entitled absolutely for an estate of inheritance in fee, according
to the custom of the said manor, of all that, &c., and that
the said C. B. shall have and be entitled in like manner to all
that, &c.

Now this indenture witnesseth, that in consideration of the
premises and of 10*s.* of lawful money, &c., to the said C. D.
paid by the said A. B., at or immediately before the execution
of these presents [*the receipt whereof is hereby acknowledged*]
he the said C. D. hath remised, released, and for ever quitted
claim, and by these presents doth remise, &c., unto the said
A. B., tenant as aforesaid, all that, &c., and the reversion,
&c., and all the estate, &c., to the use and behoof of the said
A. B., his heirs and assigns for ever, according to the custom
of the said manor, and so that neither he the said C. D.
nor his heirs, nor any other person or persons having or
claiming or to claim by, from, through, under, or in trust
for him or them, shall have any estate, right, title or interest,
of, in, or to the said hereditaments so mentioned to be released to the use of the said A. B., his heirs and assigns, but
thereof and therefrom shall be by these presents utterly precluded and barred.

[*Add a like release from A. B. to C. D., of the parts which he
is to have.*]

And each of them the said A. B , and C. D., doth hereby
for himself, his heirs, executors, and administrators, covenant,
promise, and agree to and with the other of them, his heirs and
assigns, that each of them the said A. B. and C. D. respectively, and his respective heirs, shall and will from time to

time, and at all times hereafter, upon every reasonable request, and at the expense of the party requiring the same, make, pass, execute, and perfect all and every such further and other lawful and reasonable acts, deeds, surrenders, releases, and assurances whatsoever, for the further, more perfectly or satisfactorily conveying, confirming, and assuring the said respective hereditaments to the uses and in manner hereinbefore mentioned, and according to the true intent and meaning of these presents, as by the said A. B. and C D. respectively, or their respective heirs or assigns, or their counsel in the law, shall be reasonably devised or advised and required, and that until admission shall be taken by the said A. B. and C. D. respectively, their respective heirs and assigns, to the hereditaments hereby mentioned to be released to their respective use as aforesaid, each of them and his heirs shall stand and be a trustee or trustees for the other and his heirs of such respective hereditaments, according to the true intent and meaning of these presents. In witness.

> It will frequently be requisite to insert a covenant for production of writings, when they relate to the whole property and are held by one of the parties.
> The object of the present deed is to avoid the expence of immediate admission ; but should the property be small, and the expence deemed unimportant, the simple way of partition, in all cases, will be by the parties joining in a surrender of the whole premises to the use of A. B., as to the premises to be taken by him, and to the use of C. D., as to those to be taken by him, and for admission to be taken on the surrender.

344.—By Coparceners.

When admitted together they may release as above, but not when admitted severally (see Scriven Cop. 354) ; but as most frequently some of the coperceners are married women, the only general course to be adopted will be their joining in a surrender of the whole property to the use of each party as to the premises she is to take, and for admission to be taken under such surrender.

As far as the estate clause, with the exception of the statement of consideration, the surrender can be drawn from No. 280.

The consideration clause may be stated thus :—" for the purpose of effecting the partition hereafter contained."

The uses will be as follow :—

As to, for, and concerning all that, &c. to the use of the

said A. B., her heirs and assigns for ever ; as to, for, and
concerning all that, &c. to the use of the said C. D., her
heirs and assigns for ever, &c.

The remainder of the draft will be similar to No. 276.

345.—*By Tenants in Common.*

The legal estate of tenants in common can only be effected
by a surrender of the whole copyhold to uses as to each person, as in the case of caperceners ; but with a view to save
the immediate expence of a fine, they might enter into mutual
covenants to pass such surrender whenever called on ; and to
be interested in the property until such surrender, upon trusts
agreeably to the partition ; and it might be as well to stipulate that the expense of admission by the heir of any of the
parties should be borne by such party's representatives, or
by the party requiring the surrender, as might have been
agreed on.

346.—*Deed of Covenant between Tenants in Common.*

After parties, and recitals of admission and agreement,

Now this Indenture witnesseth, that in pursuance of the
premises, and in and towards performance of the said recited
agreement, each of them the said A. B., C. D., and E. F., doth
hereby for himself, his heirs, executors, and administrators,
covenant, promise, and agree to and with the other and others
of them, their, and each of their heirs and assigns, in manner
following (that is to say), that they the said A. B., C. D., and
E. F. respectively, and their respective heirs, shall and will
at any time hereafter, whenever requested by the other or
others of them, or their respective heirs or assigns, at any
general or special court baron, to be holden for the said
manor of G., or out of court, according to the custom of the
said manor, either in person or by attorney as may be required, well and effectually surrender into the hands of the
lord or lords, lady or ladies for the time being of the said
manor, by the hands and acceptance of the steward or deputy
steward for the time being of the said manor, or otherwise
according to the custom thereof, All those, &c. [*description*]
And the reversion, &c.; And all the estate, &c. of them the said
A. B., C. D., and E. F., and their heirs, of, in, to, &c., To
the uses and in manner following, (that is to say) as to and
concerning all that, &c. to the use of the said A. B., his heirs

130

and assigns, according to the custom of the said manor; and as to, &c. [*same uses in favour of other parties.*]   And that in the mean time, and until such surrender shall be made and admission taken thereunder, they the said A. B., C. D., and E. F., and their respective heirs, shall stand and be possessed of the said copyhold hereditaments respectively, with the appurtenances, upon trust for the party and parties respectively who, under such surrender and admittance, would be entitled thereto, or as he or they shall direct or appoint, according to the true intent and meaning of these presents. And further, that all expences of and attending the making and passing such surrender shall be borne and paid equally by the said A. K., C. D., and E. F., their heirs or assigns; but the expense of admission of the heirs of any of the said parties previously to making such surrender, shall be borne by his estate, and the expence of admissions subsequent to such surrender shall be borne by the parties respectively taking admission; but all costs, charges, and expences occasioned by the refusal of any party to pass such surrender, or otherwise perform the covenant and provisions herein contained, shall be entirely borne by the party so refusing, and shall be recoverable by the other or others paying the same from such refusing party, his heirs, executors, or administrators, as and for ascertained and liquidated damages.

See remarks in No. 343 as to covenants for production of wrtings.

346.—*Value of Copyhold Enfranchisement.*

In general a fine is payable on death or alienation; and as alienation does not admit of the same calculation *a priori* as a question depending on regular intervals or on lives, the most correct way of estimating the probable number of years between each payment, is to take the average in a great number of past cases, similarly to the principle adopted in the formation of tables on the value of lives.

From such an average, taken on the fines paid during one hundred years in an extensive manor, the number of years may be fairly estimated at thirteen, including deaths and alienations.

Calculating on this basis, the value of enfranchisement to be paid by a purchaser of copyhold property, will be found by taking the present value of each succeeding fine, and taking the value of the fine to be paid by the purchaser at unity, and the fines at 13, 26, 39, &c. years, the amount will, at four per cent., be 2·462; and the fines being two years' purchase, the value would be 4·921 years' purchase, or, as the incidental rights of the lord are not brought into the calculation, the value will be fairly estimated at five years' purchase.

Of course 25 years' purchase of the quit rent must be paid in addition.

ENFRANCHISEMENTS.

347.—*Contract.*

Memorandum of agreement made, &c., between A. B., of, &c., lord of the manor of G., in the county of S., and C. D., of, &c., a copyhold tenant of the said manor, as follows :—

That on payment of £   , on or before, &c., the said A. B., shall execute a proper and effectual deed of enfranchisement of all that, &c., copyhold of the said manor of G., and to which the said C. D. now stands admitted tenant on the rolls of the said manor.

And it is hereby mutually agreed, that an abstract of the conveyance to the said A. B., of the said manor of G , shall, within fourteen days, be made at his expence, and delivered to the said C. D., but no further title to the said manor shall be required ; neither shall the said A. B. be put to any expence for requisitions on such conveyance or otherwise, or for copies of such conveyance, or in any way further than the perusal of the deed of enfranchisement, its examination with the draft, and the execution by the said A. B. ; but it is also agreed that in case the said C. D. shall, within three days after receipt of such abstract, express in writing his determination to relinquish such enfranchisement; and shall at the same time pay to the solicitor of the said A. B., the expence of preparing such abstract, at the rate of 10s. 6d. per sheet, he shall be at liberty to relinquish the contract for enfranchisement, otherwise the said C. D. shall be deemed to accept the abstract ; and in default of preparing a proper deed of enfranchisement, and paying the consideration money, by, &c., the said C. D. shall be at liberty to waive the said contract, or proceed to enforce the same.

And it is further agreed, that in case of dispute as to the propriety of the draft, the same shall, at the joint expence of the parties, be submitted to Mr.   , with a copy of this agreement, and the same as settled by him shall be deemed satisfactory.

In witnesss, &c,

348.—*Another Form, where Rent reserved, and Deed to be prepared by Steward.*

The said A. B., agrees to enfranchise all that, &c., copyhold of the said manor of G., and to which the said C. D. now stands admitted tenant, in consideration of the sum of £   , to be paid on, &c., and of a rent charge of   to be henceforth for ever payable out of the said hereditaments, and which sum and rent charge the said C. D., agrees to pay and secure accordingly.

And it is further agreed between the said parties, that no title shall be required to be shown by the said A. B., to the said manor of G., further than, &c. [*according to particular terms of contract*] and that a proper deed of enfranchisement shall be prepared by Mr. R. R., steward of the said manor, at the expense of the said C. D , [*or at the joint expence of, &c.*] and that therein shall be contained a reservation and security of such rent charge ; and that the said A. B., shall be entitled to have a duplicate of such deed, prepared at his expence, for better evidencing the claim to the said rent charge ; and the said deed of enfranchisement shall, at the expence of the said C. D., be presented and entered on the court rolls of the said manor.   In witness, &c.

349.—*Where Enfranchisement Deed to be in form previously used.*

Memorandum. Mr. A. B., lord of the manor of G., agrees to enfranchise, and Mr. C. D. [*the tenant*], agrees to accept the enfranchisement of all that, &c., on the following terms :— The consideration money to be £   , and to be paid on, &c.; the deed of enfranchisement to be conformable to the annexed draft ; and the expence of deed and presenting and enrolling to be borne by Mr. C. D. ; and Mr. A. B., not to be required to shew any title to the said manor.   Dated, &c.

350.—*Creation of Term out of Copyholds.*   (see cl. 265.)

This indenture made, &c., between [*tenant*] of one part, and [*trustee*] of other part ; whereas, &c. [*recite admission to copyhold, contract for enfranchisement, and desire to create term to protect estate against mesne incumbrances.*]

Now this indenture witnesseth that in pursuance of the
133

premises and for [*nominal consideration*] he the said [*tenant*], with the licence and consent of the said [*lord*] first obtained, hath demised, leased, and farm let, and by these presents doth, &c., unto the said [*trustee*], his executors, administrators, and assigns,

All that, &c., and the reversion, &c.

To have and to hold the said messuage, &c., with the appurtenances, unto the said [*trustee*], his executors, administrators, and assigns, from the day next before the day of the date of these presents, for and during and unto the full end and term of 1,000 years, from thence next ensuing, and fully to be complete and ended ;

Yielding and paying therefore yearly and every year during the said term, the rent of one peppercorn, if lawfully demanded ;

In trust, nevertheless, for the said [*tenant*], his heirs and assigns, to attend, wait upon, and go along with the reversion and inheritance of the copyhold tenure of and in the said hereditaments, in the mean time and until the same copyhold tenure shall be extinguished ; and from and after such extinguishment [*in trust for the person or persons to whom the freehold tenure of and in the same hereditaments shall be conveyed*] (*or*, in trust for the said [*tenant*], his heirs and assigns, according to the estates and interests which shall from time to time be existing therein,) to the end and intent that the reversion and inheritance of the said copyhold tenure of and in the said hereditaments, in the mean time and until that tenure shall be extinguished, and afterwards to the intent that the freehold tenure of the said hereditaments, so far as the said [*tenant*] shall be interested therein, shall, by means of the said term of 1000 years, be protected and defended from all incumbrances against which the said term of 1000 years can afford a protection. In witness, &c.

351.—*Deed of Enfranchisement.*

This indenture made, &c.

Between A. B. of, &c., lord of the manor of G., in the county of S. of the one part, and C. D. of, &c , a copyhold tenant of the said manor, of the other part ;

Whereas the said A. B. is seised of or well entitled to the said manor of G. for an estate of inheritance in fee simple in possession, free from all incumbrances ;

And whereas, &c. [*Recite admission.*]

And whereas, the said C. D. hath contracted and agreed with the said A. B. for the enfranchisement of the said copyhold hereditaments [*subject as hereinafter mentioned*] at the sum of £

Now this indenture ,witnesseth, that in pursuance and performance of the said recited contract, and in consideration of the said sum of [*state consideration, as in* 311.]

He the said A. B. hath granted, &c. [311, cl. 7, 8, & 9], save and except, and reserving unto the said A. B. his heirs and assigns out of this present grant, release, and assurance, the yearly rent of £   , the same to be for ever hereafter paid to the said A. B., his heirs and assigns as a free rent, and to be issuing and payable out of the said hereditaments and premises, at such times and in such manner as the like rent as a quit rent is now due and accustomed to be paid, being, &c.

To have and to hold, all and singular, &c., and, &c. [311, cl. 11], freed and absolutely acquitted, exonerated, and discharged henceforth and for ever hereafter, of and from all and all manner of customary fines, heriots, rents [*except as aforesaid*], fealty, suit of court, amercements, forfeitures, and other customary payments, duties, services, and penalties whatsoever, which by or according to the custom of the manor of G. aforesaid, the said hereditaments or any part thereof, are, is, or have, or hath been subject or liable to, or charged with, or which would otherwise be payable or to be done or performed to the lord or lords, lady or ladies, for or in respect of the same hereditaments and premises, as copyhold holden of the aforesaid manor.

Yielding, paying, and rendering nevertheless, unto the said A. B., his heirs and assigns for ever, the said yearly quit or chief rent of £   (heretofore payable in respect of the said hereditaments as copyhold), at or upon the feast of St. Michael the Archangel in every year, clear of all taxes and deductions whatsoever, the first payment to begin and be made on the feast, &c., now next ensuing. And yielding, rendering, and performing such and the like suit of court at the court baron of the said A. B., his heirs and assigns, to be holden from time to time for the said manor of G. and other services as other the freehold tenants are subject and liable to do and perform in respect of their estates lying within and holden of the same manor. And the said C. D., for himself, his heirs, executors, administrators and assigns, doth hereby grant, covenant, promise, and agree to and with the said A. B., his heirs and assigns, that in case the said yearly rent hereby reserved shall at any time or times hereafter be in arrear and unpaid, either in whole or in part, or in case the said C. D., his heirs or assigns, shall neglect or refuse to do and perform such suit and services as are hereinbefore also reserved, or intended so to be, Then, and in either of the said cases, it shall be lawful for the said A. B., his heirs and assigns, from time to time to exercise and pursue such remedies by amerciament, distress, action or suit at law or in equity, or otherwise howsoever for compelling payment and performance of the same rent, suit, and services respectively, as the said A. B., his heirs or assigns, is or may be authorized or entitled to exercise and pursue by reason of any neglect or refusal by or on the part of other the freehold tenants of the said manor to pay the rents or perform the suits or services which they respectively are subject and liable to pay and perform in respect of their estates, lying within and holden of the aforesaid manor.

> Add covenants by lord for title, &c. [311]; and if any commonable right attached to the copyhold, add a separate grant and confirmation of such right.

> This form is in part from one in Mr. Serjeant Scriven's work; but see his remarks, mentioned previously, as to reservation of services

---

· 352.—*Enrolment of Deed.*

The deed will be presented and enrolled at the next court; or a short memorandum of its contents entered on the rolls.

STAMPS.

353.—*Agreements.*

> Not under seal, where matter of value of 20*l.* or upwards, whether evidence of contract or being obligatory as written instrument; together with every schedule, receipt, or other matter indorsed or annexed, not containing more than 1,080 words   } 20*s.*
>
>   Containing more than 1,080 words . . 35*s.*
>
> And for every entire 1,080 words above first, a further progressive duty of . . . . . . } 25*s.*
>
> When divers letters are offered in evidence to prove any agreement between the parties, it will be sufficient if one be stamped with 35*s.* stamp, though the whole contain more than 1,080 words.
>
> Agreements liable to 20*s.* duty may be stamped within 21 days from date; but all other agreements must be stamped before signed, or penalty of 5*l.* paid.

354.—Conveyances.—General Stamps.

				£	s.
Consideration money		under	£20	0	10
Amounting to £20 and under			50	1	0
50	„	„	150	1	10
150	„	„	300	2	0
300	„	„	500	3	0
500	„	„	750	6	0
750	„	„	1,000	9	0
1,000	„	„	2,000	12	0
2,000	„	„	3,000	25	0
3,000	„	„	4,000	35	0
4,000	„	„	5,000	45	0
5,000	„	„	6,000	55	0
6,000	„	„	7,000	65	0
7,000	„	„	8,000	75	0
8,000	„	„	9,000	85	0
9,000	„	„	10,000	95	0
10,000	„	„	12,500	110	0
12,500	„	„	15,000	130	0
15,000	„	„	20,000	170	0
20,000	„	„	30,000	240	0
30,000	„	„	40,000	350	0
40,000	„	„	50,000	450	0
50,000	„	„	60,000	550	0
60,000	„	„	80,000	650	0
80,000	„	„	100,000	800	0
100,000	„	„	or upwards	1,000	0

Lease for year on Freehold.

Under 20*l.*—10*s.*; under 50*l.*—15*s.*; under 150*l.*—20*s.*;
150*l.* or upwards 35*s.*

Progressive Duty.

20*s.* for every entire fifteen folios beyond the first.

Stamps in special cases.

On conveyance of property of different tenures or under
different titles, the consideration money may be apportioned as the parties think fit, and the *ad valorem* stamp
in respect of each portion shall be impressed on the
conveyance of the parcels to which it relates. Thus,
in copyholds, the stamp in respect of the consideration
money apportioned for the copyhold, must be impressed
on the surrender.

Joint Purchasers.—At one sum, if conveyed by separate instruments, the consideration to be divided, and duty charged on
each instrument in respect of the portion; if conveyed by one

137

instrument, the duty to be charged on the aggregate amount.

Sub-purchasers.—The duty shall be paid on amount to be given by the sub-purchaser, and the like on apportioned amount, when subsale to several.

When *ad valorem* duty shall have been paid, and conveyance taken from seller, any further conveyance shall be liable to ordinary deed duty. (35*s.*, and 25*s.* progressive.)

Separate Contracts, and one Conveyance.—Duty to be charged on aggregate.

Equity of Redemption.—Duty to be paid on mortgage money as well as further consideration money.

Instrument on which Duty to be impressed.

When copyholds are conveyed by bargain and sale as well as surrender, the duty to be impressed on bargain and sale; otherwise on surrender, if out of court; or copy, if in court. Grants for lives are to be charged as for any greater interest.

Exemptions.

Surrenders of copyholds, under 20*s.*, per annum value.

Voluntary grants of copyholds for life or lives for pecuniary considerations, and copies of court roll thereof.

These are charged with ordinary duty.

———

355.—*Common Surrenders and Admissions.*

Surrender of copyholds or copy thereof, if passed in court, if of above 20*s.* a year value . . } 20*s.*

Copy of admission . . . . . 20*s.*

Not exceeding 20*s.* value, each . . . 5*s.*

Where both on same skin, each duty to be charged; and where more than one on same skin, separate duties to be charged.

The usual 20*s.* progressive duty is also payable.

Voluntary grant and admission, the same duty as a surrender and admission.

———

356.—*Mortgages.*

				£	£	s.
		Not exceeding		50	1	0
Exceeding	£ 50	and not exceeding	100	1	10
	100	,,	,,	200	2	0
	200	,,	,,	300	3	0
	300	,,	,,	500	4	0
	500	,,	,,	1,000	5	0
	1,000	,,	,,	2,000	6	0
	2,000	,,	,,	3,000	7	0
	3,000	,,	,,	4,000	8	0
	4,000	,,	,,	5,000	9	0
	5,000	,,	,,	10,000	12	0
	10,000	,,	,,	15,000	15	0
	15,000	,,	,,	20,000	20	0
	20,000	,,	,,	,,	25	0

If amount uncertain (*save as to expence of fire insurance or life insurance, in pursuance of annuity deed*) 25*l.*

Progressive duty of 20*s.* for every entire fifteen folios beyond first.

If for securing different sums to different persons, the separate duties, and not the aggregate, to be paid.

Where distinct deeds or instruments, *ad valorem* duty if exceeding 2*l.*, to be charged on only one, and general duty on other.

Where made as further security, where bond stamped with *ad valorem* duty previously given, no *ad valorem* duty payable, but only general duty; but if further sum secured, the *ad valorem* duty to be paid on the further sum.

Where copyholds mortgaged alone, duty to be impressed on surrender out of court, or copy of surrender in court.

Where copyholds mortgaged with other property, *ad valorem* stamp to be impressed on security relating to other property.

Exemptions from *ad valorem* duty.—Any deed or instrument for further assurance only, of property charged by deed on which is impressed the *ad valorem* duty. And see stamp act more fully, as to the stamps on additional advances.

Mortgage and Purchase.—Both *ad valorem* duties payable.

Assignment of Mortgage.—35*s.*, with 25*s.* progressive duty; and if further advance, the *ad valorem* duty to be paid on each advance.

Mortgage Bond.—20*s.*

———

357.—*Annuities.*

BONDS for Life or other indefinite Annuities.

Amount secured per annum.

	£			£	£
Under	10				1
Amounting to	10	and under	50		2
	50	,,	100		3
	100	,,	200		4
	200	,,	300		5
	300	,,	400		6
	400	,,	500		7
	500	,,	750		9
	750	,,	1,000		12
	1,000	,,	1,500		15
	1,500	,,	2,000		20
	2,000	,,			25

Progressive duty of 25*s.*

If for payment of annuity or sums of money at definite periods, so that principal amount can be previously ascertained (except upon the original creation and sale of such annuity), the same as bond for a sum equal to such total amount.

Grants of Annuities.—The same duties as on a conveyance, the consideration being the sum paid by the grantee of the annuity.

Repurchase of Annuities.—When made subject to repurchase, 35*s.*, with progressive duty of 25*s.*

358.—*Leases.*

When granted in consideration of fine, with rent, under 20*l.*, the conveyance duty on amount of fine, and where granted in consideration of a fine, and also of rent of 20*l.* and upwards, the conveyance duty for the fine, and also the duty, *post*, on the rent.

			£	£	
Yearly rent under			20	1	0
If	£ 20	and under	100	1	10
	100	,,	200	2	0
	200	,,	400	3	0
	400	,,	600	4	0
	600	,,	800	5	0
	800	,,	1,000	6	0
	1,000	and upwards		10	0

Not otherwise charged, 35*s.*

Counterpart, if duty on original not above 20*s.*, the like; and if more, 30*s.*

Progressive Duty, 20*s.*

Leases for lives not exceeding three, or for years determinable on lives not exceeding three, by whomsoever granted, and leases for term absolute, not exceeding twenty-one years granted by ecclesiastical corporations, aggregate or sole, subject to 35s. duty.

Exemptions.—Leases of waste lands to poor, not exceeeding three lives, or ninety-nine years, when fine not above 5s., nor rent above one guinea per annum, and counterparts thereof.

359.—*Settlements.*

Of any certain sums or funds.

		£.	£.	s.
If under, or under value of	1000	1	15
If 1000	and under	2000	2	0
2000	,,	3000	3	0
3000		4000	4	0
4000	,,	5000	5	0
5000	,,	7000	7	0
7000	,,	9000	9	0
9000	,,	12000	12	0
12000	,,	15000	15	0
15000	,,	20000	20	0
20000	and upwards		25	0

Progressive duty, 25s.

Duplicates, the like duties.

Exemptions from above duties

Bonds, &c., charged with *ad valorem* duties.

Appointments in execution of powers in settlement, deed, or will, to or in favour of persons specially named or described as the object of such powers.

Deeds merely declaring trusts, pursuant to previous settlement, &c.

Wills and testamentary dispositions.

360.—*Partitions.*

If no sum, or sum under £300 paid for equality of exchange, 35s., and a progressive duty of 25s. If £300, or upwards, the conveyance duty on the sum paid, and progressive duty of 20s. Duplicates to bear the same duties.

361.—*Enfranchisements.*

The same duty as conveyances on the amount paid.

PART II.

COURT-KEEPING

PRACTICE.

PRACTICE

OF

COURT-KEEPING.

---

361. In the king's manors a steward should be appointed by patent; and the steward of a manor belonging to a corporation can only be appointed by deed; in other cases a steward may be appointed by parol, but it seems he could not be appointed for a term or for life by parol. See authorities in Scriven on Copyholds, 126.

In general practice, except in the cases abovementioned, no appointment by deed takes place, but the lord merely directs the previous steward to deliver the books and papers to the successor, who then takes upon himself the office of steward; but as the form of appointment by deed may be useful, it is given in the Appendix, 441.

362. The steward, on receiving the appointment, will in the first place obtain the court books, &c. from his predecessor, and will be careful in seeing that all are delivered up. It should, however, be remarked, that as the draft courts are not paid for by the lord, the dismissed steward will seldom deliver them up; and in some cases the steward refuses to deliver up the original surrenders after they have been presented, alleging that they became useless after the presentment and entry on the court rolls.

This is however not a very honourable practice ; and it is conceived, that on the usual application to the Court of Queen's Bench for delivery of papers, a delivery of all such documents would be required ; but in a case which came within the writer's knowledge, the delivery was not enforced where a very experienced court-keeper was appointed to a stewardship ; and therefore the existence of such right to enforce may be doubtful.

363. The steward's duties will extend to taking absolute and conditional surrenders, preparing abstracts, and making searches as to copyholders' titles and customs, &c. ; taking an account of all deaths, surrenders, and other business leading to admissions ; preparing for and holding courts ; drawing courts, entering in the court books, and making copies ; receiving and handing over to the lord the fines, &c. ; preparing the yearly rental ; perusing any enfranchisement deeds, and advising on enfranchisements, and attending to any general business connected with the manor. As the practice of legal proceedings in manorial courts is now obsolete, it is deemed useless to enter into the subject of such practice here.

364. According to the usual practice, he may also appoint a deputy, either to act generally for him, or to act in any particular business ; and though formerly even the limited appointments were by deed, yet at the present time no formal appointment takes place, the authority to act as deputy being verbal, or by a letter ; and as the acts of a steward *de facto* as to any ministerial matter (forming almost the whole of the present practice) are deemed valid, even if the steward be a minor, a formal appointment would, in most cases, be a needless expence. See more fully on this subject, Scriven on Copyholds, 131.

365. Except when the custom of a manor authorizes the taking a surrender before copyhold tenants, the steward or his deputy takes all the surrenders, both absolute and conditional, unless the lord chooses to exercise his right in any particular case and take a surrender.   146

366. A steward or his deputy may take a surrender at any place, whether within or out of the manor, and hence arises a great facility in copyhold conveyances, as according to the usual practice where parties live at a considerable distance from the steward, he authorizes a professional man residing near the parties, to take the surrender as deputy, on its being delivered to the steward within a specified time, and receiving the usual deputation fee of one guinea for each deputy.

367. The mode of taking a surrender is as follows : The steward, on being required to take a surrender, will peruse it in order to see that it is worded so as to only give a customary estate, and that it does not infringe the lord's rights, as by being made without impeachment of waste, and he will also see that it is properly stamped.

Should the wife of the party join in the surrender, he will take her examination as on a freehold sale, asking her in the absence of her husband, whether she consents voluntarily to the proposed surrender (stating shortly its substance); and on her consenting he will call in the husband, and giving into the hands of the husband and wife the rod or customary symbol, and taking hold of the other end himself, will read the surrender, altering it to the second person, adding, at the end, " In token whereof you deliver me this rod," and they resign the stick to him. The parties will then sign the surrender and receipt, and the steward the surrender, retaining the original, and signing a receipt on the back of the copy to the following effect : " Received the original surrender, of which this purports to be a copy, to be presented and entered at the next court." " A. B., steward." [*Date.*] The original surrender should then be deposited with the other documents, to be presented at the next court.

368. The usual fees on a common surrender, for taking, presenting, and entering, are each 6s. 8d., being 1l.; and the fee on examination of feme covert is

6s. 8d., which is generally paid at the time of passing the surrender, being payable by the surrenderor; the other fees on absolute surrenders are however most frequently paid at the time of admission under the surrender.

369. The steward's duty out of court on warrants to enter satisfaction on conditional surrenders, will be merely the giving a receipt on the duplicate, and placing the original with the other papers for presentment at the next court. The usual fee is 13s. 4d., though, if long and special, rather more is sometimes charged.

370. On preparing abstracts of title, the steward will at the foot sign a certificate, which may be as follows: "Abstracted from the court rolls of the manor of W., this   day of, &c. A. B., steward." The usual charge is 10s. 6d. per sheet, and sometimes an extra 7s. for certificate.

371. Searches for incumbrances are frequently made by stewards at the request of parties about to advance money on a conditional surrender, and the steward certifies that there are no incumbrances within the period for which the search is made; but as with illiberal practitioners there is too frequently an attempt to curtail the fee for a long search to a common search fee of 7s., and the steward takes great responsibility upon himself in giving the certificate, it is better, when the parties live near, to allow the party to make the search himself, charging him a reasonable amount for attending with the rolls, and which might perhaps be about 7s. for each 50 or 100 pages, according to their size and the particular nature of each search.

372. A steward is often requested to certify an abstract of title prepared by another party as being correct; but as hardly a case occurs in which a dispute does not arise with respect to the fees, a steward should in most cases refuse to make such certificate, and leave the party to effect such examination on

payment of the usual search fee. This being an indirect and not very fair way of getting the advantage of a steward's abstract, and transferring the emolument into the hands of another person, it really calls for no great courtesy on the steward's part, and might perhaps justify him in refusing to allow any comparison with the rolls, offering the party a search without notes, as at the ecclesiastical courts with respect to wills.

373. When a steward is requested to certify as to the custom of a manor relative to descent, &c. it is the practice to do so, and the usual fee, as the steward is presumed to have no lengthened search to make, will be _7s._

374. The steward will, of course, take a minute of all deaths, of waste committed, and of the different documents to be presented, and business to be transacted at the next court.

On it appearing that sufficient business has arisen to render it expedient to hold a court, the steward will proceed to hold one.

375. Courts may be held at any place within the manor, but cannot be held out of the manor, except where by special custom courts for several manors may be held in one of them. See Scriven Cop. 690 ; and see _Doe_ dem. _Leech and another_ v. _Whittaker,_ 5 B. & A. 409, which case also decided, that though a steward could not grant out of the manor, a lord might, the admission being certified at the next court.

376. There are no particular times at which courts must be held ; but except in small manors there are generally three courts in a year, so as to allow all parties about a year's time for taking admission.

377. The court may be held before the steward or his deputy, or it may be held before the lord. The number of homage is in most manors two.

378. Having fixed the time at which he intends to hold a court, the steward will prepare a notice (see Form 442) to be affixed at the place where the

149

court is to be held, and frequently the court is also advertized (being a copy of the notice for a single court, and as in 443, when more than one court is to be advertized); but as notice is given to the parties deemed likely to attend, such advertisement may often be dispensed with.

Notice is sent to the bailiff of the manor, and either the steward requests two of the copyhold tenants to attend, or directs the bailiff to do so : no formal precept is issued.

The steward then writes to all the parties to whose use surrenders have been passed, and the executors, heirs, or devisees of tenants dead, apprizing them of the court, and whether it be the first, second, or third court, and requesting instructions for admissions previously to the court, so that the minutes may be prepared and the fines calculated.

379. Before the Court, the steward makes inquiries as to the value of each property to which admission is expected, and confers with the lord as to the amount of the fines to be charged, and also as to any commutation to be made for heriots, (the law as to which, see in Scriven, 423,) and which are most usually compounded for at a fixed sum.

380. He also prepares the heading of the minute book and presentment paper ; refers to the previous admissions ; and, as far as he can, makes out the minutes of the business to be transacted, the presentments, and sometimes his own bill of fees. Forms of minute book and presentment paper, will be found in Appendix, Nos. 452, &c.

381. At the time fixed for holding the court, he directs the bailiff to open the court, which he does accordingly. See form, Appendix ; and the steward then swears the homage, (see forms, Appendix 444 and 445) and enters their names in the minute book.

Having thus formed the court, he proceeds to presentments, which, from his previous memoranda are complete, except as to any deaths, &c. with which he is unacquainted, but which are known to the homage. Forms 452, &c., will shew the mode of entering the presentments.

No formal charge is made to the homage, but the steward merely goes through the presentment paper, saying " Gentlemen, you present, &c." reading the presentment paper in the second person. He then calls over the names of the tenants, and asks the homage if they have any thing further to present.

The steward then enters in the minute book a memorandum of any admissions which may have taken place before the lord since the last court.

He next proceeds to the admissions, generally taking those on proclamations or seizure first, and those on surrenders in court last; but where the minutes are not previously prepared, the admissions are often entered in the minute book in the order in which they take place; the arrangement being altered so as to follow the general rule in drawing out the court for entry in the court books.

The memorandum of any conditional surrenders, presented or taken in court, is then entered in the minute book, and the like as to warrants to enter satisfaction on any conditional surrenders.

Having thus disposed of the business which is completed by admission, or does not require admission, the steward next proceeds to the entry of absolute surrenders, presented or taken at the court, and the proclamations thereon; and afterwards the presentment of deaths with the proclamations.

He also, on the third proclamation being made, awards seizure, and issues the precept to the bailiff to seize until admission, and to make return at the following court. Entries of return of seizure, when made, are usually inserted near the beginning of a court.

Licenses are generally entered after the admissions, or conditional surrenders.

A general outline of the business at the court is thus given, and the practice will be found more minutely in the subsequent part, giving the forms of presentments, minutes, entries, &c, commencing with the more immediate presentments and admissions, and proceeding to admissions on proclamations, re-grant, forfeited conditional surrenders, &c.

It may, however, be useful to first give the mode of taking surrenders in court, and of granting admissions.

382. A surrender in Court is thus taken. On a party proposing to surrender, the steward must, under the Stamp Act, obtain from him a certificate of the consideration money, with a view to the payment of stamp duty;—the forms will be found in Appendix, Nos. 499, & 507 ; and stewards generally keep blank forms so as to save time in preparing them at the court. On the certificate being signed, the steward proceeds to the wife's examination separately from her husband, as in a surrender out of court, and then takes the surrender verbally, according to the form No. 498, using the second instead of the third person, and enters a short memorandum of the surrender in the minute book. If an absolute surrender, either admission takes place or a proclamation is made ; but on conditional surrenders, no proclamation is made, as admission is not taken ; a copy is however to be afterwards made on stamp for delivery to the mortgagee. The fees will be found in 415.

383. The mode of admission is as follows :—The steward hands the party about to be admitted the rod or other customary symbol, and after reading or stating the surrender or presentment and proclamations under which he claims, adds " Whereupon you the said A. B. pray to be admitted, &c. [*See admissions, post*, 469, &c.] " And thereupon the lord, by me his steward, grants and delivers to you seisin thereof by the rod," &c., as in admission, to the end, using the second person, and adding at the end, " In token whereof I deliver you this rod."

384. Should the party be admitted by attorney, the only difference will be the using the third person

as to the party, adding "by you his attorney." [*See form*, 479.]

Admissions are more frequently taken by attorney than personally, as no power of attorney is necessary; and when the party and his solicitor live at a distance from the manor, the expence of their attendance is saved by requesting the steward to admit the party by attorney at the next Court, and the steward upon being so instructed, admits the party by his clerk, or any other person present at the court as attorney. The additional fee on such admission, whether the solicitor or the party attends, or the admission be taken by any other person, will be 6*s*. 8*d*.

385. The admission is shortly entered in the minute book, with a reference to the book and folio where the previous admission took place, and which contains the description of the parcels; and in the margin is entered the amount of the fine, and when and where to be paid, (usually three weeks after the court,) at the place where the court was held.

Since 55 G. 3, no surrender to will is taken, except in the case of a married woman.

The fine is not payable till admission, nor is it usual to state the amount previously.

386. The steward is entitled to his fees before admission; (see Stamp Act, 48 G. 3,) but very seldom avails himself of his right; and usually either delivers his bill of fees at the court, or sends it to the party or his solicitor, shortly afterwards.

The subject of fines is fully treated of in 404; and of fees, in 411, &c.

387. Warrants to enter satisfaction on conditional surrenders, are merely presented and entered in the minute book shortly; and the like as to entry of licences to demise, pull down buildings, &c.

388. Within a reasonable time after the court, the steward draws the court fully, and as to admissions and conditional surrenders passed in court, makes stamped copies on parchment for delivery to

the parties, inserting the title of the court, adding the word "at" before the words, "a general court, &c.," omitting the names of the homage, and substituting the words "amongst other things it is thus enrolled;" then proceeding with the copy of the particular admission, adding at the end, "examined by me, A. B., steward."

389. The copies should be made out within four months, as otherwise under the stamp act, the steward would be subject to a penalty of 50*l.*; but it is too frequently the case that stewards omit to make out the copies till applied to for them.

390. The stamps will be found in Appendix 355, and it will be borne in mind that on admissions under surrenders in court, a surrender as well as an admittance stamp must be impressed.

391. In well conducted manors, a duplicate of the court books is kept; and the importance of carefully examining the courts and copies, and making a strictly accurate index, need scarcely be adverted to.

In the Appendix will be found a full set of presentment papers, and minute books for five courts, with the forms of proclamations, entries of courts, stamps, &c. See. 452, &c.

The other points connected with the steward's duties remaining to be considered, are:—the right of parties to surrender: the like as to admittance: the enforcing admittance: the fines on admittance, and heriots: the recovery of quit rents: amending court rolls: inspection of rolls: and the steward's fees.

392. *The right of parties to surrender.*—A husband may surrender to use of his wife; *Bunting* v. *Lepingwell*, 4 Co. 29, b.; Scriven, 147; and in p. 146, it is stated that it seems a surrender by husband and wife, of wife's lands, she being examined, will be good even if she he an infant. A surrender by an infant, if it appear on the face of it to be for his benefit, as to obtain renewal on copyholds for lives, will be voidable only. *Zouch* v. *Parsons*, 3 Burr. 1794, 1804; *Ashfield* v. *Jones*, 157. But an infant

cannot exercise a power when coupled with an interest. *Heacle* v. *Greenbank*, 1 Ves. 299; and 3 Atk. 695.

. A person not in seisin as contingent remainder man, or heir in life of ancestor, cannot surrender. *Doe* d. *Blacksall & al.* v. *Tomkins & ux.*, 11 East, 185. A reversioner and vested remainder man, may, however, surrender.

A surrenderee cannot surrender before admittance, nor will he forfeit by felony before admittance, but otherwise as to an heir. See Scriven, 151, 152. An heir may surrender without admittance on payment of a fine. Scriven, 346. A copyholder has not a right to surrender in a manner injurious to the lord's interest, as without impeachment of waste; and the steward may refuse to take such surrender. Scriven, 340.

393. *The like as to Admittance.*—Of course on this head the only thing to be cared about by the steward will be the obtaining as many admissions as are required, as it is no part of his duty to throw impediments in the way of admissions, except where an attempt is made to avoid an intermediate one or payment of a fine, as by surrender from an heir without payment of a fine: surrender by an unadmitted surrenderee, &c.

The right to admittance is not affected by death of the surrenderor or surrenderee. In the former case the surrenderee will be still entitled to admission, and in the latter case the heir of the surrenderee, and who will be held a trustee for the devisee of the surrenderee. See Scriven 339; but see *King* v. *Turner*, 1 Sim. & Stu. 545.

The lord is not compellable to admit by attorney. See Scriv. 349.

394. *Enforcing Admittance.*

Against the Heir.—This is by proclamations and seizure; but should the heir be beyond sea at the time of the descent and proclamations, he is not bound by a custom that land should be *forfeited* after three proclamations; but if he leave after first proclamation, or it seems after descent, unless without notice of the descent, it would seem he is bound. See Scriv. 343. But this it is presumed would not apply to a seizure *quousque,* but merely to an absolute seizure for a forfeiture.

395.—*Against Heir or Devisee being an Infant or Feme Covert.*—Where the party claims by descent or surrender to will, and does not come into court by guardian or attorney within three courts (9 G. 1, ch. 29), it shall be lawful for the lord or steward, after three courts and proclamations, to nominate and appoint at any subsequent court or courts, any fit person to be guardian for infant or attorney for feme covert, for that purpose only, and by such guardian or attorney to admit any such infant to all and every the messuages, &c., and upon such admittance to impose and set such fines as might have been imposed and set if such infant or feme covert had been of full age or sole. See 409, where an abstract of the act, and the provision for obtaining payment of the fine, are given. This act does not prevent the lord from proclamations, and seizing *quousque,* where no demand is made by the party to be admitted under the act. Scriv. 389.

396. *Of a Devisee generally.*—By proclamations and seizure, *quousque.*

397. *Of a surrenderee.*—It is only by custom that the lord can compel admission of surrenderee whilst surrenderor is living; but such custom is however very general, and the proceedings will be by proclamations and seizure, *quousque.*

398. *Of Executors.*—Of course, executors having under a properly drawn will, merely a power, are not compellable to be admitted, except, that if unable to dispose of the property by the third court, they must either take admission themselves, or allow the heir to do so, in order to avoid seizure.

On copyholds for years, the executors must be admitted.

399. *Trustees.*—Where the parties have an estate,

156

and not a simple power, they must be admitted; but the lord cannot compel all to take admission, if one offers to do so. See Scriv. 354.

400. *Of Remaindermen.*—The admittance of tenant for life being that of remaindermen, except where custom exists requiring such admission, the lord cannot compel such admission. See Scriv. 353, and cases therein cited. This custom exists in many manors.

401. *Coparceners.*—One admission only can be compelled, but of course the parties not admitted cannot accept a release from the one admitted; and on the death of the party admitted, a fresh admittance would appear requisite. The heirs of a coparcener must in all cases be admitted.

402. *Tenants in Common* must all be admitted; and on death of one, his heir's admission is compellable in the usual way by proclamations and seizure.

403. *Mortgagees.*—A fine will be due on admission under forfeited conditional surrender, and also on readmission of mortgagor. Scriv. 391; but admission of mortgagee cannot be compelled whilst mortgagor is living.

404. *The Fines on Admission.*

In some manors, and sometimes on particular copyholds of other manors, the fines are certain; in other cases, and more generally, they are uncertain, or, as they are commonly termed, fines arbitrary; but such fines must be reasonable, and two years' improved value, deducting quit rent but not land tax, is the amount recognized by the courts. See *Halton* v. *Hassell*, 2 Stra. 1042; *Grant* v. *Astle*, 2 Doug. 722; and the cases referred to in Scriven, 373.

Where several lives are admitted as joint tenants, two years are to be charged for the first life, one year for second, half-year for third, &c. *Wilson* v. *Hoare*, 1 B. & A. 350. The same principle of charging fines is usually adopted on admission of tenant for life and remainderman.

The case of *Grant* v *Astle*, and of *Lord Northwick* v. *Stanway*, 3 Bos. & Pul. 346 ; and also 6 East 56, should be seen as to assessment of fine by the lord ; and it seems from those cases he must recover all of the sum he asseses, or make a new assessment.

A separate fine should be assessed for each tenement held by a separate rent.

Should the fine not be paid at the time fixed at the court, the lord should cause a demand of payment to be made, and proceed in *assumpsit* for its recovery.

The lord will be entitled to a fine on surrender by heir, and should require payment before accepting such surrender.

In Scriven on Copyholds it is expressed as the opinion of the author, that the lord or steward may refuse to accept a surrender from the tenant till payment of the fine.

405. *The Recovery of Quit Rents.*

This will be effected by distress or action of debt, and the law is fully treated of in Scriven on Copyholds.

406. *Heriots.*

The learning on this subject will also be found in Scriven's work ; and, as it relates more to the law of copyholds than to court-keeping, it is deemed needless to enter into the subject here.

407. *Amending Court Rolls.*

The cases and points on this head will be found in Scriven's Copyholds, 258, &c. ; and in the case of *Elston* v. *Wood*, 1 Mylne & Keene, 678.

408. *Inspection of Rolls.*

An order will be made on the lord to allow usual inspection of court rolls on application of tenant in first instance, on affidavit that tenant has applied for and been refused inspection. See general rule, Moore & Scott, 430 ; and see Scriven 597, &c.

409. *Abstract of 9 Geo.* 1, *c.* 29, *intituled,*

" An Act to enable Lords of Manors more easily to recover their fines, and to exempt infants and femes covert from forfeiture of their copyhold estates in particular cases."

Sec. 1, enacts, That where any person or persons, being under the age of 21 years, or feme or femes covert, shall after 24th June, 1723, be entitled by descent or surrender to the use of a last will (see 55 G. 3, c. 192,) to be admitted tenant or tenants of any copyhold messuages, lands, tenements, or hereditaments, within England or Wales, they not having been admitted thereto, and not having paid their fines, every such infant or feme covert in their proper persons, or such feme covert by her attorney, or such infant by his or her guardian or guardians, if he or she shall have any such, or if not, then by his or her attorney or attorneys, (for which purpose such infants and femes covert shall be, and are hereby empowered by writing, under his or her hand and seal respectively, to appoint an attorney or attorneys on his or her behalf,) shall come to, and appear at one of the three next courts which shall be kept, (for the keeping whereof the usual notice shall be given,) for such manor or manors whereof such messuages, lands, tenements, or hereditaments shall be parcel, and shall there tender and offer themselves to the lord or his steward of such courts to be admitted tenants to all and every the said messuages, lands, tenements, and hereditaments, so surrendered, descended, or come to, or to the use of every such infant or feme covert; to make which appearance, and to take such admittance in behalf of such infant or feme covert, such guardian and attorney shall be, and they are hereby respectively authorized and required; and in default of the appearance of such infants or femes covert in their own persons, or by their guardians or attorneys in that behalf, and of acceptance of such admittance as aforesaid, it shall

159

and may be lawful to and for the lord or lords of every such manor or manors, or his and their steward or stewards of the courts thereof, after such three several courts have been duly holden for such manor or manors, and proclamations in such several courts been regularly made, to nominate and appoint at any subsequent court or courts to be holden for such manor or manors, any fit person to be guardian or attorney for every such infant or feme covert, for that purpose only, and by such guardian or attorney to admit every such infant or feme covert to all and every the said messuages, lands, tenements, and hereditaments accordingly, to such estates as such infants or femes covert shall be legally entitled to therein, and upon every such admittance to impose and set such fine and fines as might have been legally imposed and set, if such infant so admitted had been of full age, or if such feme covert had been sole and unmarried. Sec. 2, enacts, that upon every such admittance or admittances of any infant or feme covert as aforesaid, the fine or fines imposed and set thereupon shall and may be demanded by the bailiff or agent of the lord or lords of such manors, by a note in writing signed by the lord of such manor, or by his steward, to be left with such infant or feme covert, or with the guardian of such infant, or husband of such feme covert, or with the tenant or occupier of the messuages, lands or tenements to which such infant or feme covert was admitted, and that if in such case the said fine or fines so imposed and set be not paid or tendered to such lord or lords, or to his or their steward or stewards, within three months after such demand made, that then it shall and may be lawful to and for the lord or lords of such manor or manors where such admittance or admittances are had, to enter into and upon all and every the copyhold messuages, lands, tenements, and hereditaments, to which any such infant or feme covert shall be so admitted, and to hold and enjoy the same, and to receive the rents, issues, and profits thereof, but

160

without liberty to fell any timber standing thereon, for so long a time only, and until by such rents, issues, and profits such lord or lords shall be fully paid and satisfied such fine and fines, together with all reasonable and necessary costs and charges which such lord or lords shall have been put unto in levying and raising the same, and in obtaining the possession of such copyhold messuages, lands, tenements, and hereditaments, although such infant or feme covert shall happen to die before such fine and fines, and the costs and charges aforesaid shall be raised and collected; of all which rents, issues, and profits so to be received by such lord or lords of such manor or manors, or his or their stewards, bailiffs, or servants upon the occasion aforesaid, such lord or lords of such manor or manors, shall yearly and every year, upon demand to be made by such person or persons who shall be entitled to the surplus of the rents and profits over and above what will pay and satisfy such fine and costs and charges so received as aforesaid, or by such person or persons as shall be then entitled to such copyhold estate, give and render a just and true account, and shall pay the said surplus rents, issues, and profits, if any, to such person and persons as shall be respectively entitled to the same.

Sec. 3 enacts, That as soon as such fine or fines, and the costs, charges, and expences aforesaid, shall be fully paid and satisfied, or if after such seizure of and entry upon such copyhold lands, tenements, and hereditaments, for the purposes aforesaid, such fine or fines, and the costs and charges aforesaid, shall be lawfully tendered and offered to be paid and satisfied to the lord or lords of such manor or manors, that then and in any of the said cases it shall and may be lawful to and for such infant or feme covert, or other person entitled thereto, to enter upon and take possession of and hold the said copyhold premises according to such estate or interest as he or she shall be lawfully entitled to therein; and the lord and lords of such manor or manors shall, and is and are

161

hereby required in any of the said cases to deliver possession thereof accordingly; and if such lord or lords of such manor, after such fine or fines and the costs and charges aforesaid shall be fully paid and satisfied, or after the same shall have been tendered or offered to be paid as aforesaid, shall refuse to deliver the possession of the said copyhold premises as aforesaid, he or they shall be liable to and shall make satisfaction to the person or persons so kept out of possession for all the damages that he or she shall thereby sustain, and all the costs and charges that he or she shall be put unto for recovery thereof.

Sec. 4, enacts, That where any infant or feme covert shall be admitted to any copyhold messuages, lands, tenements, or hereditaments, if the guardian of such infant, or husband of such feme covert, shall pay to the lord or lords of any manor or manors, the fine or fines legally imposed and set upon such admittance or admittances, and the costs and charges which such lord of such manors shall have been put unto as aforesaid, that then it shall and may be lawful to and for every guardian of such infant, or husband of such feme covert, their executors and administrators, to enter into and to hold and enjoy all and every the said copyhold messuages, lands, tenements, and hereditaments, to which such infant or feme covert shall be so admitted, and the rents, issues, and profits thereof to receive and take to his and their own use, until thereby such guardian of such infant, or husband of such feme covert, their executors and administrators, shall be fully satisfied and paid all and every such sum and sums of money as they shall respectively pay and disburse upon the account aforesaid, notwithstanding the death or deaths of such infants or femes covert shall happen before such sum or sums of money so expended shall or may be so raised and reimbursed.

Sec. 5, enacts, That from and after the aforesaid 24th day of June, 1723, no infant or feme covert shall forfeit any copyhold messuages, lands, tenements, or hereditaments, within that part of Great Britain called England, and the dominion of Wales, for their neglect or refusal to come to any court or courts to be kept for any manor or manors whereof such messuages, lands, tenements, or hereditaments are parcel, and to be admitted thereto, nor for the omission, denial, or refusal of any such infant or feme covert to pay any fine or fines imposed or set upon their or any of their admittances to any such copyhold messuages, lands, tenements, or hereditaments, any law, usage, or custom to the contrary thereof notwithstanding.

Sec. 6, enacts, That if the said fine or fines imposed in any of the cases before mentioned, shall not be warranted by the custom of the manor, or shall be unlawful, that then such infant or feme covert shall be at liberty to controvert the legality of such fine or fines, in such manner as he or she might have done if this act had never been made, any thing herein contained to the contrary notwithstanding.

The Steward's Fees.

410. It is much to be regretted that a scale of fees has not been prepared by competent authority, so as to get rid of the irregularity in charging which has so long existed, particularly as the fees might be so charged as to do justice to the stewards as well as the tenants.

Mr. Serjeant Scriven, in his work on Copyholds, states that the fees are guided by custom, and in default of such a custom, on the principle of giving the steward a fair emolument for his services, as determined in the case of *Everest* v. *Glynn*, 6 Taunt. 427 ; and though the case of *Attree* v. *Scutt*, 6 East, 476, by giving separate fees for each tenant, when several admitted as tenants in common, would appear to lean to the allowance of a larger scale of fees than one based on the principle referred to ; yet on examination it will appear not to do so, as in the case of tenants in common each would require a copy admis-

163

sion; and there appears nothing in *Attree* v. *Scutt* to shew that the separate sets of fees were in respect of the presentation of death as well as the admission and copy, and consequently that the steward was only paid for his increased work in the admissions.

411. The most just way of applying the principle of making the fees equivalent to a fair remuneration for the services performed, is to so fix them that the steward should receive as much as under a fair and liberal allowance in conveyancing charges he would obtain for the same services. This mode of acting on the principle in *Everest* v. *Glynn*, will do justice to both parties; and conformably with it are the scales of fees here given; and it should be remarked, that the fees given are from actual bills of fees paid to stewards :—

412. *Fees on Absolute Surrenders out of Court.*

	£	s.	d.
Examining *feme covert* (paid by vendor)	0	6	8
Taking surrender, 6*s.* 8*d.* ; presenting, 6*s.*8*d.*; entry, (if usual length) 6*s.*8*d.*	1	0	0
If longer than usual, add 8*d.* per 72 words.			
The fees for taking, &c. are paid by purchaser on admission.			
Deputation fee, if passed before deputy steward (paid by vendor)	1	1	0

413. *Absolute Surrender in Court.*

Certificate of consideration . . . 5*s.* to	0	7	0
Examining *feme covert*, 6*s.* 8*d.* ; taking surrender, 6*s.* 8*d.*	0	13	4
Entering surrender, ... 10*s.* to	0	13	4
Paid stamp and parchment, (charged with other stamp in admission) . . .		0	0

414. *Conditional Surrender in Court.*

The same as absolute surrender, with addition of copy or stamp, according to length . . . . . 13*s.* 6*d.* to	1	1	0
And paid stamp and parchment.			

415. *Conditional Surrender out of Court.*
The same as absolute surrender.

416. *Satisfaction on Conditional Surrender.*

(If not unusually long) 0 13 4

417. *Proclamations*, each 0 6 8

Where the copyhold is extensive, 10s.
will be sometimes charged for proclamation and entry, but the usual
fee is 6s. 8d.

A fee of 3s. 4d. is sometimes charged
for reciting proclamation, but if the
fees are closely looked to, is considerably objectionable.

418. *Award of seizure and precept to seize.*

These charges generally vary with the
value of the property, and would be
in a small copyhold 6s. 8d. for each;
but the precept being a document
under seal, sometimes 1l. 1s. will be
charged for award and precept, and
in some instances 1l. 11s. 6d.; but
the former is more just, taking into
consideration the amount of work . 1 1 0

419. *Seizure and Return.*

The charges vary according to the distance, the value of the property, &c.
but may be in general fixed at . . 1 1 0

420. Presentment of death and entry
10s. or 0 13 4

421. Admission in common cases, 13s. 4d.
to 16s. 8d.; Entry and copy, each
the like, usually together 2 2 0

If by attorney, 6s. 8d. additional; and
if copy long, 3l. 3s. will frequently
be charged for these items.

Ac etiams (or different parcels,) each, . 0 6 8

Stamp and parchment (amount paid) about 1 5 0
165

	£	s.	d.
Clerk, (this fee is too often pocketed by the steward) . , . . 2s. 6d. or	0	5	0
Crier, 1s. on each proclamation, and on admission . . . . ,	0	1	0
Respiting fealty . . . . 3s. 6d. or	0	5	0
Apportionment of rent	0	6	8

422. *Surrender in Court, and Admission.*

Certificate of consideration, 6s. 8d. ; Examining feme covert, 6s. 8d.; Taking surrender, 6s. 8d. ; Entering, 10s. ; Admission, 13s. 4d. to 16s. 8d. ; By Attorney, 6s. 8d. ; Entry and copy, each, 13s. 4d. to 16s. 8d. ; Clerk, 5s. ; Crier, 1s.; Stamp and parchment, 25s.; Respiting fealty 5s.; total about   5   5   0

423. *Death presented, and Devisee admitted.*

Presenting death and entry, 13s. 4d.; Fees on surrender to will, 13s. 4d.; Clause from will, 6s. 8d. or 10s.; Admission, entry, and copy, 2l., or 3l., or 3l. 3s., according to length; other fees as before.

424. *Surrender out of Court and Admission.*

Examining feme covert, 6s. 8d., (this fee is paid by vendor) ; Taking, presenting and entering surrender, 1l.; Admission, &c. as before.

425. *Admissions, and 1st or 2d Proclamations.*

The only difference will be the addition of the charge for proclamations.

426. *Admission under Bargain and Sale from Executors.*

The only difference between this and the admission of devisee above, will be the addition of any proclamations, and the fee of 6s. 8d. for presenting; and 10s. or 13s. 4d. for enrolling in part the bargain and sale.

427. *Admission under a Bankruptcy.*

Presenting bargain and sale, 6s. 8d.; Enrolling in part, 13s. 4d.; Fees on surrender, 1l. 6s. 8d.; Admission entry and copy, two to three guineas, according to value of property, as the admission will be long. Fees for stamp, clerk, &c. as before.

428. *Admission of Infant Heir.*

The additional fee will be 13s. 4d. for appointment of guardian and entry.

429. *Admission on Re-grant.*

The only difference will be the charges for awarding seizure, precept, and returning seizure.

430. *Admission on Forfeited Conditional Surrender.*

Searching for surrender, 6s. 8d.; Reciting, 6s. 8d.; Admission, &c. as in other cases.

431. *Admission of Tenants in Common.*

Single fees for presenting death, or on surrender and proclamation, and separate fees for admission, entry, and copy.

432. *Admission of Joint Tenants.*

Usually an addition made on account of increased length. Some stewards add fees in the same way as fines, but it is presumed such a practice would not be supported.

433. *Acknowledgment of Free Tenure,*—6s. 8d. unless by attorney, and then 13s. 4d.

434. *Surrender and Release.*

Certificate of consideration, 5s.; Taking surrender and entry, 1l.; Copy, if required, 10s.; Stamp and parchment, the amount paid. If the surrender is very special, of course a proportionate alteration should be made,

435. *Licences* will be charged according to their importance, as in case of licence to fell timber, merely

167

an entry is made, but no copy, and frequently no fees are charged, or at most, only a few shillings; whilst on a valuable licence, as to work mines, not only will the entry be made, but a copy delivered to the party, as in the case of an admission; and being an important document, it will of course be framed more specially and with greater care, and consequently a fee of two guineas for licence, entry, and copy, besides the 20*s.* stamp, would be reasonable.

436. *Presenting Deeds and Enrolling.*

The steward's fee on presenting a deed will be **6***s.* **8***d.*; and for enrolling 8*d.* to 1*s.* per folio of 72 words. The former would be sufficient where only one part of the court book is kept, but where a duplicate is kept, which must be of as great advantage to the tenant as to the lord, the addition of the mere draft copy charge of 4*d.* per folio ought not to be objected to.

437. *Deputations.*

To take surrender, one deputy   . . .£1   1   0

And for each deputy, if more than one .   1   1   0

438. *Special Court.*

Some stewards will, to facilitate admissions and accommodate the parties applying, hold special courts without charging more than the expence of the court, (usually 2*s.* 6*d.* to each of the homage for expences); but of course this is entirely optional, and also the holding the special court; consequently in each case the amount of fee must be matter of arrangement with the steward; but in ordinary cases a fee of one guinea, and, under particular circumstances, a fee of two guineas would not be objectionable.

A case occurred within the writer's knowledge, where a steward modestly charged 25 guineas for holding such a court; and the solicitor of the tenant, who must be supposed not to have known much of copyhold practice, though a town solicitor of extensive business, very *liberally* paid the fee.

439. *Admission before the Lord.*

As this admission is similar to a special court as regards the convenience of the party, it is usual to add a fee of 13*s.* 4*d.*; or if of valuable property, of one guinea for attendances, making appointment with the lord, and on taking admission. The other fees will be as usual.

440. In concluding the remarks on fees, the writer cannot but express his surprise that town solicitors, even in extensive practice, should so generally have neglected to make themselves acquainted with the most simple parts of copyhold practice, or with the amount of fees which ought to be paid on admissions, —a neglect which has been most dearly paid for by their clients.

One bill of fees, which with many others, is now before the writer, most amusingly shews this :—It relates to an admission under a decree in the Exchequer, where a bill is made about four times the amount it ought to be; and the solicitor for the party, though being in a most extensive town practice, allowed all the bill, except 4*l.* or 5*l.*; and the steward wrote at the foot of his own draft—"N. B. The steward took *only*   *l.*"—underlining the "only" as an amusing annotation on the liberality of the party to whom he was opposed.

It is to be hoped that the principle of a fair and liberal, but not excessive, scale of fees will be more generally adopted, so as to satisfy the stewards as men of education and respectability, and not injure the copyhold tenants.

APPENDIX OF FORMS.

441.—*Appointment of Steward.*

KNOW ALL MEN by these presents that I, A. B., lord of the manor of W., in the county of S., have, made, ordained, constituted and appointed, and by these presents do make, ordain, constitute and appoint C. D., of &c., to be steward of the aforesaid manor of W., and the members thereof, with full power and authority from time to time to hold courts baron and customary courts for the same manor and its members, and to do all acts usual and customary to be done by stewards in relation thereunto, accounting to me from time to time for such fines, heriots, reliefs, forfeitures, amerciaments, and other manorial profits as shall be received by him or by his deputy or deputies. And I do hereby especially authorize and empower the said C. D., from time to time as there may be occasion, to make any voluntary grants of any customary or copyhold lands and hereditaments within the said manor; and any licences to demise, to fell timber, to work mines or quarries, or otherwise as he the said C. D. shall deem expedient, and either in or out of court, as fully as I myself could or might do. And also to appoint any deputy steward or deputy stewards of or for the said manor of W., or its members, either generally and with full power to hold all or any general or special courts baron or customary courts, or do such other act or acts as he the said C. D. could do as chief steward, or for transacting any limited or particular business. And I do hereby ratify and confirm all and whatsoever the said C. D., or such his deputy for the time being, shall lawfully do or cause to be done by virtue of these presents, hereby declaring that this appointment shall continue in force during my will and pleasure only. In witness whereof I have hereunto set my hand and seal this   day of, &c.

Stamp 35m.

---

171   I 2

442.—*General Notice.*

Manor of } Notice is hereby given that a general court baron
———— } and customary court will be held in and for the
said manor, on [*Thursday*] the   day of   next, at
    o'clock in the forenoon precisely, at, &c., when and where
all persons owing suit and service, claiming admittance to
any hereditaments holden of the said manor, or having any
other business to transact at the said court, are required to
attend.   Dated this ·   day of   , 1837.
                                        A. B.
                            Steward of the said manor.

443.—*Advertisement of Courts, where more than one.*

General courts baron and customary courts for the under-
mentioned manors, will be holden at the times and places
following :
    W.   H.   , on, &c , at [11] o'clock in the fore-
noon precisely, at the [*manor house*] in W.   ,
    W.   P.   , on, &c. at [11] o'clock in the fore-
noon precisely, at the [*Inn*,] in W.   when
and where all persons owing suit and service, claiming admittance to any hereditaments holden of the said manors respectively, or having any business to transact at the said
courts, are required to attend.   A. B.
    [*place and date*]   Steward.

444.—*Bailiff's proclamation on opening Court.*

Oyez. Oyez. All manner of persons that have any thing
to do at a general court baron and customary court, here about
to be holden for the manor of W.   P.   , draw nigh and
give your attendance, and you shall be heard.

445.—*Oath to Homage.*

You the homage of a general court baron and customary
court, here about to be holden for the manor of W.   P.   ,
shall diligently enquire and true presentment make, of all
matters and things which shall come to your knowledge, or
be given you in charge presentable at this court. You shall
present no one through any hatred or malice, nor leave any

one unpresented through fear, favour, affection or reward, or hope thereof, but shall present all things truly and indifferently as they shall come to your knowledge or be given you in charge, according to the best of your knowledge, understanding, and belief, So help you God.

446.—*Bailiff's Proclamation on Surrender.*

Oyez. Oyez. Let I. K. come into court and take admission to the hereditaments and premises surrendered to his use by G. H., and M. his wife, otherwise the same will be seized into the hands of the lord, according to the custom of this manor, until admission be taken thereto. This is the 1st [*2nd or 3rd*] proclamation.

The steward adds, " but no one cometh, therefore at the next court let the 2nd [*or 3rd*] proclamation be made."

447.—*The like on Death.*

Oyez. Oyez. Let the heir of C. G., or such other person or persons as claim right or title to the hereditaments holden of this manor whereof he died seised, come into court and take admittance thereto, otherwise the same will be seized into the hands of the lord for want of a tenant. This is the 1st [*2nd or 3rd*] proclamation. The steward adds as above.

448.—*The like after admittance taken to part.*

The only difference will be the insertion of the words after " he died seized," "and to which admittance remains to be taken."

449.—*On Death of a Free Tenant.*

The only difference will be the adding of the word "freely" after " holden," and the substitution of " acknowledge free tenure" for " take admittance."

450.—*Bailiff's Proclamation on dismissing Court.*

Oyez. Oyez. All manner of persons have leave to depart hence, keeping their day and hour on a new summons.

451.—*Memorandum of Presentment on Surrenders, &c.*

Manor of ⎱ We the homage of a general court baron and cus-
W. P. ⎰ tomary court, holden in and for the said manor,
the   day of, &c. present this surrender [*writing, indenture, &c.*] as part of our verdict.

A. B. ⎱ Homage.
C. D. ⎰

452.—*First Court.*

Presentment Paper.

Manor of ⎱ Presentments of the homage of a general court
W. P. ⎰ baron and customary court, holden in and for the
said manor, &c.

We present that A. B., a copyhold tenant of this manor, died since the last court, seised of certain hereditaments holden of this manor by copy of court roll.

We also present a certain absolute surrender in writing, taken out of court, before, &c., whereby C. D., a copyhold tenant of this manor, and M. his wife, out of court, surrendered certain hereditaments, therein described or mentioned, to the use of E. F., of, &c., his heirs and assigns, according to the custom of this manor.

We also present a certain conditional surrender in writing, &c. [*as in last*], subject to a condition for making the same void on payment of £   and interest, on &c., as in the said surrender mentioned.

And lastly we present all defaulters owing suit and service at this court, and amerce them 3*d.* each.

And we know of nothing further to present.

A. B. ⎱ Homage.
C. D. ⎰

MINUTE BOOK.

453.—*First Court.*

Title of Court.

Manor of ⎱ A general court baron and customary court [*of, &c.*
W. P. ⎰ *lord of the said manor*], holden in and for the said
manor, on [*Monday*] the   day of   , A. D. 1837, before A. B., gentleman, steward there.

The Homage ⎰ C. D. ⎱
              & ⎰ Sworn.
              E. F.

Absolute Surrender in Court and Admission.

At this court cometh G. H., of, &c., a copyhold tenant, and
M. his wife, and he having delivered to the said steward a
certificate of consideration, and the said M. being first separately examined and consenting, in open court surrender
All and singular, &c. [*or " all that, &c." either fully describing
the parcels or referring to the book and page where his admission
took place*]. And the reversion, &c., and all the estate, &c.,
to the use of I. K., of, &c., his heirs and assigns for ever.
And thereupon the said I. K., (by L. M., his attorney)
prayeth to be and is admitted tenant of the said hereditaments, to which the said G. H. was admitted, &c., (see book
G. 486.) to hold to the said I. K., and his heirs.   Of the
Lord, &c.   Fealty respited.
> [*Enter in margin or at foot " Fine £   , to be paid this
> day three weeks, at eleven, at, &c."*]
> [*For full entry of this admission, see* 498.]

Absolute Surrender in Court and Proclamation.

> Also at this court, &c., as above to " heirs and assigns
> for ever."   But the said I. K. cometh not to take ad-
> mission, whereupon the first proclamation is made,
> &c.   [*See Bailiff's proclamation*, 446, *and entry*, 471.]

Death presented and devisee admitted.

> Also at this court the homage present the death of
> A. G., a copyhold tenant, whereupon cometh into court
> C. G. of &c., and produceth a clause from his will,
> bearing, &c., and which will was proved in, &c.,
> whereby, &c. [*See clause from will.*]   And there-

175

upon the said C. G. prayeth to be and was admitted to the said devised hereditaments. [*Book H., p.* 394.] To hold to him and his heirs. Of the lord, &c. Fealty respited.

Fine £   to be paid, &c.

[*For entry of admission, see* 479.)

Death and first proclamation.

Also, &c., to " Tenant," whereupon at this court the first proclamation is made, &c. [See Bailiff's proclamation, 447, and entry, 464.]

Absolute surrender presented and admission.

Also at this court, the homage present an absolute surrender in writing, taken out of court, on, &c., before, &c., whereby A. H. of &c., and G. his wife, she being examined and consenting, out of court, surrendered all, &c. [*description.*] And the reversion, &c., and all the estate, &c., to the use of G. H. of, &c. his heirs and assigns for ever ; whereupon the said G. H. prayed to be and was admitted tenant to the said hereditaments [*Book H., p.* 96.] To hold to him and his heirs. Of the lord, &c. Fealty respited.

Fine £   to be paid, &c.

Form of entry, s. 493.

Absolute surrender presented and proclamation.

Also, &c., [*as in last to* " for ever."] But the said G. H. cometh not to be admitted, whereupon the first proclamation is made, &c.

See 446, and for entry, 471.

Conditional surrender presented.

Also, &c., as in last, *adding* " upon condition," to be void on payment of the sum of £   and interest, on, &c., as in the said surrender mentioned.

Form of entry, 470.

Conclusion.

Defaulters amerced 3*d.* each. (Entry 518.)

We attest the acts of this court,

W. Y. } Homage.
C. W. }

454.—*Second Court.*

The presentment paper will be in the same form as at the previous court, but in the particular courts here given there will be no presentment at the second court beyond that of the bargain and sale and defaulters.

455.—*Minute Book.*

Title of court as in first court.   (Entry 462.)

Admission on surrender in court after first proclamation.

Whereas at the last court, G. H. and M. his wife, surrendered the hereditaments in the entry of that court described or mentioned, to the use of I. K. and his heirs, and the first proclamation was made, &c. Now at this court cometh the said I. K., and prayeth to be, and is admitted tenant of the said hereditaments. [*See Book* 4, *p.* 149.] To hold to him and his heirs. Of the lord, &c. Fealty respited. [Fine £   , &c.] [Entry 498.]

Second proclamation on surrender.

Also at this court, the second proclamation is made on the absolute surrender from G. H. and M. his wife, to the use of I. K. and his heirs. [446. Entry, 472.]

Admission after death on sale by executors.

Whereas at the last court the death of I. G. was presented, and the first proclamation made, &c. Now at this court cometh A. G. of, &c , and produceth a certain indenture of bargain and sale, bearing date, &c., and made, &c., whereby L. M. and J. N., executors of the will of the said I. G., under a power therein contained, bargained and sold the hereditaments copyhold of this manor, to which the said J. G. stood admitted, to the use of the said A. G. and his heirs. And thereupon the said A. G. prayeth to be, and is admitted tenant thereof. [*See Book G.*, *p.* 63.] To hold to him and his heirs. Of the lord, &c. Fealty respited.

[Fine £   , &c.]   Entry, 500.

Death and second proclamation.

Also at this court, the second proclamation is made after the death of, &c. [417, and entry, 465.]

Admission after absolute surrender out of court and first proclamation.

Whereas at the last court it was presented that on, &c., A. P., and E. his wife, out of court, surrendered certain hereditaments, therein described or mentioned, to the use of M. N., his heirs and assigns, whereupon the first proclamation was made, &c. Now at this court cometh, &c. [*As in admission on surrender in court.*] Entry 494.

Second proclamation on absolute surrender.

Also at this court the second proclamation is made, &c. [*As on surrender in court*, 472.]

Licence.

Also at this court the lord grants license to I. G., of, &c., a copyhold tenant, to demise his copyhold hereditaments holden of this manor to, &c., for the term of   years, from, &c. Entry, 513.

Conclusion.

Defaulters amerced, &c.   [*See first court, and* 518.]

456.—*Third Court.*

Presentment paper.

Heading as at first court.

We present a certain indenture of bargain and sale, bearing date, &c., and made between, &c., whereby the hereditaments to which M. N., a copyhold tenant, stands admitted, were bargained and sold, to the use of J. G., of, &c., his heirs and assigns, and whereby an authority was given to G. K., of, &c., to surrender the same accordingly.

We also present a certain surrender made and passed by the said G. K., on, &c., before, &c., of the said hereditaments, to the use of the said I. C. and his heirs.

We also present that I. M., of, &c., an infant of the age of ten years or thereabouts, is the customary heir of I. M., deceased, a copyhold tenant of this manor, and that the said I. M., his father, died intestate.

We present all defaulters, &c., [*as before.*]

457.—*Minute Book.*

Admission after second proclamation on absolute surrender in court.

Whereas [*recite presentment of absolute surrender and proclamation.*] Now at this court, &c. [*as in admission on first proclamation at second court.*] Entry, 495. 498.

Third proclamation and award of seizure.

Also at this court, the third proclamation is made on the absolute surrender passed, &c. But the said A. G. cometh not to be admitted, whereupon at this court seizure is awarded, &c., and a precept under the hand and seal of the said steward is awarded, directing R.S., the bailiff of this manor, to seize the said hereditaments until admission, and to make return to the said precept at the next court. [*See proclamation,* 446 ; *precept,* 474 ; *and entry,* 473.

Admission after death and second proclamation.

Whereas, &c. [*recite presentment of death and proclamations.*] Now at this court cometh, &c. [*common admission according to circumstances.*] For entry see class F, 479, &c., as to devisees ; and G, 486, &c., as to heir, &c.

Third proclamation after death.

At this court the third proclamation is made after the death of , but no one cometh, &c., whereupon seizure is awarded and a precept issued, &c. [*Proclamation,* 447 ; *precept,* 467 ; *entry,* 466.]

Admission on absolute surrender out of court, and second proclamation.

Whereas, &c. [*This will be similar to that on surrender in court.*] For entry, see 495.

Third proclamation on same, and seizure awarded.

This will also be similar to that on a surrender in court. [*See* 446, *and for entry* 473.]

Admission under bankruptcy.

At this court the homage do present an indenture of bargain and sale, bearing date, &c., and made between, &c., whereby, &c. [*See presentment paper above.*] The homage also present an absolute surrender in writing, &c. [*Also, as in presentment paper above.*]. And, there-

upon the said B. G. prayeth to be, and is admitted
tenant of the said hereditaments. [*Book*   p.   .] To
hold to him and his heirs. Of the lord, &c.

   Fine *£*   , &c. [Entry, 501.]

Memorandum of presentment to be written on bargain and
sale and surrender, 451.

Admission of infant heir.

  After usual admission after death, add " Mr. E. C., of,
  &c., appointed guardian."

     [Entry, 486 and 9.]

  Defaulters amerced, &c.

458.—*Fourth Court.*

Presentment paper.

    After the usual heading,

We present a writing, bearing date, &c., under the hand of,
&c., whereby he did authorise and require the steward of this
manor or his deputy to enter satisfaction on a conditional
surrender, passed on, &c., by, &c., to the use of, &c.,
subject to a condition for making the same void on payment
of *£*   , and lawful interest as therein mentioned.

We also present that G. B., who held certain lands freely of
this manor, died since the last court seised thereof.

We also present that C. D., a copyhold tenant of this
manor, hath committed waste by pulling down a certain
messuage lately standing and being upon the hereditaments
holden of this manor, to which he stands admitted tenant.

459.—*Minute Book.*

Commencement as before.

Admission on re-grant.

  At this court R. S., the bailiff, returns that agreeably to
the precept directed to him for that purpose, he hath in
the presence of C. D. and E. F., two copyhold tenants,
seized all and singular the hereditaments whereof
A. B. lately died seised, until admission be taken
thereto, whereupon cometh into court G. B. of, &c.,
youngest son and customary heir of the said A. B.,
and prayeth the lord to regrant to him the said hereditaments, and is thereupon admitted tenant thereof.
[*See book H. p.* 10.] To hold to him and his heirs.
Of the lord, &c. Fealty respited, &c. Fine *£*   ,
&c. Entry 476, 486, or 7.

Admission on forfeited conditional surrender.

Also at this court cometh G. R. of, &c., and giveth the court to understand that the sum of £   , mentioned in the condition of a certain surrender passed to the use of him and his heirs, by &c., on, &c., was not paid agreeably to such condition, and still remains due and unpaid. And thereupon he prayeth to be, and is admitted tenant of the said hereditaments. [*See book H, p.* 17.] To hold to him and his heirs. Of the lord, &c. Fealty respited, &c. [Fine £   , &c.] [Entry 504.]

Satisfaction on conditional surrender.

Also at this court the homage present a writing, bearing date, &c., under the hand of, &c., whereby, &c. [*See presentment.*] And thereupon satisfaction is entered on the said conditional surrender, and the same is discharged accordingly. [Entry 477.]

Admission of several parties.

[The minutes will shortly state after the recitals the mode in which the parties are admitted, so as to be able to frame the entry from the minutes.] (See form, 502.)

Apportionment of rent.

At this court the annual quit rent of   , payable in respect of the entirety of the premises to which A. B. lately stood admitted tenant, and part whereof he hath surrendered to C. D., is apportioned as follows : A. B. and his heirs to pay —*s.* —*d.*, and C. D. and his heirs to pay —*s.* —*d.* [Entry 511.]

Acknowledgment of free tenure.

Also at this court the death of G. H., a free tenant, is presented, whereupon cometh into court J. M., of, &c., and acknowledges free tenure. Relief —*s.* —*d.* [Entry 512.]

Surrender and release.

Also at this court cometh I. T. of, &c., and having delivered to the steward a certificate of consideration, surrenders and releases all his estate, &c., of and in, &c., to the use of A. B., now admitted tenant thereof, his heirs and assigns for ever, so that neither the said I. T. nor his heirs may claim any right, &c. [Entry 508, &c.]

Conclusion in usual form.

181

460.—*Fifth Court.*

Presentment paper.

We present a certain indenture, bearing date, &c., and made between, &c., whereby all principal money and interest due on a certain conditional surrender, passed on, &c., by &c., and all benefit and advantage thereof, was assigned to I. K. of, &c., his executors, administrators, and assigns.

Presentment of absolute surrender in lieu of recovery, as in other presentments of surrender.

461.—*Minute Book.*

After usual title of court.

Admission after seisure.

> This will be similar to that at the last court. [Entry 485 or 497.]

Surrender in lieu of recovery.

> The homage do present a certain absolute surrender, &c. (stating the surrender shortly.) And thereupon the said   prayeth to be, and is admitted tenant of the said hereditaments. To hold to him and his heirs. Of the lord, &c. [See Entry, 519.]

Presentment of assignment of mortgage.

> Also at this court the homage present, &c. [*as in presentment paper, but see s.* 211, *as to the propriety of such assignments. Of course, if presented, a memorandum of presentment is to be entered on the deed.*]

> The entry of the assignment will be an enrolment.

Presentment of an enfranchisement.

> Also it is certified by the said steward, and presented by the homage, that on, &c., the lord of this manor did enfranchise and convey to A. B. and his heirs, all that, &c., which premises were at the date of such enfranchisement copyhold of this manor, and to which the said A. B. then stood admitted tenant.

> Amerciaments and conclusion as in other cases.

ENTRIES ON COURT ROLLS.

———

(A)

TITLE OF COURT.

462.—*General Title.*

MANOR OF } A GENERAL [*special*] *court baron* and *customary* ——————— } *court* [*of   , lord of the said manor*], holden in and for the said manor, on   , the   day of   , in the year of our lord one thousand eight hundred and thirty   , BEFORE A. B., gentleman, steward there [*or before C. D., gentleman, deputy steward of A. B., gentleman, chief steward there.*]

The Homage. }   and   { *Sworn.*

————

(B)

463.—*Entry at subsequent Court, of Reference to Admission before Lord.*

AT *this court* it is certified by the said steward, that on the   day of   last, [*W. W.*] of [*W.*] in the county of [*S. Esqre.*] was admitted tenant out of court, before the lord of this manor, on the absolute surrender of [*J. B.*] and [*L.*] his wife, to certain hereditaments in the said surrender and entry of the said admission on the court rolls of this manor described, as by the said entry of the said admission more fully appears.

————

(C)

464.—*Entry of Proclamations on Death; precept to seize, and return of seizure.*

Death presented and first proclamation.—[ALSO,] AT *this court* the homage thereof do present that A. B., a copyhold tenant of this manor, died since the last general court baron

183

or customary court holden for this manor, seised of certain hereditaments and premises holden of this manor by copy of court roll ; WHEREUPON at this court the first proclamation is made for the heir of the said A. B., or such other person or persons as claim right or title to the hereditaments and premises whereof he so died seised, to come into court and take admittance thereto, otherwise the same will be seized into the hands of the lord of this manor, for want of a tenant. *But* no one cometh to be admitted ; *Therefore*, at the next court, let the second proclamation be made, &c.

465.—*Second Proclamation.*

ALSO, *at this court* the second proclamation is made "for the heir of A. B., or such other person or persons as claim right or title to the hereditaments and premises, holden by copy of court roll of this manor, whereof he lately died seised [*if admission has been taken to part, add " and to which admission has not been taken*"], to come into court and take admittance thereto, otherwise the same will be seized into the hands of the lord of this manor, for want of a tenant. *But* no one cometh to be admitted." *Therefore* at the next court let the third proclamation be made, &c.

466.—*Third Proclamation, and Award of Seizure.*

ALSO, *at this court* the third proclamation is made, &c., [*adding the parts within inverted commas in second proclamation.*] AND THEREUPON at this court seizure is awarded, and a precept is issued under the hand and seal of the steward of this manor to R. S., the bailiff of this court and manor, and he is thereby directed that he seize into the hands of the lord of this manor the hereditaments and premises holden of this manor by copy of court roll ; and whereof the said A. B. died seised as aforesaid [*if admission has been taken to part, add " and to which admission has not been taken*",] in the mean time and until some person or persons come into court and take admittance thereto ; and that he make a return to the said precept at the next general court baron or customary court to be holden for this manor.

467.—*Form of the precept to seize* quousque.

The manor of
Woodbridge late Priory } To Robert Stevenson, bailiff of the
in the county of Suffolk. } courts of the said manor.

WHEREAS public proclamation has been made at three several general courts baron and customary ·courts, holden for the said manor, on the   day of   , the   day of   , and this   day of   , for any person or persons claiming right or title to the hereditaments and premises holden by copy of court roll of this manor, whereof A. B. lately died seised, to come into court and take admittance thereto. AND *forasmuch* as no one hath come to take up and be admitted to [*if admission taken to part, say "certain of"*] the said hereditaments and premises, IT *is commanded* and ordered that you [*Robert Stevenson*] do seize, and you are hereby authorized and required to seize into the hands of the lord of the said manor, ALL *and singular* the said hereditaments and premises of which the said A. B. so died seised [*and to which admission has not been taken*] in the mean time and until some person or persons shall take admittance thereto ; *and that* you do make return to this precept at the next general court baron or customary court to be holden in and for this manor.

Given under my hand and seal the   day of   , in the year of our lord 183   .

R. R.,   · (L. S.)
Steward of the said manor.

————

468.—*Bailiff's Return to be endorsed.*

By virtue of the within precept I have, in the presence of I. K. and L. M., copyhold tenants of the said manor, seized the within mentioned lands and premises into the hands of the lord, as commanded by the said precept.

R. S. Bailiff.

————

469. *Entry of Bailiff's return.*

ALSO, *at this court* [*Robert Stevenson*], the bailiff of the courts of this manor, returns that by virtue of a precept to him for that purpose directed at the last general court baron and customary court held for this manor, he has seized into the hands of the lord of this manor, All and singular the hereditaments and premises holden of this manor by copy of

185

court roll whereof A. B. lately died seised [*if admission taken to part,* "*and to which admission has not been taken*"], in the mean time and until some person or persons shall take admittance thereto, as by the said precept he was commanded.

(D)

470.—*Presentment of Surrenders (absolute or conditional), with proclamations, &c., on absolute surrenders.*

Presentment of Surrender.—ALSO, *at this court* it is certified by the said steward, and presented by the homage of this court, that since the last general court baron or customary court holden for this manor, namely, on the   day of   last,   A. B., of, &c., &c. [*copying surrender, but making it in the past tense instead of the present.*]

471.—*First Proclamation.*

[*If an absolute surrender, and no one comes to be admitted, add at the bottom*]
WHEREUPON at this court the first proclamation is made for the said C. D., to come into court and take admittance to the said hereditaments and premises so surrendered to his use as aforesaid, otherwise the same will be seized into the hands of the lord, according to the custom of this manor, until admission be taken thereto, &c. *But* he cometh not ; *Therefore* at the next court let the second proclamation be made, &c.

472.—*Second Proclamation.*

ALSO, *at this court* the second proclamation is made " for C. D., to come into court and take admittance to the hereditaments and premises surrendered to his use by A. B., otherwise the same will be seized into the hands of the lord, according to the custom of this manor, until admission be taken thereto, &c. ; but he cometh not ;" *Therefore* at the next court let the third proclamation be made, &c.

473.—*Third Proclamation.*

ALSO *at this court* the third proclamation is made, &c. [*parts within* " " *in second proclamation*] ; THEREFORE at this court seizure is awarded, and [*Robert Stephenson*], the bailiff of this court, is commanded by a precept under the hand and seal of the said steward, that he do seize the hereditaments and premises so surrendered to the use of the said A. B., in the mean time and until the said A. B., shall come into court and take admittance thereto ; and that he make return to the said precept at the next general court baron or customary court to be holden for this manor.

474.—*Precept.*

THE MANOR OF W. P. in the county of S. } To [*R. S.*] bailiff of the courts of the said manor.

WHEREAS public proclamation hath been, according to the custom of the said manor, made at three several general courts baron and customary courts held for the said manor, on, &c., &c., and on this   day of   , for C. D. to come into court and take admission to the hereditaments and premises holden of this manor by copy of court roll, and surrendered to his use by A. B.; AND *forasmuch* as he hath not come to take up and be admitted to the said hereditaments and premises, according to the custom of this manor, IT IS *commanded* and ordered that you R. S. do seize, and you are hereby authorised and required to seize into the hands of the lord of the said manor, the hereditaments and premises so surrendered by the said A. B. to the use of the said C. D., in the mean time and until the said C. D. shall come into court and take admittance thereto ; and that you do make return to this precept at the next general court baron or customary court, to be held in and for this manor.

Given under my hand and seal this   day of   , in the year of our lord 183 .

R. R.   (L. S.)
Steward of the said manor.

475.—*Bailiff's return to be endorsed.*

By virtue of the within precept I have, in the presence of I. K. and L. M., copyhold tenants of the said manor, seized the within mentioned hereditaments and premises into the hands of the lord, as commanded by the said precept.

R. S., Bailiff,
Sept. 11th, 1836.

476.—*Entry of Return to Precept to seize.*

ALSO, *at this court* R. S., the bailiff of the courts of this manor, returns that by virtue of a precept to him for that purpose directed at the last general court baron and customary court held for this manor, he has seized into the hands of the lord all and singular the hereditaments and premises holden of this manor by copy of court roll, and surrendered by A. B. to the use of C. D.; in the mean time and until the said C. D. shall take admission to the said hereditaments and premises, as by the said precept he was commanded.

(E)

477.—*Presentment of warrant and entry of satisfaction on conditional surrender.*

ALSO *at this court* the homage thereof do present a certain writing, bearing date, &c., under the hand of A. B., of, &c., WHEREBY he did authorize and require the steward of this manor, or his lawful deputy for the time being, to enter full satisfaction and discharge in the court books, or on the court rolls of this manor, on and for a certain conditional surrender, bearing date, &c., and made and passed [*out of court*] by C. D, of, &c., and E. his wife, of certain hereditaments and premises in the said surrender described [*or of all and singular, &c. as in warrant*], to the use of the said A. B., his heirs and assigns for ever, for securing to him, his executors, administrators, and assigns, the repayment of the sum of £   , with interest for the same, after the rate, at the days or times, and in manner in the said surrender mentioned and appointed for payment thereof, WHEREUPON satisfaction is entered on the said surrender, and the same is discharged accordingly.

[Of course this must be altered to correspond with the form of each warrant, as they are drawn in different ways.]

478. [Frequently the discharge only applies to part, sold to a certain person : the following will then be the form of conclusion.]

AND THEREUPON satisfaction is entered on the said conditional surrender, and the same is discharged accordingly, so far as the same relates to or affects the said hereditaments and premises so sold to the said (W. W.) as aforesaid.

(F)

479.—*Admissions of Devisees.*

Cl. 1. *Presentment of death and admission of devisee.*—ALSO *at this court* the homage thereof do present that A. B., a copyhold tenant of this manor, died since the last general court baron or customary court held for this manor, seised of certain hereditaments and premises holden of this manor by copy of court roll.

2. *At same court as death presented.*—WHEREUPON cometh into court [*devisee*] of, &c. [if by attorney, *add* " by E. F., gentleman," his attorney,] and produceth to the court a clause from [*or probate of*] the last will and testament of the said A. B., deceased, whereby it appears that the said will bears date on or about, &c.* and was proved on, &c. in, &c. [*stating court,*] and that the same, so far as relates to the hereditaments and premises holden of this manor, whereof the said A. B. died seised, follows in these words (that is to say.) [*Add clause from will, and parts affecting the copyholds.*]

3. AND *thereupon* the said (devisee) [*by his said attorney*] prayeth to be admitted to the said hereditaments and premises so devised to him as aforesaid (that is to say),

4. *To* ALL, &c. [*description.*]   [*State quit rent in margin.*]

5. *Which* premises the said A. B., deceased, had and took up to him and his heirs at a general court baron held for this manor, on, &c. [*or as the case may be*] on the absolute surrender of, &c. [*according to facts*] as by the entry of the said court, reference being thereunto had, will more fully appear. [*If the testator was admitted at separate times, the statement must be varied to correspond with the facts.*]

6. TO WHICH said (devisee) [*by his said attorney*] the lord of this manor, by the said steward, doth grant and deliver

---

* No actual necessity exists for stating where proved; but it is better to do so, as it may save expense afterwards in searches for wills.

seisin of the said hereditaments and premises, so devised as aforesaid, by the rod.

7. To HOLD the same, with the appurtenances, unto the said [*devisee*] and his heirs [*if only given for life, omit " and his heirs.*"] of the lord, by copy of court roll at the will of the lord, and according to the custom of this manor, by fealty, suit of court, and other the rents, duties and services therefore due and of right accustomed.

8. *And*, saving the rights of the lord, the said (devisee) is [*by his said attorney*] admitted tenant of the said hereditaments and premises, and pays on such his admittance a fine, &c. But his fealty is respited until, &c.

480.—*Admission to several copyholds in one admission.*

Clauses 1 and 2 in 479.

3. AND THEREUPON the said (devise) [*by his said attorney*] prayeth to be admitted tenant to certain of the hereditaments and premises devised to him as aforesaid (that is to say), *To* ALL, &c. [*description of first premises.*]   *Which*, &c. [*add clause* 5.]

4. AND the said (devisee) [*by his said attorney*] also prayeth to be admitted tenant to certain other of the hereditaments and premises devised to him as aforesaid (that is to say), *To* ALL, &c. [*description and clause* 5.]

To WHICH said (devisee), &c. [*adding clauses* 6, 7, *and* 8, *adding the words* " several and respective" *before* " hereditaments."]

If separate admisssions are to be made, take 1 and 2 in 479, 3 as in 480, and 6, 7, and 8 in 479, omitting the words " devised as aforesaid;" and in the same manner proceed with the admission to each estate.

482.—*Admission after first proclamation.*

WHEREAS at the last general court baron and customary court held for this manor, " the homage thereof did present that A. B., a copyhold tenant of this manor, died since the then last court, seised of certain hereditaments and premises holden by copy of court roll of this manor, whereupon at that court the first proclamation was made for want of a tenant, &c., but no one came to be admitted, &c." Now *at this court* cometh, &c. [*proceed as in* 479 *or* 480.]

483.—*Admission after second proclamation.*

WHEREAS at a general court baron and customary court held for this manor, on, &c., the homage, &c. [*as in above, between inverted commas.*]   AND WHEREAS at the last general court baron and customary court, the second proclamation was in like manner made, &c., but no one came, &c. Now *at this court* cometh, &c. [*as in* 479.]

484.—*Admission after third proclamation, and award of seizure.*

WHEREAS, &c. [*recite first and second proclamations as in No.* 483.] AND WHEREAS at the last general court baron and customary court held for this manor, the third proclamation was in like manner made, but no one came to be admitted, *whereupon* at that court seizure was awarded, &c. Now *at this court* cometh, &c. [*as before.*]

485.—*Admission after return of seizure.*

WHEREAS, &c. [*recite first and second proclamations as in No.* 483.] AND WHEREAS at a general court baron and customary court held for this manor, on, &c., the third proclamation was in like manner made, but no one came to be admitted, &c., *whereupon* at that court seizure was awarded, and R. S., the bailiff of the courts of this manor, was commanded by a precept under the hand and seal of the said steward, that he should seize into the hands of the lord of this manor, all and singular the hereditaments and premises holden of this manor by copy of court roll, and whereof the said A. B. died seised, in the mean time and until some person or persons should take admittance thereto. AND, WHEREAS, at the last general court baron and customary court held for this manor, the said R. S., bailiff as aforesaid, returned that he had seized into the hands of the lord the said hereditaments and premises in the mean time and until admission thereto, as by the said precept he was commanded.

2. Now *at this court* cometh, &c. [cl. 2, in precedent No. 479.]

3. AND *thereupon* the said (devisee) (by his said attorney) prayeth the lord of this manor to re-grant to and admit him tenant of the said hereditaments and premises so devised to him, and seized as aforesaid (that is to say),

4. *To* ALL, &c. [*description.*]
    Which, &c. [cl. 5, 479.]

5. To WHICH said (devisee) (*by his said attorney*) the lord of this manor, by his said steward, doth regrant and deliver seisin of the said hereditaments and premises so seized into the lord's hands and devised as aforesaid.

6. To HOLD, &c. [cl. 7 and 8, 479.]

(G)

486.—Admissions of Heirs.— Widow to Freebench and Husband to Curtesy.

Cl. 1. *Admission of Heir where Widow not admitted to Free-bench.*]—ALSO *at this court* the homage thereof do present that A. B., a copyhold tenant of this manor, died since the last general court baron or customary court held for this manor, seised of certain hereditaments and premises holden of this manor by copy of court roll.

2. AND THEREUPON cometh into court [*heir*] of, &c., youngest son and heir, according to the custom of this manor of the said A. B. (by C. D., gentleman, his attorney), and prayeth to be admitted tenant of the hereditaments and pre-mises holden of this manor by copy of court roll, whereof the said A. B. died seised, as his right and inheritance (that is to say),

3. *To* ALL, &c., [*description.*] [*Add rent in margin.*]

4. *Which* premises the said A. B. had and took up to him and his heirs at a general court baron or customary court held for this manor, on, &c., after the death and under the will, &c. [*as the case may be*], as by the entry of the said court, re-reference being thereunto had, will more fully appear.

5. To WHICH said [*heir*] (by his said attorney) the lord of this manor by the said steward doth grant and deliver seisin of the said hereditaments and premises by the rod.

6. To HOLD the same with the appurtenances unto the said [*heir*] and his heirs, of the lord by copy of court roll at his will, and according to the custom of the manor, by fealty, suit of court, and other the rents, duties, and services therefore due and of right accustomed.

7. *And* saving the right of the lord, the said [*heir*] is (by his said attorney) admitted tenant of the said hereditaments and premises, and pays on such his admittance a fine, &c., but his fealty is respited until, &c.

If the heir is an infant, add appointment of guardian as in 489.

If after proclamations, alter the admission according to the precedents in Class F.

487.—Admission of Heir after admission of Widow to Freebench.

ALSO *at this court*, &c. [*Cl. 1 as above.*]

AND THEREUPON, &c. [*Cl. 2, adding after "inheritance"*] ("subject to the customary dower or freebench of C., the widow of the said A. B., and to which she hath at this court been admitted tenant (that is to say),

Cl. 3. To *two equal* undivided third parts, and the remainder or reversion expectant on the decease of the said C., the widow of the said A. B., of and in the other or remaining undivided third part of ALL, &c. [*description.*]

Which, &c. [*Cl. 4 as above, and also clauses* 5, 6, 7; *and guardianship, if requisite, as in G.* 489.]

488.—*Admission of Daughters as Coparceners.*

ALSO *at this court*, &c. [*Cl.* 1, *as in* 486.]

Cl. 2. AND THEREUPON come into court [*married daughter*] wife of, &c. [*husband*] (by the said   , her attorney), and [*unmarried daughters,*] [*describing them*] (by   , their attorney), and which said [*daughters*] are the [3] only children and coheiresses, according to the custom of this manor, of the said A. B. deceased, and pray to be admitted tenants in coparcenary to all and singular the hereditaments and premises holden of this manor by copy of court roll, and whereof the said A. B. died seised as aforesaid (that is to say),

3. *To* ALL, &c. [*description.*]

4. *Which* premises, &c. [486, 4.]

5. *To* WHICH said [*daughters*] (by their said attorney) the lord, &c. [486, 5.]

6. *To* HOLD the same with the appurtenances unto the said [*daughters*] and their heirs, as tenants in coparcenary, of the lord, &c. [486, 6.]

7. *And* saving, &c. [*proceed as in Cl.* 7, *altering it to plural number.*]

> From the above and [487] the admission can be drawn if the widow is admitted to dower; and if any of the daughters are minors, a guardian can be appointed, as in 489.

489.—*Guardian appointed.*

ALSO *at this court*, because it appears to this court that the said [*heirs*] are minors, (that is to say), the said [*C. B.*] of the age of [14] years or thereabouts, and the said [*D. B.*] of the age of [12] years or thereabouts. Therefore the custody and guardianship, as well of the persons of the said [*C. B.*] and [*D. B.*], as of the aforesaid hereditaments and premises to which they have been at this court admitted tenants, is awarded and committed to [*guardian*] until the said [*C. B.*] and [*D. B.*] shall respectively attain the age of 21 years; he the said [*guardian*] answering such services as are

or ought to be performed by him as such guardian as aforesaid, according to the custom of this manor, and rendering a
full and just account when thereunto required, and the said
[*guardian*] is (by   his attorney for that purpose) admitted
guardian of the said [*C. B.*] and [*D. B.*] as aforesaid.

490.—*Admission of Widow to Freebench.*

ALSO *at this court*, &c. [486, 1.]

Cl. 2. AND THEREUPON at this court cometh [*widow*] of
&c., widow of the said A. B. (by   , gentleman, her attorney), and prayeth to be admitted tenant for her life to her
customary dower or freebench, according to the custom of
this manor, of and in the hereditaments and premises holden
of this manor, whereof the said A. B. so died seised (that is
to say),

3. To *one equal* third part (the whole into three equal parts
being divided) of and in ALL, &c. [*description.*]

4. *Which* premises, &c. [486, 4.]

5. To WHICH said [*widow*] (by her said attorney) the lord
of this manor by the said steward doth grant and deliver
seisin of the said one-third part of the said hereditaments and
premises by the rod.

6. To HOLD, &c. [486, 6, *omitting the words " and his
heirs."*]

7. [Cl. 7, *adding the words " to the said one-third part."*]

491.—*Admission of Husband as tenant by Curtesy.*

ALSO *at this court*, &c. [486.]

Cl. 2. AND THEREUPON at this court cometh [*husband*] of
&c., husband of the said A. B., and prayeth to be admitted
tenant for his life as tenant by curtesy, according to the custom of this manor, to the hereditaments and premises whereof
the said   his wife lately died seised as aforesaid (that is
to say),

3. *To* ALL, &c. [*description.*]

4. *Which* premises, &c. [486, 4.]

5. To WHICH said [*husband*] &c. [*Cl. 5.*]

6. To HOLD the same with the appurtenances unto the said
[*husband*] for and during the term of his natural life, as tenant
by curtesy, according to the custom of this manor, of the
lord, &c. [*Cl. 6.*]

7. [*Cl. 7.*]

Should there have been proclamations in any of the foregoing precedents, the admissions can be drawn on referring to the admissions of devisees [*Cl. F.*]

———

492.—*Admission of Infant or Feme Covert under* 9 *G.* 1, *on application of Party.* See abstract of act, 409.

(**a**) *When party attends personally.*—Whereas, &c., [*state presentment of death and proclamations in usual manner.*] Now at this court cometh in his (or her) own proper person, G. B., of, &c., an infant of the age of   years, (or G. B., wife of H. B., of, &c.), only child and heir (or devisee named in the will) of the said A. B. deceased, and (having produced to the court the probate of the will of the said A. B., deceased, bearing date, &c., and whereby, &c.), the said G. B., pursuant to the act of parliament for that purpose passed in the 9th year of the reign of his late Majesty King George the First, prayed to be admitted tenant, &c. [*then proceed as in other admissions, the usual appointment of guardian will be added.*]

(**b**) *When infant admitted by guardian.*]—The only difference will be the omitting the words "in his own proper person," and substituting the words "by E. T., of, &c., his guardian appointed, &c. [stating the appointment); the remainder of the admission will be similar to that by attorney, substituting the word " guardian" for " attorney."

(**c**) *When admission by attorney.*]—In this case, instead of the common form of admission by attorney, the first statement will be as follows : " by E. P., of, &c., attorney for and on behalf of the said G. B., duly appointed by the said G. B. by writing under his (or her) hand and seal, pursuant to the act, &c., and which is presented and inrolled at this court, [*then proceed as on an admission by attorney in ordinary cases.*]

The power of attorney will be enrolled by making the entry and the presentment, and *adding*, " and which said writing the said E. T. prayeth to have enrolled amongst the acts of this court," and it is enrolled as follows : " To all to whom, &c."

(**d**) *Admission of infant or feme covert under* 9 *G.* 1, *where lord appoints the guardian or attorney.*]—Whereas, &c. [*presentment of death, and three proclamations at previous courts*]. Now at this court the lord of this manor, by his said steward, doth, in pursuance of the act of parliament passed, &c., nominate and appoint E. T., of, &c., to be guardian of the said G. B. the infant (or attorney for the said G. B. the feme covert) for this purpose only ; and thereupon the said G. B., by the said E. F., his guardian (her attorney), prayeth to be admitted, &c. [*proceeding as in the other admissions.*]

———

(H)

ADMISSIONS ON SURRENDERS PASSED OUT OF COURT.

493.—Admission on an Absolute Surrender passed out of Court.

Where Surrender presented at same Court.]—Cl. 1. ALSO *at this court* it is certified by the said steward, and presented by the homage, that since the last general court baron or customary court held for this manor, namely, on, &c. A. B., of, &c. [*stating surrender in past tense.*]

2. AND THEREUPON cometh into court the said [*purchaser*] (by C. D., gentleman, his attorney), and prayeth to be admitted tenant to the hereditaments and premises so surrendered to his use as aforesaid (that is to say),

3. *To* ALL, &c. [*add description.*]

4. *Which* premises the said A. B. had and took up to him and his heirs at a general court baron held for this manor, on, &c., on the absolute surrender of E. F., &c. [*as the case may be*], as by the entry of the said court, reference being thereunto had, will more fully appear.

5. To WHICH said [*purchaser*] (by his said attorney) the lord of this manor by the said steward doth grant and deliver seisin of the said hereditaments and premises surrendered to his use as aforesaid by the rod.

6. To HOLD the same, with the appurtenances, unto the said [*purchaser*], and his heirs, of the lord, by copy of court roll at the will of the lord, and according to the custom of the said manor, by fealty, suit of court, and other the rents, duties, and services therefore due and of right accustomed.

7. *And* saving the right of the lord, the said [*purchaser*] is (by his said attorney) admitted tenant of the said hereditaments and premises, and pays on such his admittance a fine, &c.; but his fealty is respited until, &c.

494.—After First Proclamation.

Cl. 1. WHEREAS at the last general court baron or customary court held for this manor, it was certified by the steward, and presented, &c. [*stating presentment of surrender and proclamation fully, according to entry in previous court.*]

2. Now *at this court* cometh, &c. [*then proceed as in* 493.]

495.—*After Second Proclamation.*

WHEREAS at a general court baron and customary court held for this manor, on, &c., it was certified, &c. [*stating presentment of surrender as in last form.*]

2. AND WHEREAS at the last general court baron and customary court held for this manor, the second proclamation was in like manner made for the said [*purchaser*] to come into court and take admission to the hereditaments and premises surrendered to his use as aforesaid, but he came not, &c.

3. Now *at this court* cometh, &c. [*as in last precedent for remainder of admission.*]

496.—*After Third Proclamation and Award of Seizure.*

Recite presentment of surrender, and first and second proclamations, as in last form, except inserting the date of the second proclamation.

2. AND WHEREAS at the last general court baron and customary court held for this manor, the third proclamation was in like manner made, but the said [*purchaser*] came not to take admission, &c., and thereupon at that court seizure was awarded, &c.

3. Now *at this court* cometh, &c. [*as above.*]

497.—*After Seizure.*

Recite presentment of surrender, and first, second, and third proclamations, and award of seizure, &c., except that the award of seizure should be stated fully.

2. AND WHEREAS at the last general court baron and customary court held for this manor, the bailiff of the courts of the said manor returned, that by virtue of the said precept he had seized the said hereditaments and premises into the hands of the lord of this manor in the mean time and until admission should be taken thereto.

3. Now *at this court* cometh the said [*purchaser*] (by A. B., gentleman, his attorney), and prayeth the lord of this manor to re-grant to and admit him tenant of the said hereditaments and premises so surrendered to his use as aforesaid (viz.), TO ALL, &c. [*description.*]

4. *Which* premises, &c. [*Clause* 5, *as above.*]

5. To WHICH said [*purchaser*] (by his said attorney) the lord of this manor by the said steward doth re-grant and de-

197

liver seisin of the said hereditaments and premises surrendered to his use and seized as aforesaid, by the rod.

To HOLD, &c. [6 and 7, 493.]

(I)

ADMISSIONS ON SURRENDERS PASSED IN COURT.

498.—*Absolute surrender.*

Cl. 1. *Immediately on passing surrender.*—ALSO *at this court*
came A. B., of, &c., a copyhold tenant of this manor, and
(M.) his wife, and the said A. B. proposeth with the said M.
his wife to surrender the hereditaments and premises holden
by copy of court roll of this manor and hereinafter described,
to the use of [*purchaser*], his heirs and assigns. *And* in pursuance of the act or acts of parliament requiring the same,
the said A. B. doth deliver to the said steward a writing under
the hand of the said A. B., certifying that the said proposed
surrender is upon a sale to the said [*purchaser*], and that the
whole consideration on the same is the sum of £   and
no more.

2. AND *immediately* afterwards the said A. B. and M. his
wife (she being first examined by the said steward, separate
and apart from her said husband, touching and concerning her
free and voluntary consent to the making and passing the said
proposed surrender, and freely and voluntarily consenting
thereto as by law required.)

3. Do in open court, in consideration of the said sum of
£   , of lawful money of Great Britain, to the said A. B. in
hand well and truly paid by the said [*purchaser*], the receipt
whereof the said A. B. doth hereby, and by the receipt on the
said certificate acknowledge [*and in pursuance of a covenant for
that purpose contained in a certain indenture, bearing date, &c.,
and made between, &c., if so.*]

4. SURRENDER out of their and each of their hands into the
hands of the lord of this manor, by the hands and acceptance
of the said steward by the rod, according to the custom of this
manor.

5. ALL, &c. [*description*], and the reversion and reversions, remainder and remainders, yearly and other rents,
issues, and profits thereof, and of every part thereof; and all
the estate, right, title, interest, inheritance, use, trust, benefit,
property, possession, power, claim and demand whatsoever,
both at law and in equity of them, the said A. B. and M. his
wife, and each of them, of, in, to, or out of the said hereditaments and premises, and every part and parcel thereof, with
the appurtenances.

6. To THE ONLY *and absolute* USE *and behoof* of the said [*purchaser*], his heirs and assigns for ever, according to the custom of this manor.

7. AND THEREUPON, &c. [*proceed with admission as in surrender passed out of court, beginning with cl. 2.*]

If no admission taken, add first, second, or third proclamation, as the case may require; as in the case where a surrender out of court is presented.

The admission after proclamation can be drawn from precedents in class H.

[*On the copy of admission must be impressed the* ad valorem *stamp on surrender, as well as that on admission.*]

499.—*Certificate of consideration.*

Manor of Woodbridge late Priory. } To the steward of the said manor, or his lawful deputy steward.

I, A. B., of &c., do propose, with M. my wife, to surrender at a court this day holden for the said manor, to the use of [*purchaser*], his heirs and assigns, all, &c. And in pursuance of the act or acts of parliament requiring the same, I do certify that such proposed surrender is upon a sale, and that the whole consideration on the same is the sum of £   , and no more. As witness my hand this   day of   1836.

Witness.

(K)

300.—*Admission under Bargain and Sale from Executors.*

Cl. 1. [*Recite death of testator and proclamation as in admission of a devisee.*]

2. Now *at this court* cometh [*purchaser*], (by A. B. his attorney), and produceth to the court a certain indenture of bargain and sale, bearing date, &c., and made or expressed to be made between, &c., and which is presented by the homage of this court. WHEREBY after reciting, &c. IT IS WITNESSED, &c. [*stating sufficient to render the admission clear, and show the conveyance.*]

3. AND THEREUPON the said [*purchaser*], (by his said attorney,) prayeth to be admitted tenant to the hereditaments and premises so bargained and sold to his use as aforesaid (that is to say),

To ALL, &c. [*description,*] which premises the said deceased, had and took up to him and his heirs, &c. [493, 4.]

4. *To which*, &c. [*proceed as in admissions of devisee, class
F. clauses* 5, *&c., substituting* " bargained and sold " *for*
" devised."]

If the executors or either of them have been admitted for
want of sale, a surrender is usually taken. In which case, after
presenting the bargain and sale, you present the surrender, if
taken out of court, or enter it, if taken in court, and then add
in clauses 3, and subsequent clauses, the words " and
surrender," after the words " bargained and sold," when
they occur.

<hr>

(L.)

501.—*Admissions on sales of Bankrupt's Copyholds.*

By 6 G. 4, the mode of conveyance of bankrupts' copyholds is by a bargain and sale, to which the assignees and
commissioners are parties, and usually the bankrupt and
wife ; and a surrender, made by a party or parties authorized
by the commissioners, usually the bankrupt and his wife.

ALSO *at this court* the homage thereof do present a certain
indenture of bargain and sale, &c. [*stating such recitals as are
deemed requisite, and the bargain and sale, and authority to surrender.*]

AND *it is* also certified by the said steward, and presented by
the homage, &c. [*present absolute surrender passed by direction of
commissioners, or if passed in court, say,* " AND ALSO at this
court cometh, &c." *adding surrender in court in common form.*]

AND THEREUPON cometh into court the said [*purchaser*],
(by his said attorney), and prayeth to be admitted tenant to
the hereditaments and premises so bargained and sold, and
surrendered to his use as aforesaid (that is to say),

To ALL, &c. [*Then proceed as in other admissions, stating the
premises as* " *bargained and sold, and surrendered,*" *where requisite.*]

If proclamations made, the admission can be readily drawn
from the aforegoing precedents.

<hr>

(M)

502.—*Admissions of two or more persons.*

As joint tenants.—(State the will or surrender in the usual
manner.)

2. AND THEREUPON come into court the said [*A. B.*] and
[*C. D.*], that is to say, the said A. B. in his own proper person, and the said [*C. D.*] [*by   his attorney, if so*], and pray

to be admitted tenants to the hereditaments and premises so surrendered [*or devised*] to them as aforesaid (that is to say),

3. *To* ALL, &c. [*add description.*]

4. *Which* premises, &c. [*add cl. 4, as in common admission, F.*]

5. To WHICH said [*A. B.*] in his proper person, and [*C. D.*] (by his said attorney), the lord of this manor, by the said steward, doth grant and deliver seisin of the said hereditaments and premises by the rod.

6. To HOLD the same, with the appurtenances, unto the said A. B. and C. D. and their heirs, as joint tenants, of the lord, by copy of court roll, at the will of the lord, and according to the custom of this manor, by fealty, suit of court, and other the rents, duties, and services therefore due and of right accustomed.

7. *And* saving the rights of the lord, the said [*A. B.*] and [*C. D.*] are admitted tenants of the said hereditaments and premises, and pay on such their admittance, fines &c. But their fealty is respited until, &c.

***

503.—*As tenants in common.*

(After the statement of the surrender or will in the common manner.)

2. AND THEREUPON cometh into court the said A. B., and prayeth to be admitted tenant to one undivided moiety or equal half part (the whole into two equal parts to be divided), of and in all and singular the hereditaments and premises so devised [*or surrendered*] as aforesaid (that is to say),

3. *Of* and in ALL THAT, &c. [*adding description.*]

4. *Which* premises, &c. [*cl. 4, as in common admission.*]

5. To WHICH said A. B., the lord of this manor by the said steward doth grant and deliver seisin of the said moiety, of and in the said hereditaments and premises, so devised [*or surrendered*] as aforesaid by the rod.

To HOLD, &c. [*add clauses G. and H. as in usual cases.*]

[*Then admit C. D. to the other moiety in like manner.*]

If more than two are admitted, the only difference will be that the parcels will be described as " one equal undivided third," [*fourth, &c., as the case may be*], part (the whole into three equal parts to be divided), of and in, &c. [*and the grant will correspond.*]

If only one admission is to be made, it will be as in 502, substituting the words " tenants in common," for " joint tenants."

***

(**N**)

504.—*Admission under Forfeited Conditional Surrender.*

1. WHEREAS at a general court baron or customary court held for this manor, on, &c., it was certified by the then steward, and presented by the homage of that court, that, &c. [*add presentment of conditional surrender.*]

2. Now *at this court* it is presented by the homage that default was made in payment of the principal sum of £ and interest thereon, according to the provision contained in the said surrender, whereby the said surrender became forfeited and absolute at law.

3. WHEREUPON cometh into court the said [*mortgagee*], and gives the court to understand and be informed that the said principal sum of £   , together with the sum of £   , for interest thereon now remains due to him the said [*mortgagee*].

4. AND THEREUPON the said [*mortgagee*] prayeth to be admitted tenant to the hereditaments and premises so surrendered to his use as aforesaid (that is to say),

5. *To* ALL, &c. [*description.*]

6. *Which* premises, &c. [*clause* 5, *common admission, class H.*]

7. TO WHICH said [*mortgagee*], &c. [*cl.* 6 *ditto.*]

8. TO HOLD, &c. [*clause* 7 *ditto.*]

9. *And,* saving the rights of all persons, the said [*mortgagee*] is admitted, &c. [*cl.* 8 *ditto.*]

(**O**)

505.—*Admission to a Remainder or Reversion.*

[*State Surrender or will under which party claims, in usual manner.*]

2. AND THEREUPON, &c. [*clause D., as in admission under surrender or devise.*]

3. *To* ALL THAT the reversion or remainder expectant on the decease of C. D., of and in ALL *that,* &c. [*add description.*]

4. *Which* premises, &c. [*stating previous admission in common manner.*]

5. TO WHICH said [*reversioner*], the lord of this manor, by the said steward doth grant and deliver seisin of the said remainder or reversion, expectant as aforesaid of and in the said hereditaments and premises by the rod.

6. TO HOLD, &c. [*as in common admission, F. or H.*]

7. *And,* saving, &c. [*as in common admission, F or H.*] adding the words " reversion or remainder of and in the said" before " hereditaments."

1. Also, *at this court* come [*A. B.*], of, &c., a copyhold tenant of this manor, and [*M.*] his wife, and the said A. B. proposeth, with the said M. his wife, to surrender the hereditaments and premises copyhold of this manor, and hereinafter described or mentioned, to the use of [*mortgagee*], and his heirs. *And* in pursuance of the act or acts of parliament requiring the same, the said A. B. doth deliver to the steward of this manor a writing,* under the hand of him the said A. B, certifying that the said proposed surrender is not upon a sale, but by way of mortgage, and that the full consideration on the same is the sum of £   , and no more.

2. And afterwards *the said A. B. and M.* his wife (she having been by the said steward first examined, separate and apart from her said husband, touching her free and voluntary consent to the making and passing the said proposed surrender, and freely and voluntarily consenting thereto, as by law required) do, in open court, before the homage, in consideration of the sum of £   , of lawful money of Great Britain to the said A. B. in hand, well and truly paid, lent, and advanced, at or immediately before the passing the said surrender, by [*mortgagee*], of, &c., the receipt whereof the said A. B. doth hereby and by the receipt on the said certificate acknowledge, surrender out of their and each of their hands into the hands of the lord of this manor, by the hands and acceptance of the said steward, by the rod, according to the custom of this manor,

3. All, &c., [*description :* if general description, say "All *and every* the messuages, lands, tenements, hereditaments, and premises whatsoever of them the said A. B. and M. his wife, or either of them, holden of this manor by copy of court roll, with their and every of their rights, members, and appurtenances."] And the reversion and reversions, remainder and remainders, yearly and other rents, issues, and profits thereof, and of every part and parts thereof, with the appurtenances; and all the estate, right, title, interest, inheritance, use, trust, benefit, property, possession, power, claim, and demand whatsoever, both at law and in equity, of them the said A. B. and M. his wife, or either of them, of, in, to, from, or out of the said hereditaments and premises, and every part thereof, with the rights, members, privileges, appendages, and appurtenances.

* See form of certificate next page.

4. To THE USE and behoof of the said [*mortgagee*], his heirs and assigns for ever, according to the custom of this manor.

5. SUBJECT *nevertheless to* and *upon this express condition*, that if the said A. B., his heirs, executors, administrators or assigns, do and shall well and truly pay, or cause to be paid, unto the said [*mortgagee*], his executors, administrators or assigns, the sum of £   , of lawful money of Great Britain, on, &c. [*six months*], together with interest for the same at and after the rate of [5*l.*] for every sum of £100 by the year, to be computed from the day of passing this surrender, without any deduction or abatement whatsoever; *Then* this surrender to be void and of no effect, otherwise to remain in full force, power, and virtue.

[*The same stamp must be impressed on the copy of the surrender as would have been on a surrender out of court.*]

507.—*Certificate of Consideration on aforegoing Surrender.*

Manor of ⎫ To the steward of the said manor, or his lawful
W.   ⎬   deputy for the time being.

I, A. B., of, &c., a copyhold tenant of this manor, do propose with [*M.*] my wife, to surrender at a court this day holden for the said manor, all and singular the messuages, lands, tenements, hereditaments, and premises of me the said A. B., and M. my wife, and each of us, holden of the said manor [*or of* " all that, &c.," *adding description*], to the use of [*mortgagee*], of, &c., and his heirs; And in pursuance of the act or acts of parliament requiring the same, I do certify that the said proposed surrender is not upon a sale, but by way of mortgage; and that the full consideration on the same is the sum of £   , and no more.

Witness my hand this   day of   , 18 .
Witness,

(Q)

RELEASES.

508.—*By Widow of Dower or Freebench.*

1. Also at this court cometh [*widow*], of, &c., widow of A. B. deceased, late a copyhold tenant of this manor, and in consideration of the natural love and affection which she hath and beareth for [*heir*], her [*son*], [*if for pecuniary considera-*

tion, state it in usual manner] doth, in open court surrender out of her hands into the hands of the lord of this manor, by the hands and acceptance of the said steward, by the rod, according to the custom of this manor; and doth also remise, release, and for ever quit claim,

2. All the customary dower, widow's estate, or freebench right, title, and interest whatsoever of her the said [*widow*], in, to, or out of All that, &c. [*If the heir admitted at same court, say* " all and singular the messuages, lands, tenements, and hereditaments whatsoever, holden by copy of court roll of this manor, to which the said [*heir*] hath at this court been admitted tenant."

3. To which hereditaments and premises the said [*heir*] was admitted tenant at, &c., stating admission.

4. To the use and behoof of the said [*heir*] and his heirs, according to the custom of this manor, to the end and intent that the said [*heir*] and his heirs may henceforth have, hold, possess, and enjoy all and singular the hereditaments and premises hereinbefore described, freed and discharged of and from the customary dower, widow's estate, or freebench, of her the said [*widow*] in, to, or out of the same premises, or any part thereof, and of and from all actions, suits, claims, and demands in respect thereof, or in anywise relating thereunto.

509.—*Of Equity of Redemption.*

1. Whereas at a general court baron and customary court, holden in and for this manor, on, &c., [*mortgagee*] of, &c., was admitted tenant on the forfeited conditional surrender of [*mortgagor, describing him*], bearing date, &c. To all, &c. [*describing premises*], to hold to the said [*mortgagee*], and his heirs according to the custom of this manor, and now stands admitted thereto.

2. Now at this court cometh the said [*mortgagor*], and proposeth to surrender and release the said hereditaments and premises, equity and benefit of redemption, right and title of him the said [*mortgagor*] therein and thereto, unto the said [*mortgagee*] and his heirs; and in pursuance of the act or acts of parliament requiring the same, doth deliver to the steward a certificate* in writing under the hand of the said [*mortgagor*], stating that the full consideration on the said proposed surrender and release is the sum of £   , and no more.

3. And immediately afterwards the said [*mortgagor*] doth in open court, before the homage, in consideration of the

* Same as in class F., adding " release."

said sum of £   , of lawful money aforesaid, to the said [*mortgagor*] in hand, now well and truly paid by the said [*mortgagee*], the receipt whereof the said [*mortgagor*] doth hereby, and by the receipt written on the said certificate acknowledge, surrender, and also remise and release out of his hands into the hands of the lord of this manor, by the hands and acceptance of the said steward, by the rod, according to the custom of this manor.

4. All and singular the hereditaments and premises hereinbefore mentioned or described, and to which the said [*mortgagee*] was admitted tenant as aforesaid.

5. And the reversion and reversions, remainder and remainders, yearly and other rents, issues, and profits thereof, and of every part thereof, with the appurtenances, and all the estate, right, title, interest, equity, and benefit of redemption, property, power, claim, and demand whatsoever, of him the said [*mortgagor*], of, in, to, or out of the said hereditaments and premises, and every part thereof.

6. To the only and absolute use and behoof of the said [*mortgagee*], his heirs, and assigns for ever, freed and discharged of all equity and benefit of redemption, estate, right, title, claim, or demand whatsoever, of him the said [*mortgagor*] and his heirs, and all actions, suits, claims, and demands in respect thereof or in anywise in relation thereto.

Should the wife be made a party, this form will serve, altered as in the next form.

510.—*Surrender and Release by Heir or other Party possessing a R'ght.*

1. Whereas, &c. [*recite admission of party to whom release is to be made, and that he still stands admitted; and also recite such facts as may shew how the party claims, which of course must differ according to the particular circumstances of the case.*]

2. Now at this court come the said [*heir*] and [*M.*] his wife, and propose to surrender and release the said hereditaments and premises, and all their estate, right, and title therein and thereto, to the use of the said [*tenant*], his heirs and assigns; and the said [*heir*], pursuant to the act or acts requiring the same, doth deliver to the steward a writing,* under the hand of the said [*heir*], certifying that the full consideration on the said surrender and release is the sum of £   , and no more.

* As in class F., adding "release."

3. And immediately afterwards the said [*heir*] and [*M.*] his wife, (she the said [*M.*] being by the said steward first examined separate and apart from her said husband, touching and concerning her free and voluntary consent to the making and passing the said surrender and release, and freely and voluntarily consenting thereto, as by law required.)

4. Do in open court before the homage, in consideration of the sum of £   , of lawful money of Great Britain to the said [*heir*] in hand now well and truly paid by the said [*tenant*], the receipt whereof the said [*heir*] doth hereby, and by the receipt for the said sum on the said certificate in writing acknowledge, surrender out of their and each of their hands into the hands of the lord of this manor, by the hands and acceptance of the said steward, by the rod, according to the custom of this manor.

5. All, &c. [*description*], and the reversion, &c., and all the estate, &c. [506, 3.]

6. To the only and absolute use and behoof of the said [*tenant*], his heirs and assigns for ever, according to the custom of this manor, freed and absolutely discharged of and from all the estate, right, title. claim, and demand, both at law and in equity, of them the said [*heir*] and [*wife*] and each of them, of, in, to, or out of the said hereditaments and premises, and every part thereof, with the appurtenances, and so that neither he the said [*heir*], nor the said [*M.*] his wife nor his heirs, may have, claim, challenge, or demand therein or thereto any estate, right or title whatsoever, but shall for ever hereafter be therefrom by this release precluded and barred.

(R)

511.—*Apportionment of Rent.*—*Acknowledgment of Free Tenure. Licenses, and Conclusion.*

Appotionment of Rent.—Also at this court the annual quit rent payable in respect of the hereditaments holden of this manor by copy of court roll, whereto A. B. lately stood admitted, and to certain parts whereof C. D. hath at this court been admitted tenant, is apportioned as follows (that is to say) the sum of   , part thereof to be paid by the said C. D. and his heirs, in respect of the hereditaments to which he hath at this court been admitted tenant; and the sum of   , residue thereof, to be paid by the said A. B. and his heirs, in respect of the remaining part of the said hereditaments to which he still stands admitted tenant.

512.—*Acknowledgment of Free Tenure.*

Also at this court cometh A. B. of, &c. and acknowledges to hold freely of the lord of this manor, all &c. by fealty, suit of court, and the annual rent of —*s.* —*d.* ; and he giveth to the ' rd for a relief —*s.* —*d.* ; but his fealty is respited, &c.

513.—*Licence to Demise.*

Also at this court the lord of this manor doth, by the said steward, give and grant to A. B., one of the copyhold tenants of this manor, full licence, power and authority, to demise and lease to any person or persons willing to take the same as lessee or lessees to the said A. B., but not by way of mortgage, and to his or their executors, administrators, and assigns, all and singular or any of the hereditaments and premises holden of this manor, and to which the said A. B. stands admitted tenant, to hold for any term or number of years not exceeding　　　years, to be computed from the　　　day of　　　instant, saving always to the lord of this manor, and the lord and lords, lady and ladies thereof for the time being, all and all manner of fines, heriots, rents, customs, and services therefore due and of right accustomed ; and for this licence the said A. B. doth pay to the lord the sum of £　　　.

> If granted by the lord out of court, the commencement and conclusion will be like a surrender taken out of court before him, and the licence will be presented at the next court.

514.—*Licence to fell Timber.*

Also at this court the lord of this manor by the said steward doth grant to A. B., a copyhold tenant of this manor, licence to fell [8] [*oak*] trees, standing and growing (*in a certain close called the　　　, part of the*] or [*on the*] hereditaments, copyhold of this manor, to which the said A. B. stands admitted tenant [*and which trees have been marked by the steward of this manor, if so*] ; and the said A. B. payeth to the lord for a fine for this licence the sum of £

515.—*Licence to pull down Buildings.*

· Also at this court the lord of this manor by the said steward doth grant to A. B., a copyhold tenant of this manor, licence to pull down and waste a barn, standing and being in a certain close, called   , part of the hereditaments holden by copy of court roll of this manor, to which the said A. B. stands admitted tenant; and he giveth the lord as a fine for this licence, the sum of £   .

516.—*Licence to dig for Brick Earth.*

· Also at this court the lord of this manor by the said steward doth grant licence to [*A. B.*] [*tenant of this manor*], and to his undertenants, licence during his remaining a copyhold tenant of this manor, to dig brick earth, clay, sand, and gravel, on the lands and premises holden by copy of court roll of this manor, and to which he stands admitted tenant, and to manufacture the same into bricks, tiles, or pottery ware, and sell the same in such manufactured state from off the said land and premises: he and they replacing the growing soil upon the parts of the said land and premises from which the said brick earth, clay, sand, or gravel, shall be so excavated; and the said A. B. giveth to the lord for this licence a fine of £   .

517.—*Or, if Payment according to Quantity to be made.*

Also at this court the lord of this manor by the said steward doth grant licence to A. B., a copyhold tenant of this manor, and to his undertenants, during such time as he shall remain a copyhold tenant of this manor, and shall continue to pay the royalty or rent hereinafter mentioned, but not further or longer, to dig, &c. [*as in above precedent to "excavated" (if latter part to be inserted) and then add*] he well and truly paying unto the lord of this manor, his heirs and assigns, the royalty rent or payment of 6*d.* for each and every cart load or cubic yard of brick earth, clay, sand, gravel, or soil which he shall so dig out or excavate and remove from off the said land, or manufacture thereon, and delivering half-yearly, on the 6th day of January and 6th day of July, an account of the quantity so carried off or manufactured; and also on the said days paying the said royalty rent or sum then due.

209

518.—Amerciaments (not added at Special Court.)

And, lastly, the homage of this court do present all persons owing suit and service at this court, who have made default in not appearing to do the same, and do amerce them 3*d.* each.

THE END OF THIS COURT.*

[* *These words are all that are inserted at end of Special Court.*]

(S)

519.—Surrender in lieu of Recovery and Admission.

If out of court, the forms 294 & 5, making the use to the surrenderor and his heirs, will be applicable, and the re-admission will then be in the common form.

Should the surrender be passed in court, form 498 will give the surrender, by altering the statement of the consideration as in 294 ; and the admission will then be as before.

The protector's consent, where there is a protector, will be given by a separate deed, which will be presented and referred to in the entry of the surrender; and under 3 & 4 W. 4, c. 74, s. 51, the deed giving such consent must be enrolled at the court where the surrender is passed.

(T)

520.—Admission before the Lord.

[*Title*], Manor of, &c.   , the   day of, &c.

Be it remembered, that on, &c. A. B., of, &c. a copyhold tenant of the said manor, came before me, C. D., lord of the said manor, and having delivered to me, &c. [*state certificate of consideration as in surrender and admission in court, and adding the surrender and admission as being made into* " the proper hands of me the said lord"] and making the admission as being direct from the lord, instead of the steward.   [*See* 498.]

This admission will be entered in the court books, and a copy made, which will be signed by the lord, and countersigned in the margin by the steward.   The steward's fees are usually about the same as on other admissions, adding a fee for attendance on lord, making appointment for admission, &c. ; and a certificate, as in 483 must be entered at the following court.

ABSTRACT

OF THE

ACT 1st VICTORIA, c. 26,

FOR THE

AMENDMENT OF THE LAWS WITH RESPECT TO WILLS.

ABSTRACT

OF THE

ACT 1st VICTORIA, ch. 26,

INTITULED

"An act for the Amendment of the Laws with respect to Wills."—3rd July, 1837.

———

Sec. I. The words and expressions after mentioned, which in their ordinary signification have a more confined or different meaning, shall in this act, except where the nature of the provision or context shall exclude such construction, be interpreted as follows :—the word *" will"* shall extend to a testament, a codicil, an appointment by will or writing in nature of a will in exercise of a power, and also to a disposition by will and testament or devise of custody and tuition of any child by virtue of 12 C. 2, c. 24, or the Irish act, 14 and 15 C. 2. (I.) and to any other testamentary disposition; the words *"real estate"* shall extend to manors, advowsons, messuages, lands, tithes, rents, and hereditaments, whether freehold, customary freehold, tenant right, customary or copyhold, or of any other tenure, and whether corporeal, incorporeal, or personal; and to any undivided share thereof, and to any estate, right, or interest (other than a chattel interest) therein. The words *" personal estate"* shall extend to leasehold estates and other chattels real; also to monies, shares of government and other funds, securities for money (not

213

being real estates), debts, choses in action, rights, credits, goods, and all other property whatsoever, which by law devolves upon the executor or administrator, and to any share or interest therein; every word importing *singular number* only, shall extend and be applied to several persons or things as well as one, and words importing *masculine gender* only, shall extend and be applied to a female as well as male.

II. Repeals (except as the same relate to wills or estates *pur autre vie*, to which the present act does not extend) 32 H. 8, c. 1; 34 and 35 H. 8, c. 5.; 10 Car. 1, sess. 2. c. 2 (I.); sections 5, 6, 12, 19, 20, 21, and 22 of Statute of Frauds (29 Cra. 2, c. 3.); the like provisions in Irish Statute of Frauds, 7 W. 3. c. 12 (I.); section 14 of 4 & 5 Anne, c. 16, and the corresponding Irish Act, 6 Anne, c. 10 (I.); section 9 of 14 G. 2, c. 20; 25 Geo. 2, c. 6. (except as to colonies); 25 G. 2, c. 11. (I,) and 55 G. 3, c. 192.

III. It shall be lawful for every person to devise, bequeath, or dispose of by his will, executed as after required, all real estate and all personal estate which he shall be entitled to, either at law or in equity, at the time of his death, and which, if not so devised, bequeathed or disposed of, would devolve upon the heir at law or customary heir of him, or if he became entitled by descent of his ancestor, or upon his executor or administrator; and the power hereby given shall extend to all real estate of the nature of customary freehold or tenant right, or customary or copyhold, though not surrendered to the use of his will : *or though* being entitled as heir, devisee, or otherwise to be admitted, he shall not have been admitted; *or though* the same for want of a custom to surrender to will or otherwise, could not at law have been disposed of by will if this act not made; *or though* the same, in consequence of a custom that a will or surrender to will should continue in force a limited time only, or any other special custom, could not have been disposed of by will according to the powers

214

contained in this act, if act not made ; *also* to estates *pur autre vie*, whether or not any special occupant, and whether freehold, customary freehold, tenant right, customary or copyhold, or of any other tenure, and whether a corporeal or incorporeal hereditament. *Also* to all contingent, executory, or other future interests in any real or personal estate, whether the testator may or may not be ascertained as the person or one of the persons in whom the same respectively may become vested, and whether entitled thereto under the instrument by which the same respectively were created, or under any disposition thereof by deed or will : *Also* to all rights of entry for conditions broken and other rights of entry. ALSO *to such of the same estates, interests, and rights, and other real and personal estate as the testator may be entitled to at the time of his death, notwithstanding that he may become entitled to the same subsequently to the execution of his will.*

IV. Where real estate of the nature of customary freehold, tenant right, customary or copyhold, might, by custom of the manor, have been surrendered to use of a will, and the testator shall not have so surrendered the same, no person entitled or claiming by virtue of such will shall be entitled to be admitted, except on payment of all such stamp duties, fees, and sums of money as would have been lawfully due and payable in respect of the surrendering of such real estate to use of will, or in respect of presenting, registering, or enrolling such surrender, if the estate had been surrendered to use of will, and where the testator was entitled to have been admitted, and might, if admitted, have surrendered to use of his will, and shall not have been admitted, no person entitled or claiming such real estate in consequence of such will shall be entitled to be admitted by virtue thereof, except on payment of all such stamp duties, fees, fine, and sums of money as would have been lawfully due and payable in respect of the admittance of such testator, and of surrendering to use of the

215

will, or of presenting, registering, or enrolling such surrender, had the testator been duly admitted and afterwards surrendered to use of his will; all which stamp duties, fees, fine, or sums of money due as aforesaid shall be paid in addition to the stamp duties, &c., due or payable on admittance of such person so entitled or claiming as aforesaid.

V. When any real estate of the nature of customary freehold or tenant right, or customary or copyhold, shall be disposed of by will, the lord of the manor or reputed manor of which such real estate is holden, or his steward, or the deputy of such steward, shall cause the will by which such disposition shall be made, or so much thereof as shall contain the disposition of such real estate, to be entered on the court rolls: and when any trusts are declared, it shall not be necessary to enter the declaration of such trusts, but sufficient to state in the entry that such real estate is subject to the trusts declared by such will; and when any such real estate could not have been disposed of by will if this act had not been made, the same fine, heriot, dues, duties, and services shall be paid and rendered by the devisee as would have been due from the customary heir in case of descent; and the lord shall, as against the devisee, have the same remedy for recovering and enforcing such fine, &c., as now entitled to for recovering and enforcing the same from or against the customary heir in case of a descent.

VI. If no disposition by will shall be made of any estate *pur autre vie* of a freehold nature, the same shall be chargeable in the hands of the heir, if it shall come to him by reason of special occupancy, as assets by descent, as in the case of freehold land in fee simple; and if no special occupant of any estate *pur autre vie,* whether freehold or customary freehold, tenant right, customary or copyhold, or of any other tenure, and whether a corporeal or incorporeal hereditament, it shall go to the executor or administrator of the party that had the estate thereof by virtue of

216

the grant; and if the same shall come to the executor or administrator either by reason of a special occupancy or by virtue of this act, it shall be assets in his hands, and shall go and be applied and distributed as the personal estate of the testator or intestate.

VII. No will made by any person under the age of twenty-one years shall be valid.

VIII. No will made by any married woman shall be valid, except such a will as might have been made by a married woman before the passing of this act.

IX. No will shall be valid unless in writing, and executed in manner after mentioned; (i. e.) it shall be signed at the foot or end thereof by the testator, or by some other person in his presence and by his direction; and such signature shall be made or acknowledged by the testator in the presence of two or more witnesses present at the same time; and such witnesses shall attest and shall subscribe the will in the presence of the testator, but no form of attestation shall be necessary.

X. No appointment made by will, in exercise of any power, shall be valid, unless the same be so executed; and every will so executed shall so far as respects the execution and attestation thereof, be a valid execution of a power of appointment by will, notwithstanding it shall have been expressly required that a will made in exercise of such power should be executed with some additional or other form of execution or solemnity.

XI. Any soldier being in actual military service, or any mariner or seaman being at sea, may dispose of his personal estate as he might have done before the making of this act.

XII. This act shall not prejudice or affect the provisions contained in 11 Geo. 4. and 1 W. 4, c. 20., respecting the wills of petty officers and seamen in the royal navy, and non-commissioned officers of marines, and marines, so far as relates to their wages, pay, prize money, bounty money, and allow-

217   L

ances, or other monies payable in respect of services in her Majesty's navy.

XIII. Every will executed as aforesaid shall be valid without any other publication thereof.

XIV. If any person who shall attest the execution of a will shall at the time of the execution thereof or at any time afterwards be incompetent to be admitted a witness to prove the execution thereof, such will shall not on that account be invalid.

XV. If any person shall attest the execution of any will to whom or to whose wife or husband any beneficial devise, legacy, estate, interest, gift, or appointment, of or affecting any real or personal estate (other than and except charges and directions for the payment of any debt or debts), shall be thereby given or made, such devise, &c., shall, so far only as concerns such person attesting, or the wife or husband of such person, or any person claiming under such person, wife or husband, be utterly null and void, and such person so attesting shall be admitted as a witness to prove the execution of such will, or to prove the validity or invalidity thereof, notwithstanding such devise, &c., mentioned in such will.

XVI. In case by will any real or personal estate shall be charged with any debt or debts, and any creditor, or the wife or husband of any creditor, whose debt is so charged, shall attest the execution, such creditor notwithstanding such charge shall be admitted a witness to prove the execution, or the validity or invalidity thereof.

XVII. No person shall, on account of being an executor of a will, be incompetent to be admitted a witness to prove the execution, or the validity or invalidity thereof.

XVIII. Every will made by a man or woman shall be revoked by his or her marriage (except a will made in exercise of a power of appointment, when the real or personal estate thereby appointed would not in default of such appointment pass to his or her heir, customary heir, executor, or administrator, or

218

the person entitled as his or her next of kin, under the statute of distributions.)

XIX. No will shall be revoked by any presumption of an intention on the ground of an alteration in circumstances.

XX. No will or codicil, or any part thereof, shall be revoked otherwise than as aforesaid, or by another will or codicil executed in manner before required, or by some writing declaring an intention to revoke the same, and executed as a will is required to be executed, or by the burning, tearing, or otherwise destroying the same by the testator, or by some person in his presence and by his direction, with the intention of revoking the same.

XXI. No obliteration, interlineation, or other alteration made in any will after the execution, shall be valid or have any effect, except so far as the words or effect of the will before such alteration shall not be apparent, unless such alteration shall be executed as required for execution of the will; but the will, with such alteration as part thereof, shall be deemed to be duly executed if the signature of the testator and the subscription of the witnesses be made in the margin or on some other part of the will opposite or near such alteration, or at the foot or end of or opposite a memorandum referring to such alteration, and written at the end or some other part of the will.

XXII. No will or codicil, or any part thereof, which shall be in any manner revoked, shall be revived otherwise than by the re-execution, or by a codicil executed as aforesaid, and showing an intention to revive the same; and when any will or codicil partly, and afterwards wholly revoked, shall be revived, such revival shall not extend to so much thereof as shall have been revoked before the revocation of the whole thereof, unless an intention to the contrary shall be shown.

XXIII. No conveyance or other act made or done subsequently to execution of a will relating to any real or personal estate therein comprised, except an act by which such will shall be revoked as aforesaid, shall prevent the operation of the will with respect to such estate or interest in such real or personal estate as the testator shall have power to dispose of by will at the time of his death.

XXIV. Every will shall be construed, with reference to the real and personal estate comprised in it, to speak and take effect as if executed immediately before the death of the testator, unless a contrary intention appear by the will.

XXV. Unless a contrary intention appear by the will, such real estate or interest therein as shall be or intended to be comprised in any devise in such will, which shall fail or be void by reason of the death of the devisee in the lifetime of the testator, or by reason of such devise being contrary to law or otherwise incapable of taking effect, shall be included in the residuary devise (if any) in such will.

XXVI. A devise of the land of the testator, or of the land of the testator in any place or in the occupation of any person mentioned in his will, or otherwise described in a general manner, and any other general devise which would describe a customary, copyhold, or leasehold estate if the testator had no freehold estate which could be described by it, shall be construed to include the customary, copyhold, and leasehold estates of the testator, or any of them, to which such description shall extend, as the case may be, as well as freehold estates, unless a contrary intention appear by the will.

XXVII. A general devise of the real estate of the testator, or of his real estate in any place or in the occupation of any person mentioned in his will, or otherwise described in a general manner, shall be construed to include any real estate, or any to which such description shall extend (as the case may be), which he may have power to appoint in any manner he may think proper, and shall operate as an execution of such power, unless a contrary intention shall appear by the will; and in like manner a bequest of the personal estate, or any bequest of personal property described in a general manner, shall be construed to include any personal estate, or any to which such description shall extend (as the case may be), which he may have power to appoint in any manner he may think proper, and shall operate as an execution of such power, unless a contrary intention shall appear by the will.

XXVIII. Where real estate shall be devised to any person without words of limitation, such devise shall be construed to pass the fee simple, or other the whole estate or interest which the testator had power to dispose of by will in such real estate, unless a contrary intention shall appear by the will.

XXIX. In any devise or bequest of real or personal estate the words " die without issue," or " die without leaving issue," or " have no issue," or any other words which may import either a want or failure of issue of any person in his lifetime or at the time of his death, or an indefinite failure of his issue, shall be construed to mean a want or failure of issue in the lifetime or at the time of the death of such person, and not an indefinite failure of his issue, unless a contrary intention shall appear by the will, by reason of such person having a prior estate tail, or of a preceding gift, being, without any implication arising from such words, a limitation of an estate tail to such person or issue, or otherwise: Provided, that this act shall not extend to cases where such words as aforesaid import if no issue described in a preceding gift shall be born, or if there shall be no issue who shall live to attain the age or otherwise answer the description required for obtaining a vested estate by a preceding gift to such issue.

XXX. Where real estate (other than or not being a presentation to a church) shall be devised to any trustee or executor, such devise shall be construed to pass the fee simple or other the whole estate or interest which the testator had power to dispose of

221

will, unless a definite term of years, absolute or byterminable, or an estate of freehold, shall thereby de given to him expressly or by implication.

beXXXI. Where real estate shall be devised to a trustee, without any express limitation of the estate to be taken, and the beneficial interest in such real estate, or in the surplus rents and profits thereof, shall not be given to any person for life, or shall be given to any person for life, but the purposes of the trust may continue beyond the life of such person, such devise shall be construed to vest in such trustee the fee simple, or other the whole legal estate which the testator had power to dispose of by will, and not an estate determinable when the purposes of the trust shall be satisfied.

XXXII. Where any person to whom real estate shall be devised for an estate tail or an estate in quasi entail shall die in the lifetime of the testator leaving issue who would be inheritable under such entail, and any such issue shall be living at the time of the death of the testator, such devise shall not lapse, but shall take effect as if the death of such person had happened immediately after the death of the testator, unless a contrary intention shall appear by the will.

XXXIII. Where any person being a child or other issue of the testator to whom real or personal estate shall be devised or bequeathed for any estate or interest, not determinable at or before the death of such person, shall die in the lifetime of the testator leaving issue, and any such issue of such person shall be living at the death of the testator, such devise or bequest shall not lapse, but shall take effect as if the death of such person had happened immediately after that of the testator, unless a contrary intention shall appear by the will.

XXXIV. This act shall not extend to any will made before 1st January, 1838, and every will re-executed or republished, or revived by any codicil, shall for the purposes of this act be deemed to have

222

been made at the time at which the same shall be so re-executed, republished, or revived; and this act shall not extend to any estate *pur autre vie* of any person who shall die before the 1st January, 1838.

XXXV. This act shall not extend to *Scotland*.

XXXVI. This act may be amended, altered, or repealed by any act or acts to be passed in this present Session of Parliament.

INDEX.

M

INDEX.

227　　　　　　　M 2

228

L.

M.

N.

P.

E. Spettigue, Printer, 67, Chancery Lane.